HUMAN RIGHTS IN THE FIELD OF COMPARATIVE EDUCATION

COMPARATIVE AND INTERNATIONAL EDUCATION:
A DIVERSITY OF VOICES
Volume 21

Scope

Comparative and International Education: A Diversity of Voices aims to provide a comprehensive range of titles, making available to readers work from across the comparative and international education research community. Authors will represent as broad a range of voices as possible, from geographic, cultural and ideological standpoints. The editors are making a conscious effort to disseminate the work of newer scholars as well as that of well-established writers. The series includes authored books and edited works focusing upon current issues and controversies in a field that is undergoing changes as profound as the geopolitical and economic forces that are reshaping our worlds. The series aims to provide books which present new work, in which the range of methodologies associated with comparative education and international education are both exemplified and opened up for debate. As the series develops, it is intended that new writers from settings and locations not frequently part of the English language discourse will find a place in the list.

THE WORLD COUNCIL OF COMPARATIVE EDUCATION SOCIETIES

The WCCES is an international organization of comparative education societies worldwide and is an NGO in consultative partnership with UNESCO. The WCCES was created in 1970 to advance the field of comparative education. Members usually meet every three years for a World Congress in which scholars, researchers, and administrators interact with colleagues and counterparts from around the globe on international issues of education.

The WCCES also promotes research in various countries. Foci include theory and methods in comparative education, gender discourses in education, teacher education, education for peace and justice, education in post-conflict countries, language of instruction issues, Education for All. Such topics are usually represented in thematic groups organized for the World Congresses.

Besides organizing the World Congresses, the WCCES has a section in *CERCular*, the newsletter of the Comparative Education Research Centre at the University of Hong Kong, to keep individual societies and their members abreast of activities around the world. The WCCES comprehensive web site is http://www.wcces.com.

As a result of these efforts under the auspices of the global organization, WCCES and its member societies have become better organized and identified in terms of research and other scholarly activities. They are also more effective in viewing problems and applying skills from different perspectives, and in disseminating information. A major objective is advancement of education for international understanding in the interests of peace, intercultural cooperation, observance of human rights and mutual respect among peoples.

Series Editors:

Suzanne Majhanovich and Allan Pitman

The WCCES Series was established to provide for the broader dissemination of discourses between scholars in its member societies. Representing as it does Societies and their members from all continents, the organization provides a special forum for the discussion of issues of interest and concern among comparativists and those working in international education.

The first series of volumes was produced from the proceedings of the World Council of Comparative Education Societies XIII World Congress, which met in Sarajevo, Bosnia and Herzegovina, 3-7 September, 2007 with the theme of *Living Together: Education and Intercultural Dialogue.* The series included the following titles:

Volume 1: Tatto, M. & Mincu, M. (Eds.), *Reforming Teaching and Learning*
Volume 2: Geo JaJa, M. A. & Majhanovich, S. (Eds.), *Education, Language and Economics: Growing National and Global Dilemmas*
Volume 3: Pampanini, G., Adly, F. & Napier, D. (Eds.), *Interculturalism, Society and Education*
Volume 4: Masemann, V., Majhanovich, S., Truong, N., & Janigan, K. (Eds.), *A Tribute to David N. Wilson. Clamoring for a Better World*

The second series of volumes has been developed from the proceedings of the World Council of Comparative Education Societies XIV World Congress, which met in Istanbul, Turkey, 14-18 June, 2010 with the theme of *Bordering, Re-Bordering and new Possibilities in Education and Society.* This series includes the following titles, with further volumes under preparation:

Volume 1: Napier, D. B. & Majhanovich, S. (Eds.), *Education, Dominance and Identity*
Volume 2: Biseth, H. & Holmarsdottir, H. (Eds.), *Human Rights in the Field of Comparative Education*
Volume 3: Ginsburg, M. (Ed.), *Preparation, Practice and Politics of Teachers*

Human Rights in the Field of Comparative Education

Edited by

Heidi Biseth
Buskerud University College, Norway

and

Halla B. Holmarsdottir
Oslo University College, Norway

SENSE PUBLISHERS
ROTTERDAM / BOSTON / TAIPEI

A C.I.P. record for this book is available from the Library of Congress.

ISBN 978-94-6209-150-4 (paperback)
ISBN 978-94-6209-151-1 (hardback)
ISBN 978-94-6209-152-8 (e-book)

Published by: Sense Publishers,
P.O. Box 21858, 3001 AW Rotterdam, The Netherlands
https://www.sensepublishers.com/

Printed on acid-free paper

TABLE OF CONTENTS

ACKNOWLEDGEMENTS

The editors of this volume would like to convey their immense appreciation to the many people who have contributed greatly in bringing this volume to completion. All the chapters in this collection originated as paper presentations at the XIV World Congress of Comparative Education Societies held in Istanbul, Turkey on June 14-18, 2010. The Congress was hosted by the World Council of Comparative Education Societies (WCCES) and by the local organizers TÜKED (Turkish Comparative Education Society) and Boğaziçi University. We would like to thank all parties involved in the XIV World Congress, and in particular the Congress Convenor Professor Fatma Gök and the other members of the Local Organizing Committee and in particular Meral Apak and Soner Şimşek for their assistance to us in reconnecting with presenters to develop their papers into chapters for the volume.

We would also like to thank all the contributors to this volume for their enthusiasm and hard work, particularly with regard to refining their contributions in light of our feedback as editors, but also the feedback of the individual reviewers. All this diligence and dedication has allowed us to bring together a volume focusing on Human Rights and Education from a number of perspectives, not only methodological and theoretical, but also geographical. This is something that was also reflected in the broader Congress theme *Bordering, Re-Bordering and New Possibilities in Education and Society*, which was particularly significant given Istanbul's geographical position, straddling both the 'East' and the 'West'. Through this volume we believe the different authors have been able to start a discussion on how we envision the role of human rights in education within the field of comparative education and the ways in which local understandings can bring to light the trends, effects and influences that exist in the different contexts globally.

Further, we are especially grateful to the manuscript reviewers who provided meticulous and constructive feedback to the chapter authors and to us as editors: Jennifer Chung, Kendra Dupuy, Bjørn Flatås, Greta Gudmundsdottir, Stephan Hamberg, Janicke Heldal-Stray, Jessica Hjarrand, Lihong Huang, Berit Johnsen, Kimmo Kosonen, Lars Leer, Lars Gunnar Lingås, Hanna Lomeland, Simen Mæhlum, Jennifer R. Olson, Anatoli Rapoport, and Ådne Valen-Sendstad. We are above all grateful to Michel Lokhorst and the staff of Sense Publishers, Rotterdam, Netherlands who took responsibility for the production process and to the publications committee of the WCCES, especially Suzanne Majhanovich, for both their encouragement and support in bringing this volume to completion.

HEIDI BISETH AND HALLA B. HOLMARSDOTTIR

1. HUMAN RIGHTS IN THE FIELD OF COMPARATIVE EDUCATION

Mapping Ways of Understanding Human Rights

INTRODUCTION

This volume consists of a selection of nine papers presented at the *Fourteenth World Congress of Comparative Education*. The Congress was organized by the Turkish Comparative Education Society and held at Boğaziçi University located in Istanbul, Turkey, in June 2010. The theme of the Congress "*Bordering, Re-bordering and new Possibilities in Education and Society*" was particularly significant given Istanbul's geographical position, straddling both the 'East' and the 'West'. The 'East/West' rivalry ever so present in terms of identity can also be found in local as well as global inequalities or as Edward Said reminds us the way in which 'Western' culture "gained in strength and identity by setting itself off against the ['East'] as a sort of surrogate and even underground self" (Said, 2003, p. 3).

A common European identity is seen as imperative in terms of the EU, thus in the case of Turkey there has been a questioning that Turkish-EU relations amount to a clash of civilizations. Nevertheless it is pertinent to point out that the process of membership is complicated by a clash of two conflicting definitions of what Europe is and should be. From the Turkish side demands have been placed on inclusion into Europe and the need to recognize the distinct cultural identity inherent in Turkey, while a minimalist discourse has portrayed Europe at the center of civilization requiring Turkey to assimilate. More importantly the debate has been over Turkey's ability to adhere to and fulfill its obligations on some of the most important EU values. The values that EU citizens feel are most important to them personally are Peace (52%), Human Rights (41%) and Respect for Human Life (43%) (European Commission, 2006). These themes also permeated some of the fourteen Congress thematic groups. It is from the parallel sessions within these thematic groups that the nine papers have been identified.

MAPPING WAYS OF SEEING HUMAN RIGHTS IN EDUCATION

According to Paulston and Liebman (1996) "the writing and reading of maps … [addresses] questions of location in the social milieu" (p. 7). Thus social cartography illustrates the use of metaphor as a visual way of constructing meaning, a visual dialogue. However, maps are never neutral documents. Since the process of mapping encourages personal interpretation of specific criteria in

H. Biseth & H.B. Holmarsdottir (eds.), Human Rights in the Field of Comparative Education, 1–11.

representing spatial relationships among differing ideas, social cartography relies heavily upon the use of the visual metaphor as an explanatory device to bring about further discussion (Holmarsdottir, 2011). Our intention in conducting the following mapping is to place each of the nine papers within a framework inspired by the work of Dembour (2006). Likewise, we find it important to point out that in this mapping exercise it is not our intention to suggest that our views are necessarily shared in the broader social context, but it is simply to visualize the discourses in the field in order to initiate a dialogue between researchers from various disciplines. Moreover, our intention is to clarify the ways in which we understand and talk about human rights within the field of comparative education and in doing so we also attempt to shed light on the issues within human rights to which we are silent, issues that we should conceivably be discussing.

This mapping exercise is based on Marie-Bénédicte Dembour's (2006) attempt to describe and categorize the ongoing discourses on human rights. There is no single answer to the question: what are human rights? The answer depends on whom you ask. The schools presented by Dembour can be contested and are not the only way of understanding and describing the ways in which we talk about human rights. Nevertheless we consider this a fruitful exercise as it sheds light on the fact that we do not always mean the same thing when talking about human rights. Dembour (2006) chooses to divide the ongoing human rights discourses into the natural school, the protest school, the deliberative school, and the discourse school.

Natural scholars understand human rights as entitlements we have solely because we are born as human beings. It follows from this that human rights are believed as held universally by all human beings. This tends to be a dominant understanding. The presumed consensus among states, through for example the signing of the UN Universal Declaration of Human Rights (UN, 1948), is considered as evidence of the entitlements. An interesting aspect of the arguments presented by natural scholars is that their stand is rarely made explicit. It is more of an underlying assumption, something taken for granted. In addition, there is a possession paradox in that we need human rights the most when we do not have them or our rights are violated. This questions the notion of human rights as something possible to possess.

Protest scholars do not see human rights as individual entitlements but rather as claims and aspirations. They often start from the premise that human rights are potentially universal, but from there onwards they focus on human rights as a political norm which we all have to strive to reach by securing the rights of our fellow human beings. These scholars tend to be preoccupied with marginalized groups and the struggle for human rights. There is always yet another fight to be had. In other words, protest scholars disagree with natural scholars in that we have human rights. In their perspective it is not possible to have them, the only option is to fight for them to be fulfilled so that all people can enjoy them equally. This makes human rights only potentially universal, dependent on the results of our efforts towards the realization of their fulfillment.

Deliberative scholars see human rights as procedural principals to be used in order for a society to function well. Although deliberative scholars do not believe in human rights in the way natural and protest scholars do, they are committed to them. The use of concepts like 'adjudication' indicates that deliberative scholars understand human rights as only existing through human rights law and thus use, for example, international human rights legislation extensively in their arguments. Deliberative scholars' focus on human rights as 'thin' principles of procedures, which provides scholars with far less expectations of what human rights can achieve compared to natural and protest scholars.

Discourse scholars are fundamentally skeptical of human rights. This does not imply that they find human suffering acceptable, but they do not necessarily see human rights as the means of alleviating human suffering. Discourse scholars have a clear understanding of human rights as a social construct existing only through its linguistic encapsulation. This implies that human rights are not inherently good and we need to scrutinize the ways in which human rights are understood and used. Dembour, herself a discourse scholar, describes this position as something that brings intellectual discomfort. The other schools have less uncomfortable positions, yet we need to engage in the discomfort in order to continue the search for better ways of living our lives together.

The four different schools of thought can be visualized in this way:

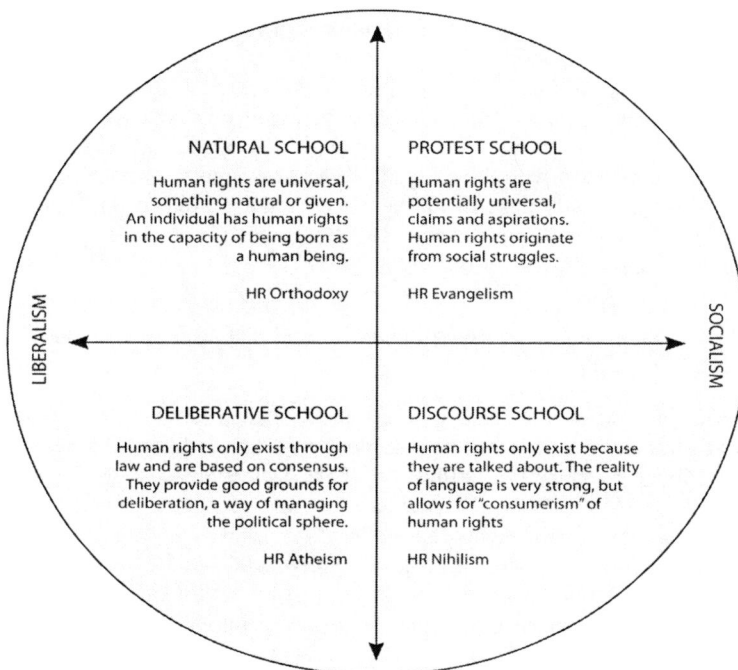

Figure 1. Dembour's Matrix

Based on the above description of Dembour's classification of human rights discourses, our intention is now to present the contributions in this volume and at the same time identifying the arguments they use and in doing so we position them in Dembour's matrix.

The Educational Rights of Asylum-Seeking and Refugee Children within the Neo-Liberal State and Inclusive Schools in the UK

In this chapter Madeleine Arnot, Halleli Pinson and Mano Candappa outline what can happen when asylum-seeking and refugee children cross territorial and symbolic borders into liberal democratic educational systems. It revisits the findings of a recent study on the political and economic conditions affecting asylum-seeking and refugee children in the UK, contrasting inhospitable immigration policies that deny these children's human rights with inclusive schooling approaches (Pinson, Arnot & Candappa, 2010). By drawing on rights-based approaches and on more radical interventions on behalf of the refugee child, teachers' responses to such hostile agendas challenge government actions.

With a focus on how teachers want to 'rehumanise' their students and the need of a culture of social morality, these authors can be placed among protest scholars. However, their use of international human rights instruments, such as the UN Universal Declaration on Human Rights (UN, 1948), the Convention of the Right of the Child (UN, 1989) and the Convention Relating to the Status of Refugees (UN, 1951) to argue their case for the inclusion of refugee children in regular UK schools is similar to that of deliberative scholars. In this case the international legislative measures are used when judging the practice in the UK, and the lack of access to education is not found to be in compliance. Thus, on the one hand these scholars are concerned with the struggle for human rights for asylum-seeking and refugee children, clearly linked with the protest school, while also recognizing the principals of procedures involved and as such they can simultaneously be placed in the deliberative school.

The Protection of Children's Rights in Latin America: Perspectives on the Right to Education

Paulí Dávila and Luis Mª Naya focus their chapter on how the defense of children's human rights has had an important evolution in Latin America in recent decades, above all since the ratification of the Convention on the Rights of the Child (CRC) (UN, 1989). Most countries in the region found a way of implementing children's rights and education rights through some genuine documents such as the Codes of Children. Since 2000, most of these Codes have been reformed. In this paper the authors have carried out a textual analysis of these documents. They focus on how Latin American countries have implemented the right to education during the last decade. In their analysis they employ Katarina Tomaševski's (2006) categories of Availability, Accessibility, Acceptability, and

Adaptability. At the legal level, these categories provide a tool to verify the compliance of indicators with the right to education.

The Codes of Children are documents described as important steps in the implementation of the CRC in the region and documents that are complementary to the national educational legislation. In Latin America legal texts alone are seen to be able to secure the implementation of rights but the authors are clear, however, that the Codes of Children alone do not guarantee compliance with children's rights as described in the CRC. The protection of children's rights also relies on measures to implement them on the ground.

The authors signal a substantial reliance on the CRC as crucial in protecting the rights of children in addition to the development of subsequent legal documents in Latin American countries. It seems as if the authors consider human rights as existing through the rule of law. In a Dembourian perspective these arguments place Dávila and Naya in the deliberative school of thought.

The Right to Education in Latin America (2005-2010): Analysis of the Latin American Conferences on Education

Ana María Montero Pedrera is conducting a documentary analysis of the right to education in Latin America based on documents presented by the Organization of the Latin American States for Education, Science and Culture (OEI). The international human rights instruments have a firm footing in Latin America and the author claims that the most lasting evidence of the advance of the right to education is the progressive expansion of the school system. It seems as if the Latin American countries mostly adhere to the demands and pressure present when international conventions and treaties are ratified.

The core of this chapter engages in the human rights instruments as they are represented in international conventions and covenants. The point of departure seems to be that these instruments can be used as a political framework to secure a better life for children through providing access to education. In seeing human rights as a device when discussing issues of distribution of societal wealth, Montero Pedrera represents a typical deliberative scholar.

Tensions between National Citizenship and Human Rights: Perspectives in Greece and Turkey

Citizenship education often includes human rights perspectives. Sevincer and Biseth point out, however, that national citizenship and human rights can also represent opposing perspectives. Citizenship education policies and programs tend to remain predominantly national and often nationalistic in practice (Reid & Sears, 2009). This tendency is particularly marked in new and aspirant nation-states and in post-conflict contexts where there are political pressures to stress unity, even to the extent of denying past conflicts and overstating current societal political consensus. Greece and Turkey have both emphasized a sense of shared national unity as a pivotal trait of citizenship education. However, the national homogenization projects are currently challenged by increasing diversity in society. This is a factor contributing to tensions existing between human rights and national civic values. The simple coexistence of these perspectives is considered by the authors as problematic and they suggest another possibility in trying to integrate these aspects in social life.

The line of arguments presented in this chapter indicates authors who take as a point of departure the given nature of human rights, something inherent in each individual. This places them among natural scholars in Dembour's model although the authors express their knowledge of the limitations of such a position.

Interpreting Children's Rights: A New Challenge for Education

Catarina Tomás and Mariana Dias analyze how specific characteristics of Portugal, such as demographic composition, unemployment and poverty, affect children's rights. The gap between the legal frameworks and social practices are described as rather wide in the Portuguese context with discourses on childhood being of a decorative character. The authors have used national and international statistics to map out life conditions of children in Portugal since the transition to democracy in 1974. Some children experience social exclusion, others are particularly vulnerable if coming from ethnic minorities or having special educational needs. In order to provide for equal educational access for all and the opportunity of achieving good results, more efforts on the protection of children's rights are required.

Advocating for children's right to education and a political process can have a visible impact on the life of children, Tomás and Dias present arguments indicating that human rights represent an existing framework which is valid and relevant only if we fight for the rights to be realized. This line of thought is well established within the protest school of Dembour.

Culturally Responsive Pedagogy and Human Rights: Identifying Global Values in the Classroom

In this chapter, Susan J. Courey and Pam LePage take as a point of departure that every child has the human right to education, training and information. Children also have other fundamental human rights that are dependent upon the realization of the human right to education. This particular human right is explicitly set out in the Universal Declaration of Human Rights (UN, 1948), the International Covenant on Economic, Social and Cultural Rights (UN, 1966), and the Convention on the Rights of the Child (UN, 1989). In order to realize human rights in general, the authors argue that we must bring the human rights movement into classrooms around the world, that teachers must think and talk explicitly about values that are shared across vast cultural and geographical gulfs, as well as across the boundaries created by income and wealth inequalities, and that we must be concerned with the fundamental values that follow from our acknowledgement of the intrinsic dignity of humans. Culturally responsive pedagogy is a platform from which teachers can model and discuss the values inherent in the human rights movement. It requires teachers to effectively educate students that vary in culture, language, ability, and many other characteristics. Teachers utilize both empirically sound and culturally responsive pedagogy to design classrooms that welcome and support all types of students. In this chapter Courey and LePage define culturally responsive teaching and present ways to create culturally responsive classrooms.

Courey and LePage handle human rights in this chapter mainly on an individual level when focusing on the role of pre-service teachers in special education. They call for teacher students in special education to have a thorough understanding of the history of human rights in addition to the theory and politics behind human rights. Special education teachers are described in this chapter as human rights defenders by the very fact that they engage in this particular profession, and thus partake in fulfilling the educational rights of children with disabilities. However, a point is made about the pre-service teacher in this profession as having a rather shallow understanding of human rights. Furthermore they have a tendency to limit their focus to their own classrooms, not necessarily having a wider perspective including global citizenship as a frame of reference. The authors claim that a wider outlook will enable pre-service teachers to become capable and willing to critically reflect on their roles as globally competent and culturally responsive educators:

> We want to inspire them [the students] to become agents of change by being more than culturally competent; we want them to help their students to understand the importance of human rights in a global community.

In order to inspire their students, Courey and LePage have created a program for culturally responsive pedagogy and human rights. In seeing themselves as teacher educators and their students as activists of human rights, Courey and LePage clearly situate their arguments in the protest school of thought as presented by Dembour (2006). In calling for a more in-depth understanding of human rights among the pre-service teachers, it seems as if the students initially take for granted their human rights. This locates the students closer to the natural scholars, whereas Courey and LePage express a deeper desire to change the students' attitudes in the direction of protest scholars that see as their mission to uphold and defend human rights in their work.

Moroccan Children's Rights in an Educational Space

In spite of Morocco's ratification of the Convention of the Rights of the Child (CRC) (UN, 1989) and recognition of education as a right for all children, the diglossic language situation in which most Moroccan children live sometimes threatens their educational attainment. The mismatch between the language of everyday life and the language of the school is perceived by the author, Mina Afkir, as a risk to the child's right to education.

Moroccan Arabic is the language used in everyday communication, but it is not considered viable in the educational space inside school. This situation complicates access to both the written and oral Standard Arabic, Afkir argues. The Moroccan children thus experience a form of marginalization in communicative events as

Standard Arabic, not Moroccan Arabic, is defined as the hegemonic communicative tool (see e.g., van Dijk, 2000). The Standard Arabic functions as the formal and prestigious language whereas the vernacular, Moroccan Arabic, is limited to informal conversations (see e.g., Holmarsdottir, 2005). This situation creates a need for people to master Standard Arabic in order to effectively have a say in civil society or in matters of government policy, and experience freedoms of expression, of association, and of assembly (Beetham, 2000).

The author starts out the chapter with referring to the CRC and other legislative measures used by the Moroccan Government to improve the rights of children. Such a point of departure indicates that the author can be placed among deliberative human rights scholars as she uses arguments of linguistic rights coming to life through legislative measures. On the other hand, she pinpoints the gap between policy and practice, disclosing a challenging situation in the Moroccan educational space. Human rights are thus judged to be more like aspirations than possible to measure as actually achieved. When Afkir in addition focuses on a matter of what can be seen as social injustice and a condition that needs to be changed, her perspective on human rights are similar to those of protest scholars.

The Role of Inter-School Collaboration in Promoting Inter-Group Relations: The Northern Ireland Perspective

The aim of this chapter by Karen Carlisle and Joanne Hughes is to arrive at an understanding of the factors that enable, enhance and inhibit schools in a deeply divided educational context to work together in a spirit of cooperation to deliver both educational outcomes for pupils and enhance inter-group relations. The chapter considers the policy impetus for curricular collaboration within a system of religiously separate education in Northern Ireland, all of which provides an interesting dimension for exploring inter-school collaboration.

Northern Ireland is a post-conflict and divided society and one approach to enhance inter-group relations in this society is via inter-school collaboration, according to the authors. Joint activities among school staff, cooperation among teachers on school curriculum, and joint school trips are measures discussed as effective in achieving the goal. Building of trust within the school community can also be said to have a spill-over effect into the local community since it facilitates interaction among parents of cultural, social, political, religious and economically diverse backgrounds. As the efforts described in the chapter do not engage in issues on identity, they offer only a limited scope for improving inter-group relations. These issues need to be brought into the open in order to reduce the potential for inter-group tensions, according to the authors.

This chapter does not explicitly engage in a human rights discourse, but the way the topic is presented makes it relevant to theme of this volume. The paper this chapter is based on was presented at the Congress in a session entitled "Pedagogy of/for conflict resolution and understanding" in the thematic group on "Education, Conflict and Transitions within and between Societies". The authors are preoccupied with how contact across differences may promote social cohesion and in particular the role of education in improving inter-group relations. Entering into a debate on how to overcome tensions in a post-conflict society, how to achieve peace and equal opportunities for all, is a characteristic of how protest scholars argue their case for human rights, according to Dembour (2006).

Refugee Education as a Gauge of Liberal Multiculturalism: Iraqi Students in Jordan and the United States

Bruce A. Collet presents an interesting analysis of education for Iraqi refugees in Jordan and the United States, and how multiculturalism as public policies can be used as a facilitator for human rights fulfillment. The multicultural aspect of this chapter is related to refugees, not immigrants or indigenous populations often in focus when discussing this topic. When he additionally links multiculturalism and human rights, Collet's chapter is an original contribution in the discussion of human rights within the field of comparative education.

The analytical framework based on Kymlika's perspectives on multiculturalism is presented as "part of a larger human rights revolution concerning both racial and ethnic diversity" in Collet's chapter. As human rights are presented as values in which there is consensus and the research presented engages with a marginalized population, the text can safely be placed within Dembour's protest school. The rather substantial reliance on human rights instruments in the argument, however, indicates that the author judges human rights as political tools in a society, and, hence, it is possible to see a fluctuation towards the deliberative school.

SOME CONCLUDING THOUGHTS ON THE MAPPING

Through the mapping exercise conducted in this chapter, certain trends in the way we tend to discuss human rights within our field emerges. First of all several of the authors focus on marginalized groups in their work, using the human rights framework as an argument in promoting a more just society. Authors with such a focus can be situated among protest scholars. Another line of argument represented is that of the deliberative school. Human rights are seen as a political tool, particularly among those with a strong focus on the human rights legal framework. Human rights are presented, either implicit or explicit, as a leverage to implement international obligations in education. Some authors are also placed among the natural scholars who take as a point of departure the inherent nature of human rights. The illustration below also illustrates how difficult it is to place our arguments limited to one school only. The schools are not presented as rigid categories by Dembour (2006) and she is aware of the rather porous borders between the schools of thought she has sketched out. It is not in itself an aim to position authors within one school only, but the model serves as a tool to disentangle the underlying presupposition of human rights in our discussions on education.

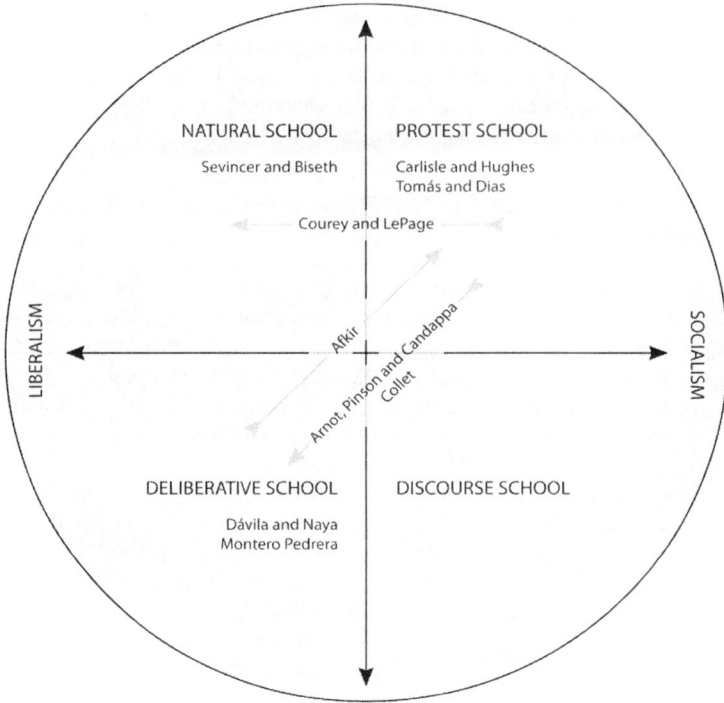

Figure 2. Mapping the Chapters

What also becomes clear when conducting such an analysis is the lack of possible arguments to place within the discourse school of thought. Our engagement in human rights seems to focus on using these rights as leverage to promote our arguments about education, not engaging in a more philosophical debate about human rights and the link between education and human rights. As human rights can be used as an ethical lingua franca as well as standards for conduct, engaging in themes at the same level as discourse scholars can provide fertile ground and a way of nuancing our understanding of human rights. The UN Universal Declaration on Human Rights (UN, 1948) is an exceptionally far sighted moral catalogue (Hamelink, 2000). Since we experience a huge gap between morality and reality, an engagement in the ethical perspectives of human rights can help us on the way to closing this gap. Currently ethical reflections about human rights tend to be blurred and vague in the field of comparative education.

REFERENCES

Beetham, D. (2000). *Democracy and human rights*. Cambridge: Polity Press.

Dembour, M.-B. (2006). *Who believes in human rights? Reflections on the European convention*. New York: Cambridge University Press.

European Commission (2006). *Eurobarometer 66*. Retrieved from http://ec.europa.eu/public_opinion/archives/eb/eb66/eb66_highlights_en.pdf.

Hamelink, C. (2000). Human rights: The next fifty years. In R. Phillipson (Ed.), *Rights to language: Equity, power, and education* (pp. 62-66). Mahwah, NJ: Lawrence Erlbaum Associates.

Holmarsdottir, H. B. (2005). *From policy to practice: A study of the implementation of the Language-in-Education Policy (LiEP) in three South African primary schools*. Doctoral dissertation, University of Oslo. Oslo: Unipub.

Holmarsdottir, H. B. (2011). Mapping the dialectic between global and local educational discourses on gender equality and equity. In J. C. Weidman & W. J. Jacob (Eds.), *Beyond the comparative: Advancing theory and its application to practice* (pp. 193-215). Rotterdam: Sense Publishers.

Paulston, R. G., & Liebmann, M. (1996). Social cartography: A new metaphor/tool for comparative studies. In R. G. Paulston (Ed.), *Social cartography: Mapping ways of seeing social and educational change* (pp. 7-28). New York: Garland Publishing.

Pinson, H., Arnot, M., & Candappa, M. (2010). *Education, asylum and the 'non-citizen' child: The politics of compassion and belonging*. London: Palgrave MacMillan.

Reid, A., Gill, J., & Sears, A. (Eds.). (2009). *Globalisation, the nation-state and the citizen: Dilemmas and directions for civics and citizenship education*. London: Routledge.

Said, E. (2003). *Orientalism*. London: Penguin Books.

Tomaševski, K. (2006). *Human rights obligations in education. The 4-As scheme*. Nijmegen: Wolf Legal Publishers.

UN (1948). UN Universal Declaration of Human Rights. Retrieved from http://www.ohchr.org/en/udhr/pages/introduction.aspx.

UN (1951). Convention relating to the Status of Refugees. Retrieved from http://treaties.un.org/pages/ViewDetailsII.aspx?&src=UNTSONLINE&mtdsg_no=V~2&chapter=5&Temp=mtdsg2&lang=en.

UN (1966). International Covenant on Economic, Social and Cultural Rights. Retrieved from http://www2.ohchr.org/english/law/cescr.htm.

UN (1989). Convention on the Rights of the Child (CRC). Retrieved from http://www.ohchr.org/english/law/crc.htm.

van Dijk, T. A. (2000). Discourse and access. In R. Phillipson (Ed.), *Rights to language: Equity, power, and education* (pp. 73-78). Mahwah, NJ: Lawrence Erlbaum Associates.

AFFILIATIONS

Heidi Biseth
Faculty of Teacher Education
Buskerud University College, Norway

Halla B. Holmarsdottir
Faculty of Education and International Studies
Oslo and Akershus University College, Norway

MADELEINE ARNOT, HALLELI PINSON AND MANO CANDAPPA

2. THE EDUCATIONAL RIGHTS OF ASYLUM-SEEKING AND REFUGEE CHILDREN WITHIN THE NEO-LIBERAL STATE AND INCLUSIVE SCHOOLS IN THE UK

INTRODUCTION

The notion of the child as an active participant in society was enshrined in the United Nations Convention on the Rights of the Child (CRC) (UN, 1989). This concept shaped the 'general principles' of what should constitute the treatment of children and their participation in society, where nation-states as signatories to the CRC are the prime guarantors of children's rights to protection, provision, and participation. The CRC recognised the particular vulnerabilities of asylum-seeking and refugee children, whose circumstances might compromise their rights, and ensures that children's rights are independent of their parents' immigration status or circumstances (Boyden & Hart, 2007). As such, the refugee child carries different contradictions from those of the refugee adult. Within the changing image of asylum, the asylum-seeking and refugee child is positioned within two contradictory discourses: a political-economic discourse which distinguishes between genuine and 'bogus' asylum-seekers and the discursive idea of childhood vulnerability and the commitment of governments to help protect children's rights (Giner, 2007). This distinction is captured by the weak-strong dialectic of the neo-liberal state, where the strong arm of the state is represented by its immigration policy which aims to reduce the numbers of the 'undeserving' from entering the country or from benefiting from its sources once inside, and the weaker arm is represented by its official central government education policy which by and large avoids directly addressing the education of asylum-seeking and refugee children.

Historically, modern education systems were projects of state-formation and the expansion of education is usually associated with the development of a welfare state and the social rights of the citizen. Consequently, the arrival of asylum-seeking and refugee children has major implications for the education system both in terms of funding and resources. Their presence challenges the somewhat delicate balance between diverse and often contradictory educational agendas such as the promotion of an inclusive ethos, cultural diversity, and social justice, at the same time as promoting academic standards and performance in a competitive school environment. To a great extent, the presence of these children and their complex needs puts to the test school ethos and teachers' professional experience and

H. Biseth & H. B. Holmarsdottir (eds.), Human Rights in the Field of Comparative Education, 13–29.
© *2013 Sense Publishers. All rights reserved.*

knowledge. Ultimately educational responses to asylum-seeking and refugee children – the ways in which their needs and rights are perceived, the support offered them, and the way teachers and schools define their responsibility towards them – are integral to the promotion of social justice.

This chapter considers how these tensions affect asylum-seeking and refugee children's rights and what happens when they cross borders into the state and into the education system. Their rights to education are enshrined in the Universal Declaration of Human Rights (UN, 1948), the UN Refugee Convention (1951) and the CRC (UN, 1989). They are additionally granted "appropriate protection and humanitarian assistance in the enjoyment of" their rights as set forth in the CRC and in other international human rights or humanitarian instruments (UN, 1989, Article 22). Below we explore the tension between these universal rights and the forms of immigration control which shapes their education and how this has affected teachers in the UK education system who have needed to respond to such children in their schools. The first section discusses the ways in which the UK government as a strong neo-liberal state now controls asylum-seeking children through immigration policy whilst the second section explores the 'weaker' side of the neo-liberal state leaving it up to local education authorities (LEAs) and schools to deal with such children and their rights. The final section explores some of the ways in which at this level – LEAs and schools – asylum-seeking and refugee children's educational rights are addressed.

THE ASYLUM-SEEKING CHILD AS IMMIGRANT

Our research indicated the extent to which the educational rights of asylum-seeking children in the UK have been substantially influenced by the country's immigration policy. The extensive state activity in the past two decades in the area of asylum and immigration (including seven Acts and two White Papers) has, in effect, co-opted other arms of the state (the educational system being one) into immigration enforcement (Cohen, 2002). As we argued in our book, *Education, Asylum and the 'Non-citizen' Child* (Pinson, Arnot, & Candappa, 2010), changes in immigration policy have far-reaching effects on the work of teachers and the ways in which schools and students engage with the issue of asylum emotionally, morally and politically.

Although there are no official figures on how many asylum-seeking and refugee children there are currently in the UK, there are some indications to be found in official statistics. For example, among the 28,300 applications made in the UK in 2007, apparently some 3,535 were unaccompanied children under 17 and of the 4,870 applications with dependents, 80 per cent were children under 18 (Home Office, 2008). Unfortunately, and indeed significantly, there are no accurate national and local demographic data on the numbers of asylum-seeking and refugee children attending British schools, which in fact attest to the weak educational arm of the state. However, Rutter (2006) estimates that, in 2005, there were at least 60,000 refugee and asylum-seeking children of compulsory school age residing in the UK.

Immigration and asylum legislation in the past decade had the explicit aim of ensuring that control over migration was more effective and that entry was more difficult. With each piece of immigration legislation, the UK government has not only tightened controls over those entering the UK, but added more restrictions to the entitlements of asylum-seekers and their access to different social services – a policy that has directly affected all asylum-seeking and refugee children in the country. Indeed, one of the major trends in the seven pieces of asylum legislation has been that the weight has shifted from controlling the entrance to the soil to monitoring those who gained entrance. The changes in the image of asylum-seekers, their criminalisation and also concerns about the security and social cohesion of British society, have all contributed to a politics of belonging which is not only concerned with who and how many enter the country, but also with their entitlements and integration once inside.

During the 1990s, the strategy adopted by the UK government was to remove those asylum-seekers from the welfare state. By the beginning of the 21st century, asylum-seeking families were to find that access to social and welfare rights (including education), had become much less attainable. Consequently, serious concern was expressed about this aggressive exclusion of asylum-seekers from welfare support and its ramifications for asylum-seeking children and their well-being. Voluntary organisations such as the Refugee Council, Save the Children, UNICEF, and the Children's Society, as well as researchers in the field warned that such restrictions would have far-reaching effects on asylum-seeking children and especially on levels of child poverty in this group. By removing asylum-seeking families from the welfare state, the government has been heavily criticised by children's advocates for adopting a position which treats asylum-seeking children first and foremost as migrants rather than as children (Crawley & Lester, 2005). Significantly, through its actions the UK government made the education needs and the rights of asylum-seeking children irrelevant to their approach to immigration and even integration.

At the same time, such educational rights were curtailed. For example, when the UK government ratified the CRC, it entered the maximum three reservations permitted. Notably, the UK would only apply the Convention insofar as it coincided with immigration and nationality legislation. In practice, this reservation meant that asylum-seeking children did not have to be fully protected (Giner, 2007), and could therefore legitimately suffer discrimination. This exclusion also allowed for the absence of immigration authorities such as the Immigration and Nationality Directorate and the National Asylum Support Service from Section 11 of the Children Act 2004[i] which lists all the authorities responsible for safeguarding of children. In practice this has meant that this duty was not to be fully extended to asylum-seeking and refugee children (Anysley-Green, 2006; Crawley, 2006; Joint Chief Inspectors, 2005). The exclusion of immigration agencies from this section of the legislation also meant that the well-being of asylum-seeking children could be compromised and overridden. This exclusion symbolically supports the precedence which immigration control had over the best interests of the asylum-seeking child. The Children's Minister at the time, in her submission to a House of Commons committee in 2005, made it clear that such safeguarding notions did not or should not apply to asylum-seeking children. This effectively meant that children currently in the UK were to be divided into two tiers, "one tier for children for whom their best interests are the paramount consideration, and another for those whose best interests are a secondary consideration".[ii]

Within this framework the use of three practices of immigration control – dispersal, detention and deportation – became the normalised way of managing asylum-seekers (Bloch & Schuster, 2005). Below we identify some of the important implications for asylum-seeking children's rights.

Dispersal as a Form of Social Exclusion

Dispersal policy was first introduced by the Immigration and Asylum Act 1999. By 2000, asylum-seekers were dispersed across the UK away from London and the south-east of England. The official rationale was that avoiding cluster areas and sharing the economic burden of catering for the needs of asylum-seekers, would render these families and individuals less visible and would therefore contribute to better ethnic relations. However, in practice, the Immigration and Asylum Act 1999 turned dispersal into yet another form of exclusion, taking from asylum-seekers the right to choose where to live and often removing them from social and familial networks. In reality "... asylum seekers have found themselves in areas outside urban centres where they lack support services and that are ethnically homogenous ... where they become targets for abuse and violence" (Bloch & Schuster 2005, p. 507). Consequently, many asylum-seekers decided to opt-out from the dispersal programme, thus losing any rights to state housing or benefits and often living in great poverty (Bloch & Schuster, 2005).

From an educational perspective, dispersal as temporary 'integration' strategy for asylum-seeking students was and is extremely problematic both to schools and the dispersed child. The findings from our study of local education authorities (Arnot & Pinson, 2005) as well as findings of other studies (e.g., Ofsted, 2003) suggest that often insufficient notice of the arrival of asylum-seekers was given to LEAs. Asylum-seekers with families were dispersed to areas where there may not have been any school placement for the children, where the schools may not have had adequate resources and funding to meet their educational needs and where schools may have had very little experience for example of: non-White students; those with English as an Additional Language; or new arrivals who appeared at unusual times in the school year. The school community could be predominantly White, often putting the children at greater risk of being racially bullied. Racial harassment is not just about subtle forms of indifference and instances of 'taking the mick'. As a number of refugee researchers have revealed (e.g., Candappa Ahmad, Balata, Dekhinet, & Gocmen, 2007; Rutter, 2003), such harassment of asylum-seeking and refugee youth can also be violent.

Detention: The Erosion of Human Rights

By the 1990s, detention of asylum-seekers was normalised and used more frequently (Bloch & Schuster, 2005). Unlike the legitimation of dispersal policy, the UK government made little attempt to justify its policy of detaining asylum-seeking children and their families in prison-like centres. The White Paper Secure Borders, Safe Haven (Home Office, 2002) articulated that "detention has a key role to play in the removal of failed asylum-seekers and other immigration offenders" (p. 66). However, de facto, many adult and child asylum-seekers were detained even when their applications were still pending and they had entered the country legally. They were detained for longer periods (often for over two months) and around 10 per cent found themselves in detention for longer than six months (Wolton, 2006).

Between 2001 and 2010 restrictions on the detention of families had been lifted, allowing the government to detain families not just immediately prior to their removal from the country but for longer periods. As a result, families could be detained at any stage and for unlimited time, just like single adults (Bloch & Schuster, 2005; Crawley, 2005). By 2005 the UK had the capacity to detain 2,644 asylum-seekers including 456 family detention spaces.[iii] Detention quite clearly succeeds in excluding asylum-seeking children from mainstream education and their families from society. The then Children's Commissioner for England, Sir Al Anysley-Green critically observed that:

> the detention of families was not reserved for use as a genuine 'last resort' as required by the United Nations Convention on the Rights of the Child (UNCRC) or 'exceptionally' as required by the United Nations Rules for the Protection of Juveniles Deprived of their Liberty (UNJDL). Rather, it appeared to be used as routine procedure where a family did not apply for voluntary departure after the failure of their appeal. (11 Million, 2009, p. 15)

Home Office statistics indicated that 1,065 children were in detention in 2009 (CYPNOW, 2010). However, Crawley and Lester's (2005) estimate suggests a higher figure: that around 2,000 children a year are held in detention centres for purposes of immigration control. These authors found that half the asylum-seeking children were detained for more than 28 days, and that their length of detention varied from seven days to almost nine months.

The Children's Commissioner and Her Majesty's Inspectorate of Prisons (HMIP) as well as children's rights activists were extremely concerned about the conditions in which children are held. In their inspection report, HMIP (2005) used strong language to describe the inadequacy of conditions for children:

> [W]e continue to find that decisions to detain children are made without taking account of their interests, and that there are no independent assessments of the welfare needs of detained children. (p. 7)

Aynsley-Green's review also found major healthcare shortcomings at the detention centres, including, "inadequacy of clinical care; poor care provided to children and adults with mental health needs ..." (11 Million, 2009, p. 6). School inspectors expressed concern about whether the wellbeing of children in detention centres was safeguarded (Ofsted, 2008). It argued that immigration authorities did not take into account the educational needs of detained asylum-seeking and refugee children or their individual special needs in the decision to detain their families. Again these children's educational and other needs were being marginalised by central government immigration policy.

Against this background, in May 2010 the new Coalition Government announced that children would no longer be detained for immigration purposes. However, over a year and a half later this commitment has not yet been realised, and a new family detention centre euphemistically named 'pre-departure accommodation', which could see over 6,000 children a year detained has been opened (NCADC, 2011). Whilst this centre provides various facilities such as indoor and outdoor play areas, a computer zone, extensive gardens and is being run with the support of a children's charity, it continues to be prison-like. The site is surrounded by a 2.5-metre perimeter fence with an extra internal barrier creating a 'buffer' between occupants and the outside world, with occupants under constant supervision by staff from the multinational security company G4S. Commentators widely see it as 'detention re-packaged' (NCADC, 2011) and a continued erosion of children's rights.

Deportation: The Ultimate Exclusion

The third aspect of immigration control focuses on measures which have also evoked immense criticism – deportation. In its implementation it could be seen not just to ignore human rights but also as creating the conditions for greater fear and trepidation on the part of asylum-seeking children. Deportation, the physical exclusion of a person from the territory of the state, is a policy which embodies some of the paradoxes faced by nation-states in the global era. On the one hand, deportation is a mechanism central to the sovereignty of the state and its ability to protect its borders (Gibney & Hansen, 2003). On the other, it can often be seen as breaching both the ethos and the provision of basic human rights. Yet raising the number of successful removals has become one of the main targets of the UK government in recent years. Its rationale emphasises the need for deportation in order to secure national borders: "Swift removal is central to the credibility of our immigration system ..." (Home Office, 2005, p. 30). Paradoxically it is easier to deport those who entered the country legally than those who find it harder to disappear under immigration control's radar – mainly families. Significantly, in the decision to deport families with children, the government's target of successful removal of failed asylum-seekers takes precedence over the educational needs of the asylum-seeking child. The deportation of families and children especially those who are enrolled into the school system has been extensively criticised as disrupting their education. Most of the opposition to deportation comes from children's rights activists, but also from those who are in direct contact with those families – schools, teachers, students and local communities – who are directly affected by the removal of the child. It is to local education responses that we now turn.

Local Educational Responses

According to Section 14 of the Education Act 1996, local authorities have a legal obligation to provide education for all children aged 5-16[iv] and therefore, by implication, legally all asylum-seeking children should have access to education. Also formally, under the Children Acts of 1989 and 2004 (UK Legislation, 1989; 2004), all children are eligible for health-care, education and support from children's services, by virtue of being children. This legislation on the face of it confirms that asylum-seeking and refugee children should be given the same opportunity to benefit from education as any other child in the UK.

However, central government responses we have outlined towards asylum-seeking children have put local government in a particularly difficult position. LEAs have been held responsible for the educational, social, physical and psychological well-being of asylum-seeking youth in their region often without the necessary experience, expertise, guidance or resources. The weak arm of the state – its official education policy in relation to asylum-seeking and refugee children – is reflected in the lack of binding central policy, the decision not to collect data on asylum-seeking and refugee children which renders them invisible, and in line with neo-liberal policy discourses, focuses on achievement as the main indicator for successful integration.

Asylum-seeking and refugee students have rarely been identified by central educational policy frameworks as a distinct category with specific educational needs that attract special support and funding arrangements. Their statistical invisibility within educational policy has serious consequences. Arguably it aids integration and could be connected to genuine concerns about possible stigmatisation, hostility and discrimination against asylum-seekers, but it can also leave those committed to helping asylum-seeking and refugee children without government support and advice. Such invisibility can explain the lack of specific funding arrangements to help schools and community agencies working with refugee communities and young people and cater for their complex needs. In our research, LEAs, especially in dispersal areas reported inadequate funding for the support of asylum-seeking and refugee pupils. Indeed, DfES (the Department for Education and Skills) policy has been to mainstream asylum-seeking students within existing funding policies focusing in particular on minority ethnic students' achievement and the broader social policies associated with supporting vulnerable children.

The guidance given to LEAs and schools by central government emphasises the need to ensure the educational achievement of asylum-seeking and refugee students, and learning is defined as the main path to integration. For example, induction into a welcoming environment is defined as important if such students are to "become effective learners" (DfES, 2002, p. 17). However, in a competitive situation, asylum-seeking and refugee children might be regarded as a potential threat to school standards and records of achievement (McDonald, 1998). Aware of this danger, refugee advocates fought for the right of schools to be given the option of excluding asylum-seeking and refugee students (if they had been less than two years in the country) or any student with English as additional language from the school's examination results. The argument put forward was that without this option asylum-seeking and refugee students might find that they are located in lower achieving schools. The decision not to count such students in school league tables could have a positive effect and even encourage schools to accept and welcome them – on the other hand the implications of the decision to omit asylum-seeking and students from performance results might give the impression that such students are only temporarily in the country and therefore have less status in the school. Their integration may be perceived by schools to be relevant only once they cease being asylum-seeking.

This complex story of asylum-seeking and refugee children's rights to an education has implications for UK schools and teachers. Below we describe how the teachers in three case study schools who had most knowledge of the issue and worked directly with such children saw the rights of these children. Their understanding reveals their difficulty as caring professionals in colluding with current state immigration policy.

TEACHERS' RESPONSES TO ASYLUM-SEEKING AND REFUGEE CHILDREN

In 2006-7, two of us (Arnot and Candappa) conducted a study entitled Schooling, Security and Belonging[v] which explored the nature of asylum-seeking and refugee students' school experiences, and how teachers and 'citizen' students respond to their presence (for more details see Pinson et al., 2010). Using a maximal variation sample so as to access schools in very different social environments, we focused on three secondary schools (all non-denominational and mixed-gender) with contrasting demographics, which were known for their inclusive practice. Fairfield, an ethnically mixed school, had small numbers of asylum-seeking and refugee students; Fordham, a large predominantly White school, without a strong history of anti-racist or multicultural work had small numbers (under 10) of unaccompanied asylum-seeking students; City School by contrast was a typical inner-city multi-ethnic, multi-faith mixed school with a strong history of work on anti-racism and other equality policies, and where around 10 per cent of students came from asylum-seeking and refugee families. As part of the study, we wanted to understand the values and practices that guided their work in supporting asylum-seeking and refugee students and promoting inclusivity.

We focused on four or five key members of teaching or support staff in each school who worked closely with asylum-seeking and refugee students, or had an overview of school policy in relation to them. Individual semi-structured in-depth interviews were conducted with a total of 13 staff, for example, headteachers, citizenship teachers, language support teachers, and pastoral care staff. We cannot generalise findings to all schools or all inclusive schools, or even to all teachers within the case study schools. We were aware that a different image might have emerged had we interviewed other teachers who might be less sympathetic to asylum-seeking students' needs. However, from evidence from our previous studies (Arnot & Pinson, 2005; Candappa & Egharevba, 2000; Candappa et al., 2007) as well as from exchanges on the electronic discussion list *refed* (groups.yahoo.com/group/refed/)[vi] we would argue that the teachers we interviewed are among a core of educationalists committed to social justice for refugees.

Teacher interviews focused on the sorts of values ascribed to in relation to asylum-seeking and refugee students, and whether the school was considered a safe place in which these students could feel they belonged and could prosper academically. The findings we consider here represent a small slice of our data; these we discuss more fully in our book (Pinson et al., 2010).

LEAs, schools and teachers in these three state schools were well aware that they had to cater for asylum-seeking and refugee children who are legally entitled to education. At the same time, they had to face the challenges of countering the effects of a hostile media and government policy that affected asylum-seeking and refugee children's lives. Our research demonstrated, that political distinctions between different categories of migrant children such as the 'deserving' or the 'undeserving' which are anti-educational in their discriminatory ethos and practice, were indeed rejected by schools and teachers. In our case study schools, all children were assumed to be equally entitled to respect and to receive help in reaching their full potential. As Watters (2011) points out, these actions demonstrate how "meso-level actors circumvent and undermine macro-level actors in the immigration sphere" (p. 326). Below we illustrate this point by focusing on the ways in which teachers in our three case-study schools defined the schools' inclusive ethos against the backdrop of exclusionary immigration policy, and how an awareness of the tension between immigration policies and their educational ethos sometimes leads to the politicization of teachers.

At a professional level, teachers were aware that their ethic implied 'equal treatment for all'. As Sheena McGrath (the Inclusion Coordinator at Fordham School) commented:

> they are just children with English as an additional language, or they're asylum-seeking and refugee children, or they're looked after children, or they're abused children, they will come to you with a level of need at any time, and my response is to react to the need that is expressed in the best way I can.

From the perspective of teachers closest to asylum-seeking and refugee students, all children as young citizens were deserving of their commitment, attention and resources. As Jenny Douglas (Headteacher, Fordham) commented:

> we have never, ever questioned a refugee or asylum seeker who's come in. We've never thought 'shall we have this kid or not?' They just come, and we integrate them straightaway.

Similarly City School explicitly distanced itself from the actions of the state, as Maureen Hunter (Assistant Headteacher and Head of Inclusion) explained:

> I don't think we've ever refused somebody admission if we've got a place, simply because they haven't had the right documentation. ... Because to be honest even if it turned out that they were here illegally, in a way that's not our concern ... We would still not refuse because we honestly don't know the circumstances and that's not for us, the school, to judge.

Such a strong open-door stance dovetails with ethical concerns of schools to promote notions of community and social integration:

> I think there is a wider compassion in the school ... I think that it's not about this is a refugee we need to help – it's about this is what we would do for a member of our community ... Which is quite nice, because that's integration, really. (Jane Brush, Assistant Head, Pastoral, Fordham)

Although only a small sample of teachers, those we interviewed were aware of the lack of legal entitlement to support of asylum-seeking and refugee students (such as in the case of minority ethnic children), yet nevertheless they wished to ensure that such students received a just entitlement:

> ... dozens of other children ... have equally desperate needs ... [but] nobody has said to me 'oh, those boys don't deserve that degree of support', ... [statemented children] have a legal entitlement to a certain number of hours' support ... asylum-seeking and refugee children don't have that legal entitlement ... [But] once they're in our school, they have an equal right to fulfil the school's aims which are presumably about each child fulfilling their potential. So if it takes a higher level of support for us to do that, we should, where possible, be offering that. (Sheena McGrath)

Some schools take an overt stand against social exclusion and discrimination. The Head of Fairfield School, Philip Watson, for example, saw the moral/ethic and political stance of the school as linked to equality and justice. Being a global multi-ethnic school, inclusion was a value he brazenly faced parents with at the open evening, saying:

> We are genuine multi-class, multi-cultural comprehensive school. Every child here has equal value, and one way we make that absolutely clear is by opening our doors to refugees and asylum-seekers ... But if you don't want your child to be sitting beside such students in class, befriending them, accepting them, making them welcome, but above all learning from them, then perhaps it is definitely not a good idea to come to [our school].

The more critical teachers used media representations as a means of teaching young people about democracy and civic action in the most active sense: campaigning and taking action politically against injustices for those without protection. For example, teachers in Fairfield used the media to illustrate the 'dehumanisation' of asylum seekers in the UK:

one of the examples I give is how, when you see pictures of all these poor people abroad looking so forlorn and upset and on the run ... everyone feels a lot of pity for them ... But then, as soon as they arrive on British soil, they're suddenly dehumanised people. (Greg Smith, Assistant Head, Fairfield)[vii]

The language of human rights was used particularly in the context of citizenship education and global citizenship courses. Rights discourse is familiar to British youth particularly in schools with strong egalitarian, socially inclusive ethics, or where there is a trained specialist teacher in citizenship education interested in refugee studies. Greg Smith comments:

So students are very conscious of their rights. But they also therefore apply that idea to other people. [...] So they pick up that they have rights, but they also apply that to issues like those seeking refugee status or asylum-seekers ... and they get in a conversation, they would argue that people have rights here, international rights.

This involvement of teachers with the issue of immigration redefines the relationship of teachers to the state. Teachers' involvement in protecting asylum-seeking and refugee youth, encouraging their abilities and helping them settle, positions teachers in opposition to state immigration policy. In contrast with the country's borders, crossing into the school system is something which the schools we visited were clear about – they adopt an ethos of inclusion and integration which is very different than that of central government. Greg Smith continued:

I don't think there's an attitude that, this student's case might come up, you know, in immigration or something, they might be sent back ... That concept, we don't even talk about that. It's not our business to talk about that.

The presence of asylum-seeking and refugee students similarly politicised a Glasgow primary school in Candappa et al.'s (2007) recent study. Despite having policies on anti-racism and bilingualism, the headteacher described becoming aware of what she called 'another layer':

We have now learned about a whole additional layer ... we've all become much more aware of the immigration system, and how that affects our families, and in some cases some of that has been a revelation to us ... particularly the dawn raids and the fact that that's happening with very young children in the midst of it, I find hard to believe that it's happening around me, in the country where I have always lived. (Siobhan Cameron, Glasgow primary headteacher)

Her politicisation came through witnessing children's trauma from their past life and from the UK deportation policy. She was well aware of the importance of schooling children:

... amongst our first group we had a little boy [whose mother had died] ... He had a further trauma, seeing his father marched off in handcuffs in a dawn raid ... So when we do identify children who seem to be quite traumatised, there is help for them ... And he, yes, he grew up to be a very responsible young boy who had ... very strong sense of justice and fair play. (Siobhan Cameron)

An example for the politicization of teachers can also be found in the Declaration on the Deportation of Children and Young People from Schools and Colleges under Immigration Act Powers produced by the Schools against Deportation campaign. Their website (www.ncadc.org.uk) is devoted to what are called 'images of resistance', in effect teachers working in alliance with other educational groups, in action against the state. The Declaration (SAD, 2005) begins:

We, teachers, headteachers, lecturers, teaching assistants, students, young people, trade-unionists, mentors and others working in the education system are concerned about the damaging impact which the threat of deportation or actual deportation can have on children and young people studying in schools and colleges. Deportation affects a child's educational progress, health and well-being. We are also deeply concerned about the detrimental effect on the wider school or college community when personal relationships are disrupted and friends are separated.

Teachers' involvement in anti-deportation brings them into contact with immigration authorities, police, and a range of other professional bodies and individuals. Their action is tipped towards three types of protection: needing to protect the asylum-seeking and refugee child from unfair actions; to protect other pupils from distress and feelings of grief at the loss of their friends; and to protect the reputation of the school's caring ethos. In this case, teachers want to 'rehumanise' their students. Mark Krantz from Manchester, for example, writes about how his pupils confront democracy when they explore the ways in which media and politicians create a culture of rejection and hostility. Similarly, anti-deportation campaigns such as that run by Forest Gate pupils in London created a common legacy that is political, practical and personal. In Rosie Mason's view:

The campaign gave those pupils involved the opportunity to experience the democratic process directly, and its success, real confidence from realising how they could control it. ... The result has been the after-school club which provides a space for pupils from Forest Gate school and beyond – to both enjoy activities ... and to have a safe place of their own to informally discuss issues that there is not time for at school.

As we noted, such action of teachers is significant morally and politically since it unites concerns about child-centred compassionate approaches to all students with egalitarian concerns about peace, equity and fairness. Public pressure, on the UK government to address the welfare of refugee and asylum-seeking youth, particularly from public service professionals and human rights agencies, has grown substantially in recent years challenging inhumane, immoral immigration policies which do not support families. The aim is to offer children fundamental rights, and to encourage a culture of social morality. New political alliances have been formed and new information sources provided to stimulate action (e.g., Children's Rights Alliance for England, refugee education electronic list). Caught up in the government's immigration and asylum policy by default, teachers engage at different levels to fight the deportation of asylum-seeking students and their families. Expert commentators such as refugee education consultant Bill Bolloten suggests that these alliances and campaigns represent a new form of politics which does not fit easily into existing party political frameworks, nor has it been led by professional organisations. What is interesting about actions such as the schools anti-deportation campaigns is that they do not appear to use the conventional language of politics nor to have been generated or supported by the traditional Left.

RIGHTS OF REFUGEE AND ASYLUM-SEEKING STUDENTS WITHIN THE SCHOOL SYSTEM

The promotion of a neo-liberal economy has led the UK government to encourage the idea that only some immigrants can contribute to the economy and could in the future adjust to neo-liberal conditions i.e., by becoming consumer citizens (Bauman, 2004). The 'unwanted' are those who the government now represents as an economic and social burden as well as potentially even a threat to the economic order (bogus asylum-seekers, terrorists, criminals). As a result the concept of asylum has been transmogrified into this economic policy which in effect, has closed the space within which the genuine asylum-seekers who flee persecution can fit. Yuval-Davis (2005, p. 520) warned that a politics of belonging based on economic rather than humanitarian principles would invite 'cherry picking' of refugees based on their alleged work skills and potential of integration rather than their real need of protection. By 2008 she went further suggesting that, in a globalised world, universal rights "tend to be restricted to those who have skills to offer to countries of immigration" (Yuval-Davis, 2008, p. 106). Human rights, it seems, are for those who already have the rights of citizenship within their home country or the state in which they reside. Increasingly there is a denial of the rights of economic and social well-being, health, and protection to 'non-citizens'.

In contrast, within our case study schools, the presence of asylum-seeking and refugee children exposes the commitment of schools and teachers to the social values of inclusion. From the perspective of those teachers who work closely with asylum-seeking and refugee students, all children were deserving of their attention and resources. Their education matters as much as that of other children in their class. As a result, consciously or not, these teachers challenge the hierarchical structure of rights ingrained in state politics of immigration and belonging. Public pressure was put on the UK government from such teachers and other 'caring professions' such as social workers to address the welfare of refugee and asylum-seeking youth. In 2008 the UK government officially declared that it had withdrawn its reservation to the CRC which gave primacy to immigration policy over children's rights. It has now accepted that the Convention applies to asylum-seeking and refugee children, over and above immigration policy. There is a new space in which the more universal model of human rights could override the exclusive authority of the nation-state, and the asylum-seeking child's social rights can be restored. However, the extent to which this change of heart over the CRC by the UK government will affect the boundaries of national citizenship (Bhabha, 2005) is a moot point. The tension between the economic logic and other political, civil and ethical logics such as human rights is likely to remain.

The inclusive local authorities and schools we researched provided evidence that a wide variety of mechanisms to support asylum-seeking and refugee students have been put in place. The strong positive caring discourse used by teachers who were directly involved with asylum-seeking and refugee children revealed the powerful commitment to ensure inclusive education as a principle, irrespective of the child's origins or history. However, such strong child-centred approaches, as Boyden and Berry (2004) in Children and Youth on the Front Line, contend, may support the view that asylum-seeking and refugee children need only to be treated as individuals with human rights and with individual educational needs. This caring ethos, whilst appearing beneficial might fail to recognise (and hence depoliticise) the very real experiences of government, forced migration and settlement, of surviving loss, death, and destitution may not sufficiently emphasise the structural features of migration or children's resilience and agency. Further, an individualising approach with its emphasis on 'vulnerability', if used, does not of itself encourage an active engagement in issues of human rights and social justice.

Even the more 'radical' response in the shape of anti-deportation campaigns might also be problematic in terms of asylum-seeking and refugee children's rights and agency. Such campaigns, Fekete (2009) suggests, are valuable since they reconnect Europeans to their history of combating poverty, authoritarianism and displacement in the Second World War era, "reinvigorating Europe's humanitarian tradition and breathing fresh life into degraded concepts such as solidarity" (p. 187). However, at the same time the Western modernist notions of childhood which in the past shaped the British humanitarian response to refugee children also constructs them as "passive" and their life circumstances as simply "a regrettable modern tragedy" (Myers, 2009, p. 30). This discursive formation might still be patronising to asylum-seeking and refugee children, rendering their 'extraordinary' childhoods as significant not because it was painful for 'them' but because it disturbs 'our' notion of childhood. Consequently, society attempts to 'normalise' their special circumstances with the result that their special circumstances can be ignored (Burman, 1994).

It is not therefore just the case that the government immigration policy carries a huge threat to the safety and well-being of asylum-seeking and refugee children. A caring ethos can also distance the asylum-seeking and refugee child from the circumstances that forced them to flee and, in turn, paradoxically exempts 'us' from the responsibility of considering issues such as community conflicts and displacements. By focusing on individuals, Boyden (2009) warns us that "attention is diverted away from the wider structural conditions that produce and reproduce forced migration ..." (p. 272). In this global context, the role of the educational system (despite being the weaker arm of the state) is now the focal point for those who wish to retain the ancient ethos of asylum, over and against state hostility to the asylum-seeking child. At the same time, the educational system needs to reflect critically on both the nature of its response, the consequences of its pedagogical approach and the requirements that are associated with the concept of human rights, in this case, of a group of children with access to few rights other than education.

NOTES

[i] Section 55 of the Borders, Citizenship and Immigration Act 2009 which introduced a new duty on the UK Borders Agency to safeguard children came into force in November 2009.
[ii] Bill Bolloton, refugee education consultant, personal communication
[iii] These centres include Yarl's Wood in Bedfordshire, Oakington in Cambridgeshire, Dungavel in Lanarkshire and Tinsley House near Gatwick. In 2011 the family unit at Yarl's Wood was closed following scathing criticisms.
[iv] With the exception of those who reside in removal centres in which case education would be provided by the centre
[v] Funded by the Faculty of Education, University of Cambridge, Research Development Fund
[vi] refed is a mailing and discussion list set up to promote discussion of practice issues to support teachers and other professionals who work with refugee and asylum-seeking young people and their families, through the exchange of ideas and resources.
[vii] In Fairfield, other pedagogical means were also called into the task of developing compassion. The GCSE citizenship curriculum module called 'Participating in Society', encourages students to understand other people's realities, to become involved in international and national charities (e.g. Oxfam, UNICEF, Islamic Relief). Other opportunities were Red Nose Day, Refugee Week, and modules such as Is Britain a Fair Society?

REFERENCES

11 Million (2009). *The arrest and detention of children subject to immigration control: A report following the Children's Commissioner for England's visit to Yarl's Wood Immigration Removal Centre*. London: 11 Million.

Arnot, M., & Pinson, H. (2005). *The education of asylum-seeker and refugee children. A study of LEA and school values, policies and practices*. Cambridge: Faculty of Education, University of Cambridge.

Aynsley-Green, A. (2006). Memorandum from the Office of the Children's Commissioner to the Joint Committee on Human Rights on the Treatment of Asylum-seekers. Retrieved from www.childrenscommissioner.org/adult/news/news.cfm?id=1964&newsid=51

Bauman, Z. (2004). *Wasted lives: Modernity and its outcasts*. Cambridge: Polity Press

Bhabha, J. (2005). Rights spillovers: The impact of migration on the legal system of Western states. In E. Guild & J. Van Selm (Eds.), *International migration and security: Opportunities and challenges* (pp. 28-50). New York: Routledge.

Bloch, A., & Schuster, L. (2005). At the extremes of exclusion: Deportation, detention and dispersal. *Ethnic and Racial Studies, 28*(3), 491-512.

Boyden, J. (2009). What place the politics of compassion in education surrounding non-citizen children? *Educational Review, 61*(3), 265-276.

Boyden, J., & Berry, J. (2004). *Children and youth on the front line: Ethnography, armed conflict and displacement*. Oxford: Berghahn Books.

Boyden, J., & Hart, J. (2007). The statelessness of the world's children. *Children & Society, 21*(4), 237-248.

Burman, E. (1994). Innocents abroad: Western fantasies of childhood and the iconography of emergencies. *Disasters, 18*(3), 238-253.

Candappa, M., & Egharevba, I. (2000). Extraordinary childhoods: The social lives of refugee children. *Children 5–16 Research Briefing*, Number 5, Swindon: ESRC.

Candappa, M., Ahmad, M., Balata, B., Dekhinet, R., & Gocmen, D. (2007). *Education and schooling for asylum-seeking and refugee students in Scotland: An exploratory study.* Edinburgh: Scottish Government.

Cohen, S. (2002). The local state of immigration controls. *Critical Social Policy, 22*(3), 518-543.

Crawley, H. (2005). *Developing DFiD's policy approach to refugees and internally displaced persons.* Thematic Paper II: The UK, the EU and Forced Migration. Oxford: Refugee Studies Centre.

Crawley, H. (2006). *Child first, migrant second: Ensuring that every child matters.* ILPA Policy Paper. London: ILPA.

Crawley, H., & Lester, T. (2005). *No place for a child. Children in UK immigration detention: Impacts, alternatives and safeguards.* London: Save the Children.

CYPNOW (2010). Detention pledge met with caution. *Children & Young People Now*, 25 May 2010, Retrieved from http://www.cypnow.co.uk/news/ByDiscipline/Social-Care/1005290/News-Insight-Joint-working-Detention-pledge-met-caution/.

DfES (2002). *Educating asylum-seeking and refugee children: Guidance on the education of asylum-seeking and refugee children.* London: DfES Publications.

Fekete, L. (2009). *A suitable enemy: Racism, migration and Islamophobia in Europe.* NYC: Pluto Press.

Gibney, M., & Hansen, R. (2003). *Deportation and the liberal state: The forcible return of asylum seekers and unlawful migrants in Canada, Germany and the United Kingdom.* Geneva: UNHCR.

Giner, C. (2007). The politics of childhood and asylum in the UK. *Children & Society, 21*(4), 249-260.

HMIP (2005). *Report of an announced inspection of Yarl's Wood Immigration Removal Centre.* 28th February-4th March 2005, London: HMIP.

Home Office (2002). *Secure borders, safe haven: Integration with diversity in modern Britain.* London: The Stationery Office.

Home Office (2005). *Controlling our borders: Making migration work for Britain.* Press Release Search, ON-line Report. Retrieved from http://press.homeoffice.gov.uk/press-releases/Controlling_Our_Borders_Making_.

Home Office (2008). *Managing our borders.* London: The Stationery Office.

Joint Chief Inspectors, The (2005). *Safeguarding children: The second Joint Chief Inspectors' Report on arrangement to safeguard children.* Retrieved from www.hmica.gov.uk/files/safeguards_imagefree.pdf.

Kirp, D. L. (1980). *Doing good by doing little.* Berkeley: University of California Press.

McDonald, J. (1998). Refugee students' experiences of the UK education system. In C. Jones & J. Rutter (Eds.), *Refugee education: Mapping the field* (pp. 149-170). Stoke-on-Trent: Stylus Publishing.

Myers, K. (2009). The ambiguities of aid and agency: Representing refugee children in England 1937–38. *Cultural and Social History, 6*(1), 29-46.

NCADC (2011). *Barnado's to help run new family detention centre.* NCADC News, National Coalition of Anti-Deportation Campaigns, 10.3.2011.

Ofsted. *Inspecting schools: Framework for inspecting schools.* London: Ofsted Publications Centre.

Ofsted (2008). *Safeguarding children.* London: Ofsted Publications Centre.

Pinson, H., Arnot, M., & Candappa, M. (2010). *Education, asylum and the 'non-citizen' child: The politics of compassion and belonging.* London: Palgrave MacMillan.

Rutter, J. (2006). *Refugee children in the UK.* Buckingham: Open University Press.

Rutter, J. (2003). *Supporting refugee children in 21st century Britain.* Stoke on Trent: Trentham Books.

Sales, R. (2002). The deserving and the underserving? Refugees, asylum seekers and welfare in Britain. *Critical Social Policy, 22*(3), 456-478.

Schools against Deportations – SAD (2005). *Declaration on the deportation of children and young people from schools and colleges under immigration act powers.* Retrieved from www.irr.org.uk/sad/schools_petition.pdf, or www.schoolsagainstdeportations.org.

UK Legislation (2004). *The Children Act 2004* (2004 Chapter 31).

UK Legislation (1989). *The Children Act 1989* (1989 Chapter 41).

UN (1989). *Convention on the Rights of the Child (CRC).* Retrieved from http://www.ohchr.org/english/law/crc.htm.

UNDHR (1948). *UN Universal Declaration of Human Rights.* Retrieved from http://www.ohchr.org/en/udhr/pages/introduction.aspx.

UN Refugee Convention (1951/1967). The 1951 UN Convention relating to the Status of Refugees and the 1967 Protocol, available at http://www.unhcr.org/.

Watters, C. (2011). Education, migration and the 'failure' of multiculturalism. *British Journal of Sociology of Education, 32*(2), 319-327.

Weiner, M. (1995). *The global migration crisis.* New York: Longman.

Wolton, S. (2006). Immigration policy and the crisis of British values. *Citizenship Studies, 10*(4), 453-467.

Yuval-Davis, N. (2008). Racism, cosmopolitanism and contemporary politics of belonging. In S. Davison & J. Rutherford (Eds), *Soundings on race, identity and belonging: A soundings collection* (pp. 101-113). London: Lawrence and Wishart.

Yuval-Davis, N., Anthias, F., & Kofman, E. (2005). Secure borders and safe haven and the gendered politics of belonging: Beyond social cohesion. *Ethnic and Racial Studies, 28*(3), 513-535.

AFFILIATIONS

Madeleine Arnot
Faculty of Education
University of Cambridge, UK

Halleli Pinson
Department of Education
Ben-Gurion University of the Negev, Israel

Mano Candappa
Institute of Education
University of London, UK

PAULÍ DÁVILA AND LUIS Mª NAYA

3. THE PROTECTION OF CHILDREN'S RIGHTS IN LATIN AMERICA

Perpectives on the Right to Education[i]

In recent decades, the defence of children's human rights has had an important evolution in Latin America, above all since the ratification of the Convention on the Rights of the Child (CRC) (UN, 1989). Most countries in the region found a way of implementing child and education rights through some genuine documents such as the Code of Children. Since 2000, most of these Codes have been reformed. In this paper we have carried out an analysis of these Codes. We have focused on how several Latin American countries have implemented the right to education during the last decade. The aim of this chapter is to analyze the implementation process of the CRC in Latin America from the Right to Education standpoint, taking the Code of Children as a documentary corpus. To do this, we used Katarina Tomaševski's (2005, 2006) categories of analysis (Availability, Accessibility, Acceptability, and Adaptability). At the legal level, these categories allow us to verify the compliance of indicators with the right to education.

THE CRC AND THE COMMITTEE ON THE RIGHTS OF THE CHILD

The concern for the protection of children in Latin America has been an evident phenomenon throughout the twentieth century (Romero, 2007). The ratification of the Convention on the Rights of the Child (CRC) in 1989 gave a new impetus by recognizing children's rights. It became a legislative framework of basic reference. As it is known, the CRC is an international treaty with 54 articles that describes human rights of all children less than 18 years of age. The treaty requires the implementation of these articles in light of its guiding principles and, as a legal instrument it gives expression to the rights of children. The CRC supports a unique combination of virtues: stresses and defends the role of family in children's lives, i.e., the obligation of States and the responsibility of parents in providing care to their children; promotes respect for children; supports the principle of non-discrimination; and, finally, establishes clear obligations on the part of States (UN, 1989). The recognition of the CRC is almost universal.

The Committee on the Rights of the Child, based in Geneva, has little real power since States are not bound by its recommendations. The Committee comprises 18 members with expertise in child rights. Two years after accession into the Committee, all States must submit an initial report. Subsequently, they

H. Biseth & H. B. Holmarsdottir (eds.), Human Rights in the Field of Comparative Education, 31–46.
© *2013 Sense Publishers. All rights reserved.*

must submit periodic reports every five years. The Committee's work is complex because it must examine the reports of States on the development of the Rights of the Child, as well as those relating to the Optional Protocols and the alternative reports of the various NGOs. Then, the committee must make a series of general comments on the issues raised in the public session. Its meetings are held in Geneva, three times a year. Besides the aforementioned work, the committee members conduct internal technical meetings prior to each public session that often result in the publication of the "General Comments" on the application of certain articles of the CRC.

All Latin American countries signed the CRC in a very short time. Most signed in the first two months after its approval, while others reaffirmed their accession throughout 1990. Also, most Latin American countries submitted their mandatory reports within the deadline period. However, some countries have strikingly delayed their submission; for instance, Brazil submitted its first report with more than a ten year delay. In other cases, for example, Cuba, Guatemala, Ecuador, Panama, Dominican Republic, and Venezuela the delay was shorter. Thus, from 1992 to 2010, a significant corpus of documents that collects substantial information on the situation of children in Latin America has been generated. The information comes from three sources: (1) the reports of States, (2) the reports of NGOs working with children and working in the region, and (3) the concluding observations of the Committee on the Rights of the Child. The most substantial of these three sources is that of the Committee, since it synthesizes information from the other two and also offers a list of observations and recommendations for each country. Our research is focused on the analysis of the Right to Education included in the Codes of Children.

Balance of the Convention on the Rights of the Child: Advances and Problems

The Latin American and Caribbean Network for the Defence of the Rights of Children and Adolescents has made a balance of the treaty in the region in the last twenty years. It provides three levels of analysis: (1) advances related to the CRC, (2) setbacks affecting the rights of children, and (3) major problems related to compliance with the rights of children (REDLAMYC, 2009). Advances operate in the field of legislative reforms and the rhetoric that has accompanied the discourse on the rights of children in recent years, i.e., construction of new conceptual or legislative changes, elaboration of reports, incorporation of child rights into the Inter-American Human Rights System, etc. Setbacks, though scarce, have relevance because they affect the difficulty of carrying out the plans promoted by the countries. In practice, these reforms do not conform to the approach of children's rights, or to the criminalization of juvenile justice systems. Instead, problems related to the implementation of these advances are the main issue: the persistence of inequality, discrimination, violence against children, migration, lack of coordination among institutions for children, lack of official data, inadequate resources, acceptance of the CRC language, low level of implementation of the Committee's comments, and the poor diffusion of the reports of the Committee.

In Latin America there is a widespread belief that the legal texts alone have the power to change the situation of child rights (Barrios, 2006). In the end, this ambiguity is solved with a rhetoric that rarely has to do with practices and public policies, as can be appreciated in the Codes. In this sense, the final reflections from this study made by REDLAMYC are conclusive: we must move from words to action, strengthening capacity for mobilization of social movements from different Latin American childhoods. We must collectively construct a new agenda in which the monitoring systems and the public investment are based on compliance with the CRC.

Observations and Recommendations of the Committee of the Rights of the Child

As noted above, another possible way to understand the situation of the rights of children and adolescents is to examine the final reports of the Committee on the Rights of the Child, which take into consideration the reports submitted by States (Committee on the Rights of the Child, 2006). In this regard, we reviewed the Committee's recommendations and observations between 2000 and 2010. The result can be summarized in the existence of five areas of concern: (1) lack of harmonization between national legislation and the CRC, (2) concern about the uncertainty of the general principles of the CRC, (3) persistence of poor treatment, abuse, and corporal punishment, (4) abuse of detention in juvenile justice system, and (5) lack of information on CRC and lack of professional training. The interest of referring to these observations and recommendations made by the Committee is that they have been taken into account in order to write or modify the Codes of Children between 2000 and 2010.

Thus, regarding the first area of concern, it is surprising that all the countries analyzed by the Committee in the last decade received comments related to the compliance with Codes or integral laws for children. These observations refer to the slow pace of implementation of institutions such as child advocates (Argentina and Bolivia), the lack of coordination among agencies concerned with children (Costa Rica, Ecuador, El Salvador, and Uruguay) or some laws relating to children that do not conform to the CRC (Brazil, Colombia, Ecuador, El Salvador, Honduras, Mexico, and Uruguay).

With regard to the second area, and concerning the general principles (according to the CRC these principles are: non-discrimination, best interests of the child, participation, and survival), the Committee notes that countries such as Bolivia, Brazil, Colombia, Nicaragua, Paraguay, Peru, and Uruguay are not particularly sensitive to the best interests of the child, and demands a better definition and involvement of professionals. Similarly, in Costa Rica, the principle of non-discrimination does not apply to indigenous children. The Committee, when making these observations, is especially cautious about using the following topical phrase: "though the Committee welcomes the advances [...] recommends [...]." As the Committee has no sanctioning function, the language that is used is politically correct. In relation to the third area (maltreatment, abuse, and corporal punishment, both at school and family environment), the Committee refers to the cases of

Bolivia, Brazil, Costa Rica, Ecuador, Honduras, Uruguay, and Venezuela. And it repeatedly refers to the cases of Bolivia and Honduras. Despite the difference of five years between one report and another, this situation indicates that there seems to be no improvements in these two countries. Regardless of the prohibition in most Codes, it appears that its implementation is ineffective.

Juvenile justice is the fourth area of concern, especially since the socio-educational measures are not enforced with the required rigor. Instead, they opt for detention or imprisonment, as is the case of Bolivia, Ecuador, Nicaragua, and Peru. Finally, the Committee, for the fifth area emphasizes that campaigns to disseminate the Codes and the CRC must be carried out, and professionals in the field of childhood must be trained (Brazil, Ecuador, Honduras, and Uruguay).

In view of this balance made by REDLAMYC, the consequences of the CRC within the legislative framework and the degree of compliance by Latin American countries with it are obvious. However, one of the most genuine forms of implementing the CRC in the region has been the development of the so-called "Codes of Children", which come into existence in the first third of the twentieth century, and are viewed as a miniature CRC.

THE CODES OF CHILDREN IN LATIN AMERICA

Overall, when the majority of the States implement the CRC in their own national policies, they tend to do it through a scattered legislation. In Latin America, however, the situation is quite different as all the countries have chosen a common legislation of the rights of children, allowing for a holistic analysis of them. In this sense, the methodological analysis of the Codes has been done taking into account the underlying categories of the definitions that the CRC has highlighted for each right (Davila & Naya, 2007a).

Following tradition, during the last twenty years, the countries of the region have developed Codes of Children, according to the framework outlined by the CRC. The implementation of this international treaty is best seen through these Codes. Therefore, Codes accounted for the recognition of the responsibilities of the state, society, and family in public policies to meet the needs and rights of children.

In the 90's, the implementation of the CRC in this process meant a "rupture" with the past. It was a new conception aimed at defending the rights of children in a context of democratic renewal. Thus, the CRC "hit Latin America in a time when an important discussion on the scope and potential of the new democracies of Latin America was taking place" (Beloff, 2008, p. 10, our translation). This has been a renewal of the protection of child rights from the perspective of human rights. It was also a process of modernization, which had already been produced in some countries of the area regarding juvenile criminal justice. Beloff asserts that in the late 90's there was a turn caused by two events: (1) two courses, one organized by UNICEF on children's issues and the other one on human rights organized by the Inter-American Institute of Human Rights in Costa Rica, widely recognized in the region, and (2) the decision of the Inter-American Court of Human Rights on the case of the Street Children (Villagrán-Morales and others) vs. Guatemala, in which the Court, pursuant to Article 19 of the American Convention on Human Rights, interpreted the State's obligations regarding the protection of the right to life and dignity. The ruling of the Court[ii] held that the State of Guatemala was responsible for the deaths of five street children at the hands of the police; the State violated the right to life and took no special measures of protection by compensating the families of victims. The court forced the State to investigate the events.

Most existing Codes were enacted from the year 1999 onwards, when the Inter-American system gained a certain prestige and was a reference for the countries in the region. The existence of a Rapporteurship on the Rights of the Child depending on the Inter-American Commission on Human Rights is a sign of the interest in the region. Only Brazil, Honduras, and Panama have Codes prior to 1998. All other countries enacted them at a later date or reformulated Codes that were previously in force. Cuba and Chile are special cases. Their Codes are prior to the CRC, which illustrates that legal protection was present and included in national legislation

Table 1. Codes of Children in Latin America and year of adoption

Year	Country	Code
1978	Cuba	Code for Children and Youth
1979	Chile	Organic Law of Creation of National Youth Service
1990	Brazil	Statute of the Child and Adolescent
1995	Panama	Family Code
1996	Honduras	Code of Childhood and Adolescence
1998	Nicaragua	Code of Childhood and Adolescence
1998	Costa Rica	Code of Childhood and Adolescence
1999	Bolivia	Code of Children and Adolescents
2000	Mexico	Law for the Protection of the Rights of Children and Adolescents
2000	Peru	Code of Children and Adolescents
2000	Venezuela	Organic Law for the Protection of the Child and Adolescent
2001	Paraguay	Code of Childhood and Adolescence
2003	Guatemala	Law on Protection of Children and Adolescents
2003	Dominican Republic	Code for the System of Protection of the Rights which sets the text of its Organic Law
2004	Uruguay	Code of Childhood and Adolescence
2005	Argentina*	Law on Integral Protection of the Rights of Children and Adolescents. In 1997, the Law on Protection of Children, Adolescents, and Families was adopted.
2006	Colombia*	Code of Childhood and Adolescence. In 1990, the Juvenile Code was adopted.
2009	El Salvador*	Law on Integral Protection of Children and Adolescents (it was enacted in 2010). In 1993, the Law of the Salvadoran Institute for the Integral Development of Children and Adolescents was adopted.

Source: Instituto Colombiano de Bienestar Familiar (2009).
(*) Countries that have renewed their Codes.

prior to the CRC. The case of Panama is also special because its Code is a Family Code.

In most of the Codes that were enacted in the last decade, there is a greater involvement of the State regarding its obligations. It guarantees fundamental rights, and adapts them to international treaties of the inter-American system and of the international one. From 1999 on, "in Latin America nobody queries the fact that the protection of childhood must be considered from an approach focused on citizenship and the protection of the human rights of children" (Beloff, 2008, p. 10, our translation). In this sense, there are some decisions of the Inter-American Court of Human Rights wherein the inter-American system for the protection of children's human rights is strengthened.

Given that all countries of the region adopted the CRC, the Codes of Children have become the best way to express the national commitment to the CRC. Thus, we might almost say that they are the manifestation of the CRC in each country. They are a point of reference for public administration and legislators. This is why it is important to analyze these laws, since they allow us to see the degree of their implementation in national legislation.

It should also be noted that most of the Codes, apart from comprising the civil and protection rights, emphasizes two issues: (1) the inclusion of Family Codes, and (2) the processes relating to juvenile justice, formerly known as the Juvenile Codes. Thus, there are some laws that incorporate children's rights, family rights and their obligations, and due process relating to the child in conflict with the law. In this sense, most of the Codes, in their early versions, indicate that the aim is the integral protection of all children and adolescents. Hence, we refer to the Codes as a compendium of rights guided by a comprehensive policy for children that, at least in terms of the legality of each country, has a high recognition, which in most cases is due to the constitutional recognition of children's rights (SITEAL, 2009a).

THE GENERAL PRINCIPLES OF THE CRC AND THE CODES OF CHILDREN

Now that we have identified the basic elements of the CRC and the Codes of Children in Latin America, this section is intended to analyze the congruence between the CRC and the Codes. The aim is to confirm the level of implementation of the CRC through the Codes. The CRC is, as the Committee on the Rights of the Child has pointed out, stretched by some general principles which also affect to education (Committee on the Rights of the Child, 2003). These principles are: non-discrimination, best interests of the child, participation, and survival.

The Codes of Children, when elaborated, took into account the CRC's content, i.e., its general principles and the rest of the articles relating to the respective rights. In this sense, it is instructive that many Codes make specific reference to the CRC, indicating compliance with it and considering it as a framework for the development of the Codes itself.

As regards the general principles, most Codes explicitly refer to the first principle (non-discrimination and equal opportunities), and collect a variety of situations in which it might be applied (gender, ethnicity, disability, etc.). The

Codes of Argentina and Costa Rica make an explicit mention to non-discrimination in education because of gender, age, race or ethnic origin, socioeconomic reason or any other reason that violates the human dignity. With regard to the best interests of the child, there are three different views present in Latin America. The first group of countries (Argentina, Brazil, Ecuador, El Salvador, Mexico, Nicaragua, Panama, Peru, Dominican Republic, Uruguay, and Venezuela), restricts the interpretation of this general principle. In the case of Argentina, the term "best interest" is replaced by "maximum satisfaction" which can lead to an erroneous interpretation as the term "maximum satisfaction" is very ambiguous from a legal point of view. In the second group of countries, (Colombia and Costa Rica), the interpretation is broader and more detailed. In the case of Colombia, it is stated that if there is a conflict of interest the most favourable rule for boys, girls and adolescents will be carried out. According to Costa Rica, it is guaranteed that in every public action this principle will be taken into account. Finally, in the third group of countries (Paraguay and Guatemala), the principle of the best interest of the child is merged with non-discrimination. In both countries it is stated that in carrying out this principle, account will be taken with respect towards family ties, education and ethnic, religious, cultural and linguistic origins. Participation is an essential principle for the education of citizens, but has not been taken into account, since it is not mentioned in the Codes of Bolivia, Brazil, Costa Rica, Guatemala, Honduras, Mexico, Panama, Peru, and Uruguay. Among the Codes that do mention participation, two interpretations should be distinguished. On the one hand, there are those who include the right to be heard (Argentina, El Salvador, Nicaragua, Dominican Republic, and Venezuela) and, on the other hand, there are those who indicate effective participation in various areas (Colombia, Ecuador, El Salvador, Dominican Republic, and Venezuela). As it can be seen, the latter three countries make reference to both areas. They state that participation should occur at all levels: community, family, school, court, etc. Thus, these countries combine their Codes much better in the spirit of the CRC than other Latin American countries. Finally, as regards the general principle of survival, all the Codes make reference to it, but differentiated it into two aspects: firstly, the right to health and, secondly, the right to life. The nuances with which these rights are developed are very broad. Issues such as nutrition, pregnant teenagers, health care, and the characteristics of a dignified life, which, in many cases, is associated with a healthy environment, must be taken into account. In contrast to this discourse, we can see that the situation in the countries of the area is very uneven For example, a child born in Bolivia has 4.8 times more likely to die in his/her first year of life than one born in Costa Rica. Though in Chile and Cuba the rates are considerably lower (SITEAL, 2009b). This right is important for education as the school is the only space where children have access to feeding, health-care, vaccination, or sex education in order to avoid early pregnancy.

The Right to Education in the Codes of Children in Latin America

In this section we will take a more comprehensive look at the right to education in the Codes of Children. In most Latin American countries the right to education is part of their own constitutions (Georgetown University Political Database of the Americas, 2006) and, therefore, what is reflected in the Codes should be complemented with national education laws. There are several well-known organizations and institutions in the region (UNESCO, UNICEF, Latin American Campaign for the Right to Education; Organization of Iberoamerican Countries for Education, Science and Culture) which work in the field of the Right to Education and its enforceability. In this sense, the written reports highlight the existing distance between the educational reality and the legal recognition of the Right to Education (Campaña Latinoamericana por el Derecho a la Educación, 2010; REDLAMYC, 2009; SITEAL, 2009a, 2009b).

Our approach to the analysis of the right to education in the Codes is based on Articles 28 (right to education) and 29 (aims of education) of the CRC, and our analytical view is based on Katarina Tomaševski's 4-As (i.e., Availability, Accessibility, Acceptability, and Adaptability) (Tomaševski, 2005, 2006). They allow us to analyze the various indicators that form these rights (Davila & Naya, 2007a, 2007b). This framework allows us to understand what affects the governments' obligations towards parents (Availability); towards the several social and personal situations of children (Accessibility); towards educative goals which take into account the Human Rights (Acceptability) and respond to the existing diversity in our classrooms (Adaptability). We think that this framework combines the Right to Education with all the Rights of Children in the educational environment. For this reason, we insist on the educative reading of the Right of the Child. However, it is necessary to distinguish between the Right to Education, in the terms that has usually been defined in the international legal documents which have been agreed upon; and the rights in education, which mean a complementary approach where Human Rights and the suitability to each individual of education are privileged. Some of the latest proofs of the validity of this interpretative framework are gathered in the work of the United Nations Rapporteur for the Right to Education, Vernor Muñoz, who focused his analysis of the Right to Education on girls in particular (Muñoz, 2006, 2011).

The Right to Education

In Table 2 we can observe several indicators which define the 28th article of the CRC: access to free and compulsory Primary Education, access to Secondary and Professional Education, and access to Higher Education.

All countries recognize the right to education in their Codes with regard to compulsory and free primary education. However, "certain elements of flexibility present in their respective constitutions, and the lack of coherent public policies in this area, have opened the door to be ignored in practice" (Barrios, 2006, p. 201).

Countries such as Paraguay and Uruguay do not mention this right in their Codes, although, in fact, it is recognized in their education systems.

Table 2. Access to education (Article 28 of the CRC)

	Free and compulsory primary education	*Secondary Education /Professional*	*Higher Education*
Argentina	Yes	No	No
Bolivia	Yes	Progressive development	Yes
Brazil	Yes	Progressive development	No
Colombia	Yes	No	No
Costa Rica	Yes	Yes	No
Ecuador	No	Yes (Free Secondary Education)	No
El Salvador	Yes	Free Secondary Education and Special Education	No
Guatemala	Yes	Compulsory and free up to high school	No
Honduras	Yes (Secular)	Progressive	No
Paraguay	No	No	No
Peru	Yes	No	No
Dominican Republic	Yes	Yes	No
Uruguay	No	No	No
Venezuela	Yes	No	No

Yes: this category is mentioned in the Code
No: the Code does not mention this category

Secondary and professional education has no relevant role in the Codes. In some cases, there exists progressive development at these levels, as in Bolivia, Brazil, and Honduras. Other countries such as Ecuador, El Salvador, Guatemala, Nicaragua, and Dominican Republic, clearly specify that access to these studies is warranted. Also, most countries include in their Codes the need for guidance in educational and professional issues, but countries like Argentina, Costa Rica, El Salvador, Ecuador, Guatemala, Panama, Paraguay, and Uruguay fail to do so. Finally, the Codes of Bolivia and Nicaragua only say that higher education is accessible on the basis of the ability of students.

On the other hand, although the reality of education in these countries reports high levels of truancy (Itzcovich, 2009), the truth is that only Bolivia, Costa Rica, El Salvador, Nicaragua, and Dominican Republic mention the need to take specific measures for students to stay at school. The Code of Nicaragua is one of the clearest examples of the presence of this indicator. Article 47 states that the State shall take measures to encourage regular school attendance, lower repetition and dropout rates, and to ensure educational methods that leave no student excluded from compulsory primary and secondary schools.

Finally, most countries, except Argentina, Guatemala, and Panama, include in their Codes issues related to school discipline, which, according to the CRC, must be consistent "with the child's human dignity". In this regard, the Codes indicate more or less accurately the sense of disciplinary measures and prohibit the "physical and psychological abuse and any form of cruel and degrading punishment", such as, for example, the Code of El Salvador states. However, the reality of education in this country contrasts with their good intentions, as evidenced by the recommendations of the Committee on the Rights of the Child made to States. For example, the Committee advised Guatemala to urgently develop a campaign to combat child abuse in schools, since this country does not include school discipline in its Code (Hodgkin & Newell, 2007).

Table 3. Elements of the right to education (Article 28 of the CRC)

	Educational Guidance	*Absenteeism*	*School Discipline*
Argentina	No	No	No
Bolivia	Yes	Yes	Yes
Brazil	Yes	No	Yes
Colombia	Yes	No	Yes
Costa Rica	No	Yes	Yes
Ecuador	Yes	No	Yes
El Salvador	No	Yes	Yes
Guatemala	No	No	No
Honduras	Yes	No	Yes
Paraguay	No	No	Yes
Peru	No	No	Yes
Dominican Republic	Yes	Yes	Yes
Uruguay	No	No	No
Venezuela	Yes	No	Yes

From the aforementioned analytic perspective, it is clear that the Codes highlight aspects related to the first two of Tomaševski's 4-A's, i.e., Availability and Accessibility. This confirms the recognition of the right to education in this type of legislation. However, as we will discuss in the analysis of Article 29, the "private school" also appears as an indicator. Something similar happens with the indicator of "school discipline", which corresponds more to an educational purpose than to the right to education.

The Aims of Education

The aims of education (Article 29 of the CRC) refer to the development of the child's personality, talents and mental and physical abilities to their fullest potential. It also aims to inculcate in children respect for human rights, their parents, their cultural identity, their national values, and the pursuing of a free society. Finally, it includes respect for the environment. In addition, this same article, in line with Article 28, does not restrict the freedom of individuals to establish and direct educational institutions, as some Codes do.

Table 4. Elements of the aims of education (Article 29 of the CRC)

	Development of the child's personality	Respect for Human Rights	Respect for Parents and Others	Values Education	Environment	Private School
Argentina	No	Yes	No	Yes	Yes	No
Bolivia	No	Yes	No	No	No	No
Brazil	No	Yes	No	Yes	No	No
Colombia	Yes	Yes	No	Yes	Yes	Yes
Costa Rica	Yes	Yes (Rights of the Child)	Yes	Yes	Yes	No
Ecuador	Yes	Yes (Rights of the Child)	Yes	Yes	Yes	Yes
El Salvador	Yes	Yes	Yes	Yes	Yes	Yes
Guatemala	Yes	Yes	No	No	No	Yes
Honduras	Yes	Yes (Rights of the Child)	Yes (Identity)	Yes	No	No
Paraguay	Yes	Yes	No	No	No	No
Peru	Yes	Yes (Rights of the Child)	Yes	Yes	Yes	No
Dominican Republic	Yes	Yes	Yes	No	No	Yes
Uruguay	No	No	No	No	No	No
Venezuela	No	No	Yes (Identity)	Yes	No	No

Yes: this category is mentioned in the Code
No: the Code does not mention this category

The Committee on the Rights of the Child has been particularly concerned about this article, and, in 2001, it made a general comment indicating the interpretation to be given to it (Committee on the Rights of the Child, 2001). This article is interpreted broadly, since it refers to specific aspects of child development, aspects of curriculum, and the fact that education must respect human rights. Most countries mention these aims and highlight citizenship education. With regard to the development of the child's personality, all Codes, except those of Argentina,

Bolivia, Brazil, Panama, Uruguay, and Venezuela, claim that education should aim at "personality development", depending on the age and characteristics of children. Respect for human rights and fundamental freedoms also have a recognized role. All countries except Brazil, Panama, Uruguay, and Venezuela, refer to it. In addition, Costa Rica, Ecuador, Honduras, Nicaragua, Paraguay, and Peru consider it necessary to include the rights of the child. In this sense, the programmes including human rights education into the school curriculum has become compulsory in the region, as evidenced by studies on Human Rights Education (Gutierrez, 2006; Magendzo, 2010). Respect for parents, respect for cultural identity, respect for language are contained in most Codes. Respect of "national values" is also part of this set of rights. To further strengthen this indicator, many countries include these values as a duty. Thus, most Codes include a chapter on the duties of children, an issue that is not in the CRC. Expressions such as "to honour the country and its symbols", "respecting parents", "meeting the educational requirements" are duties included in most Codes. This fact turns rights into obligations, for example, when including rituals and national values of education such as a national anthem or a flag greeting. Finally, it is encouraging to note the reference to environmental protection in certain Codes, such as those of Argentina, Colombia, Costa Rica, Ecuador, El Salvador, Honduras, and Peru that consider respect for environment as part of the education syllabus. We cannot forget that the protection of the environment is more and more a demanded right. Also, some countries refer to other issues related to education and, for example, focus on the procedures for challenging the assessments of students in their schools, even including some functions of teachers and management teams. In some cases, due to the characteristics of each country, the codes emphasize the importance of rural education (as in Bolivia) or it includes nutrition in the public school system (El Salvador and Honduras). With all this, they want to respond to the need of having a suitable education according to the geography of the country or to the shortage of food in some underage population groups.

Proposals for school integration of children with disabilities are seen in the Codes of Argentina, Bolivia, Brazil, Colombia, Ecuador, El Salvador, and Honduras. This reinforces the principle of non-discrimination (Amadio & Opertti, 2010; Davila, Naya & Lauzurika, 2010). However, there remains a traditional meaning of children with disabilities far from the actual term of inclusive education, which is defined by UNESCO as "a process of addressing and responding to the diversity of needs of all learners through increasing participation in learning, cultures and communities, and reducing exclusion within and from education [...]" (UNESCO, 2005, p. 13).

The fact that these rights are included in the Codes is an indicator that takes into account the rights to education and, therefore, the other two As of Katarina Tomaševski's scheme (Acceptability and Adaptability) are satisfied. As a result, it can be concluded that, in legal terms, the Codes are consistent with the CRC and, in some cases, offer indicators to analyze both the right to education and the rights in education. Therefore, problems of Latin American children do not come from laws, but rather from the gap produced by inequalities and social exclusion.

CONCLUSION: THE EDUCATION AND THE CODES IN LATIN AMERICA

Codes of children in most Latin American countries, following a long tradition, were acquired with the ratification of the CRC, a new perspective within the rights of the child, and became the interpretative framework and the prime directive of integral public policies for children. The Codes are laws with constitutional range that protect together the series of rights under international treaties and they are the regulatory frameworks for implementation. In this first decade of the 21st Century, by implementing the principles of the CRC in a consistent manner, this tradition continues.

From the analysis of these Codes, based on the general principles of the CRC and the indicators of the right to education, we see that the implementation conforms to this international treaty. Most Codes refer to the CRC as an interpretive framework of their national laws. Most Latin American countries develop the right to education in their Codes, although they put more emphasis on access to education rather than on other indicators of this right. There are important differences in policies against truancy and school discipline. Therefore, this right is formally recognized throughout the region, as regard the obligations and responsibilities of the state, but when it comes to other educational aspects of the Codes more doubts arise. However, it must be pointed out that the Right to Education is not an enforceable right to States, so some difficulties can appear in terms of fulfilment of this Right (Campaña Latinoamericana por el Derecho a la Educación, 2010; Latapí, 2009). Thus, we can say that availability and accessibility are more evident than acceptability and adaptability. As for the aims of education, the relevance that the Codes give to children's personal development and to a set of values related to family and identity can be appreciated. The importance that is given to the Human Rights Education, which is widespread in Latin America, can also be appreciated. As seen from this overview, we may conclude that the richness of nuances expressed in the Codes of children in Latin America is an example of the educational awareness of legislators in the region. It is a coherent discourse and, in many cases, it is adjusted to the text of the CRC. In this sense, we can say that it has surpassed the traditional approach that viewed children as under-aged, and the approach of human rights and children as subjects of law has been assumed. Therefore, the Codes have meant progress in all countries of the region. There are countries where there is a greater congruence with the CRC (Brazil, Bolivia, Colombia, Guatemala, Uruguay, and Venezuela). The other countries are more ambiguous when it comes to translating the basic principles and their implementation. All analyzed Codes embody the principles of the CRC in a "politically correct" language. However, as it has been pointed out before, some of the Codes are not totally harmonized with the CRC.

Our study has been focused on a textual analysis of the Codes of Children and it is not a research of their actual implementation. The countries of Latin America defend in their Codes a discourse which guarantees the rights of children before the law and they are confident that the law is enough to change the situation of children and adolescents. The value attached to education in the different areas that we have analyzed (the general principles of the CRC, the right to education, and the aims of education), is a sign of confidence in the written word and it confirms that the educational horizon is the best investment to protect and defend the rights of children.

NOTES

[i]   This chapter is part of research funded by the Ministry of Science and Technology (Project no. SEJ2007-66225/EDUC). The authors are members of the Group for Historical and Comparative Studies in Education – Garaian of the University of the Basque Country, recognized by the Basque Government with the registry number IT 298/10 and of the Unit of Training and Research "Education, Culture and Society" (UFI 11/54), funded by the University of the Basque Country.

[ii]   One can consult the complete Judgement in http://www.corteidh.or.cr/docs/casos/articulos/seriec_63_ing.doc.

REFERENCES

Amadio, M., & Opertti, R. (2010). Educación inclusiva, cambios de paradigma y agendas renovadas en América Latina (Inclusive education, paradigme-change and renewed agenda in Latin America). In P. Dávila & L. M. Naya (Eds.), *Infancia, derechos y educación en América Latina* (Children, rights and education in Latin America) (pp. 227-248). San Sebastián: Erein.

Barrios, A. G. (2006). El derecho humano a la educación en América Latina: entre avances y desafíos (The human right to Education in Latin America: between advances and challenges). In A. E. Yamin, (Ed.), *Los derechos económicos, sociales y culturales en América Latina. Del invento a la herramienta* (The economic, social and cultural rights in Latin America: From the invention to the tools) (pp. 195-214). México: Plaza y Valdés y Ottawa: IDRC International Development Research Centre.

Beloff, M. (2006). Los nuevos sistemas de justicia juvenil en América Latina (1989-2006) (The new juvenile justice systems 1989-2006). *Justicia y Derechos del niño, 8,* 9-50.

Beloff. M. (2008). *Fortalezas y debilidades del litigio estratégico para el fortalecimiento de los estándares internacionales y regionales de protección a la niñez en América Latina* (Strengths and weaknesses of the strategic dispute for the strengthening of international and regional protection standards of the childhood in Latin America). Retrieved from http://www.observatoriojovenes.com.ar/almacen/file/Fortalezas%20y%20debilidades_%20Mary%20Beloff.pdf.

Campaña Latinoamericana por el Derecho a la Educación (2010). *Justiciabilidad del derecho a la educación* (Justiciability of the right to education). Retrieved from http://www.campanaderechoeducacion.org/justiciabilidad/index.php.

Committee on the Rights of the Child (2001). *The aims of education.* General Comment no. 1 CRC/GC/2001/1.

Committee on the Rights of the Child (2003). *General measures of implementation for the Convention on the Rights of the Child.* General Comment no. 5 CRC/GC/2003/5.

Committee on the Rights of the Child (Comité de Los Derechos del Niño) (2006). *Compilación de observaciones finales del Comité de los Derechos del Niño sobre países de América Latina y el Caribe (1993-2006)* (Compilation of Concluding observations of the Committee on the Rights of the Child about the Latin American and Caribbean countries (1003-2006). UNICEF, Santiago de Chile, Retrieved from http://www.unicef.cl/unicef/public/archivos_documento/196/compilacion_1993_2006.pdf.

Dávila, P., & Naya, L. M. (2007a). Educational implications of the Convention on the Rights of the Child and its implementation in Europe. In A. Alen (Ed.), *The UN Children's Rights Convention: Theory meets practice* (pp. 243-266). Antwerpen: Intersentia.

Dávila, P., & Naya, L. M. (2007b). Education and the rights of the child in Europe. *Prospects, 37*(3), 357-367.

Dávila, P., Naya, L. M., & Lauzurika, A. (2010). Las personas con discapacidad, el derecho a la educación y la Convención sobre los Derechos del Niño en América Latina (The persons with disability, the right to education and the Convention on the Rights of the Child in Latin America). *Revista Latinoamericana de Inclusión Educativa, 4*(2), 97-117.

Instituto Colombiano de Bienestar Familiar (2009). *El Derecho del Bienestar Familiar* (The Right of the Family Wellness). Bogotá: Avance Jurídico Casa Editorial.

Instituto Interamericano de Derechos Humanos (2009). *Informe Interamericano de la Educación en Derechos Humanos* (inter-american report on human rights education). San José de Costa Rica: Instituto Interamericano de Derechos Humanos.

Georgetown University Political Database of the Americas (2006). *Constitutions and comparative constitutional study.* Retrieved from http://pdba.georgetown.edu/Constitutions/constudies.html.

Gutiérrez, J. C. (2006). *Memorias del Seminario Internacional los Derechos Humanos de los Niños, Niñas y adolescentes* (Report of the International Seminar on the Children's Rights). México: Monterrey.

Hodgkin, R., & Newell, P. (2007). *Implementation handbook for the Convention on the Rights of the Child.* Ginebra: UNICEF.

Itzcovich, G. (2009). *Escolarización de niños y adolescentes: acceso universal y permanencia selectiva* (Education of children and adolescents: universal access and selective retention). Buenos Aires: SITEAL.

Latapí, P. (2009). El derecho a la educación: Su alcance, exigibilidad y relevancia para la política educativa (The right to education: Its scope, enforceability and relevance for the educational policy). *Revista Mexicana de Investigación Educativa, 14*, 255-287.

Magendzo, A. (2010). Pensando y rescatando conceptualizaciones de la Educación en Derechos Humanos en Iberoamérica (Thinking and rescuing conceptualizations of Human Right Education in Latin America). In P. Dávila & L. M. Naya (Eds.), Infancia, derechos y educación en América Latina (Children, rights and education in Latin America). (pp. 305-316). San Sebastián: Erein.

Muñoz, V. (2006). *Girl's right to education.* Report submitted by the Special Rapporteur on the right to education. Commission on Human Rights. Sixty-second session. United Nations. E/CN.4/2006/45.

Muñoz, V. (2011). *El derecho a la educación: una mirada legislativa comparada. Argentina, Uruguay, Finlandia y Chile* (The right to education: A comparative review of selected legislations, Argentina, Uruguay, Finland and Chili). Santiago de Chile: UNESCO.

REDLAMYC (2009). *Estudio de balance regional sobre la implementación de la Convención sobre los Derechos del Niño en América Latina y el Caribe. Impacto y retos a 20 años de su aprobación.* (The regional study evaluation about the implementation of the Convention on the Rights of the Child in Latin America and the Caribbean. Impact and challenges 20 years after of its approval). Montevideo: Red Latinoamericana y Caribeña por la Defensa de los Derechos de los Niños, Niñas y Adolescentes (REDLAMYC) & Save the Children-Suecia.

Romero, S. (2007). Un siglo de legislación sobre infancia en América Latina. Un cuadro cronológico (One century of the legislation on the childhood in Latin America. A chronological framework). In P. Rodríguez & M.E. Mannarelli (Eds.), *Historia de la infancia en América Latina* (History of the childhood in Latin America) (pp. 615-632). Bogotá: Universidad del Externado.

SITEAL (2009a). *Primera infancia en América Latina. La situación actual y las respuestas desde el Estado* (Early childhood in Latin America. Actual situation and answers from the State). Madrid: OEI /IIPE/UNESCO.

SITEAL (2009b). *Sistema de información sobre la primera infancia* (Information system on early childhood). Madrid: OEI.

Tomaševski, K. (2006). *Human rights obligations in education. The 4-As scheme.* Nijmegen: Wolf Legal Publishers.

Tomaševski, K. (2005). El derecho a la educación, panorama internacional de un derecho irrenunciable (The right to education, an international outlook of a non-negotiable right). In L. M. Naya (Ed.), *La educación y los derechos humanos* (Education and human rights: International panorama on an inalienable right). San Sebastián: Erein.

UNESCO (2005). *Guidelines for inclusion: Ensuring access to Education for All.* Paris: UNESCO.

UN (1989). *Convention on the Rights of the Child (CRC).* Retrieved from http://www.ohchr.org/english/law/crc.htm.

AFFILIATIONS

Paulí Dávila
Department of Theory and History of Education
Faculty of Education
University of the Basque Country, Spain

Luis Mª Naya
Department of Theory and History of Education
Faculty of Education
University of the Basque Country, Spain

ANA MARÍA MONTERO PEDRERA

4. THE RIGHT TO EDUCATION IN LATIN AMERICA
(2005-2010)

Analysis of the Latin American Conferences on Education

INTRODUCTION

In this chapter an analysis is conducted on the right to education in Latin America as presented in documents generated by the Organization of the Latin American States for Education, Science and Culture (OEI). This agency is an international organization with an intergovernmental character, for the cooperation between Latin American countries, in the field of education, science, technology and culture in the context of integral development, democracy and regional integration.

The OEI was founded in 1949 with this name: "Office of Latin American Education", as an international agency. Later, in 1957, it turned into an intergovernmental organization constituted by sovereign states. In 1985 its name was changed into OEI, preserving its initials and extending its targets.

The States that signed the current articles of association of the OEI together with Spain and Portugal are: Argentina, Bolivia, Brazil, Chile, Colombia, Costa Rica, Cuba, Dominican Republic, Ecuador, El Salvador, Guatemala, Equatorial Guinea, Honduras, Mexico, Nicaragua, Panama, Paraguay, Peru, Puerto Rico, Uruguay and Venezuela. The OEI headquarter is in Madrid and liaises with regional offices in Argentina, Colombia, Mexico and Peru and with a Technical Office in Chile.

Inside the OEI there are three major lines of action that focuses its actions across the General Assembly:
- Integration and economic, political and cultural cooperation.
- Education, science, technology and culture as vehicles of democratization, development and social justice.
- Cultural identity and principles as consolidation of a proper space in concert of international relations.

The Latin American Summits of state's presidents and governments and the Latin American Conferences of Education (LCE) are two events of major relevance in the initiatives of integration and cooperation, which are canalized across the OEI, to comply with the goals, targets and intentions of this international organization.

A summit of Heads of State was held in July 1991. From 1991 until 2010 it has been an annual meeting. The two first meeting, in Guadalajara (Mexico) and Madrid (Spain) are considered the founding summits. The recognition of a union of

H. Biseth & H. B. Holmarsdottir (eds.), Human Rights in the Field of Comparative Education, 47–61.
© *2013 Sense Publishers. All rights reserved.*

historical and cultural affinities, which favor the unity and development based on dialogue, cooperation and solidarity, constitutes the fundamental starting point. These fundamental issues construct a philosophical frame that sustains the principles that will be continued for future actions and the justification of those intended actions. At every summit a commitment is renewed to promote the common cultural heritage, democracy, respect of human rights and fundamental freedoms, protection of national sovereignty, its political system and its institutions.

These conferences of Heads of State occupy an important place in the political space of the member countries of OEI, facilitating dialogue at the highest political level and a fertile environment for cooperation programs.

The Latin American Conferences on Education (LCE) are carried out in different locations in Latin America and held prior to the summits of Heads of State. The LCE is defined as the organ of consultation of the OEI about Education, Science and Culture and has as a goal to analyze topics of special interest for the member states of the Organization (Martínez Usarralde, 2005). The LCE serves as preparation to the summits of Heads of State because it gathers recommendations from the ministers, who later will play an important part in shaping the documents of the Declarations of the Summits (Bello, 2003).

Until 1995, when the 5th LCE and the 5th Summit took place, there was no continuity in the initial intention of the role of the LCE. From 1995 onwards, however, we find basic documents prepared by specialists of the region, which are preparatory instruments and serve as consultation documents. The important point is that the documents gather expert opinions of the region.

This current study is conducted since these conferences are scantly studied, both in the Spanish arena and in the international one. I emphasize the studies of Vidal Araya (2007), Stramiello (2003, 2006), Sanz Fernández (1997), Bidegaray (2011), Marchesi, Tedesco, and Coll (2009), and Ravela (2007), who focus on aspects of general character related to the right to education. In this analysis I intend to unravel how the right to education as a human right is discussed in the OEI documents.

THE RIGHT TO EDUCATION

The right to education is a recognized human right and it is reflected in the right to a compulsory and free primary education for all children and through an obligation to develop an accessible higher education system. Also it includes the obligation to eliminate the discrimination in all levels of the educational system, to comply with minimal standards and to improve the quality (Pisa Tolosa, 2011). These issues are of high significance and reflected in numerous international documents,[1] such as:
– Universal Declaration of Human Rights (UN, 1948)
– Convention for the Protection of Human Rights and Fundamental Freedoms (Council of Europe, 1950)
– Convention against Discrimination in Education (UNESCO, 1960)
– International Covenant on Civil and Political Rights (UN, 1966a)

- International Covenant on Economic, Social and Cultural Rights (UN, 1966b)
- Declaration of the Rights of the Child (UN, 1989)

This last document on the above list recognizes in article 13 the right of every person to education. The governments are expected to respect it, to protect it and, especially, to fulfill it. An abyss exists still today between the judicial rhetoric and reality. The right to education has the peculiarity of being an intrinsic human right and an indispensable way of realizing other human rights (UN, 1966b). This right is independent of particular factors like judicial status, gender, sexual orientation, ethnic group or nationality.

The Education Secretaries assembled in the LCE of 2007 gather, in the Declaration of Buenos Aires, an analysis of the right to education and observe that advances are made in the Latin American countries, particularly in the struggle against illiteracy and in the efforts to increase the educational coverage at all levels of the educational system. At the same time as the years of compulsory education were increasing, investments were realized to improve the infrastructures and the sanitary and nutrition conditions of children. Furthermore, educational reforms, the new project of curricula, progress of the formation of the professorship, the introduction of mechanisms of institutional evaluation and of rationalization and progress of the educational administration have taken place.

The Constitutions of Latin American countries have progressed significantly in the recognition of the right to education, but, at the same time, homogeneity does not exist in its treatment. Bolivia is the only country that mentions the right to education as a fundamental right. Brazil, Colombia, El Salvador and Peru treat it like a social right; Mexico like an individual guarantee. Argentina, Honduras, Paraguay, Uruguay and the Associate Free State of Puerto Rico recognize the right to education, but they do not make any distinction between individual and social rights. Panama groups individual and social rights under the same heading and does not detail the characteristics of the right to education. Finally, the new Ecuadorian Constitution includes it together with other rights that are sketched out in the International Covenant on Economic, Social and Cultural Rights. There are other countries in which the Constitutions do not recognize the right to education as a fundamental right, like Peru, Uruguay and Ecuador. In other cases, the right to education is defined in similar terms. In this context, Fernández Santamaría (2003) indicates that it seems suitable that the international cooperation in educational matter is a real point from which "the Latin-American societies, and its respective governments, could face to its commitment with the development, with the overcoming of the poverty, with the harmonization between the construction of solid democracies and with the progress of the quality of life for the set of the population" (p. 147).

One of the most lasting examples of the advances of the right to education in Latin America has been the progressive expansion of the school systems in all the countries of the region. The growth of national systems of education is wide and the generalization of schooling has been gradual and systematical during the whole second half of the 20th century. In other words, this period has been marked by an intense growth of school systems with a focus on including those traditionally excluded from education such as: ethnic minorities, the disabled, women, and the poor.

It is thought that the growth of school systems, as well as the judicial recognition of the right to education, are insufficient factors to celebrate the full implementation of the right to education as a fundamental human right. Nevertheless, even being insufficient, these two factors have been fundamental to cover the demand for the enlargement of the right to education in each of the different countries.

Although the expansion of education systems and the judicial recognition of the right to education are characteristics of all the countries, full implementation is not a fact. Nevertheless, the topic of the right to education is constant in every LCE. States are encouraged to handle it as a priority matter in their politics, and three aspects stand out as given particular emphasis:
– The quality of basic education,
– The renewal of secondary, technical and professional education, and
– The expansion and diversification of higher education.
This focus is a way of fulfilling the ends of the OEI, which are "the development and the scientific exchange of the member states, in order to help to raise the cultural level of its inhabitants like persons, to form them integrally for the productive life and for the tasks that the integral development needs and to strengthen the feelings of peace, democracy and social justice" (Stramiello, 2003, p. 198).

Prior to 2005 four of the LCE signal a significant emphasis on the right to education, as visible in the conference titles:
– The 5th LCE, Argentina, 1995, was entitled   Education as a Development factor[ii]
– The 6th LCE, Chile, 1996, was entitled Education, Democratic Governance and Educational System Governance[iii]
– The 8th LCE, Portugal, 1998 was entitled The Latin American educational systems in the context of the globalization. Questions and opportunities[iv]
– The 9th LCE, Cuba, 199 was entitled Educational quality: development and integration before the challenge of the globalization[v]
The last one has a synthesis character regarding the education conferences realized up to this moment. In all the conferences it also appears the important commitments acquired in other meetings are taken into consideration:

1) The Conference on Education for All in Jomtien (Thailand, 1990).[vi]
   –   The need to generalize the access to education of young people and adults
   –   To attend on the educational quality
2) World Forum on Education for All in Dakar (Senegal, 2000).[vii] The Goals of education for all imply expiring with all the collective commitments, so that as soon as possible, and no later than 2015, education for all has become a reality. To answer problems like illiteracy, drop-out, ethnic or gender discrimination, offering a quality education for all.

3) World Forum on Education. Mark of regional action (Santo Domingo, 2000).[viii]
  − It ratified the continuity to the efforts realized by the countries;
  − To fulfill the commitments dependent on the previous decade;
  − Achievements and hanging topics are indicated
4) Declaration of Cochabamba (Bolivia, 2001).[ix] It was convened by UNESCO and focused on the Main Project of Education started in 1981. They repeat the targets of the project as for education for all and quality of the same one, at the time that they point out worries that these targets have not been achieved entirely. This Conference admits, in the frame of international agreements, that some achievements are registered:
  − Expansion of the basic cycle
  − Women's education
  − A focus on populations with special educational needs
  − Information systems and evaluation
  − Bilateral and multilateral cooperation

In order to reach the goals in the Frame of Action of Dakar and Santo Domingo, the Education Secretaries of the region approved the Regional Project of Education for Latin America and the Caribbean region (2002-2017). This is an attempt to promote cooperation between the countries and the changes in the politics and educational practices. The aim is to reach the goals across five strategic points: contents and practices, teaching formation, educational institution, continual training, and social responsibility (Macedo, 2005). In most of the documents cited above the concepts of quality education, education for all and education as a way to develop democracy appear.[x] Before analyzing the topics of the conferences between 2005 and 2010, it is necessary to clarify the meaning of these concepts.

According to Marqués Graells (2011), the OECD defines quality education as education which "assures to all the young people the acquisition of the knowledge, capacities workmanship and attitudes necessary to prepare them for the adult life" (p. 1). Nevertheless it is necessary to bear in mind that in preparing for an adult life in a rural context can be rather different that preparing for an adult life in a rapidly changing urban context. A quality school is considered as a school that promotes the progress of its students in its intellectual, social, moral and emotional aspects, however the socioeconomic level, family environment and previous learning are aspects that can also play a role. An effective school system is the one that promotes the aptitude of the schools to reach these results. This document analysis will unravel how the right to education is framed in the program of *Education for All* across the LCE.

ANALYSIS OF THE TOPICS RAISED IN THE LCE (2005-2010)

Suggestions are proposed in the Declarations to the situations analyzed in the LCE. These do not include legal obligations for the States. They reflect, however, that the States agree at the moment of these suggestions, without them being legally binding, but more as moral obligations. Certain declarations have a strong moral value and contain suggestions of action. This provides an invitation to the States to take initiatives of some kind. In this way, the recommendations have the intention of influencing the development of national legislation and practices.

In the table below I list the conferences from 2005 through 2010. Then I describe how the conferences focused on education as a human right before I go on to make an analysis.

LCEDATE	PLACE	TOPIC
15th - July, 2005 Education	Toledo (Spain)	Latin American agreement on
16th - July, 2006 spread	Montevideo (Uruguay)	Latin American of the knowledge
17th - July, 2007 politics	Valparaiso (Chile)	Social cohesion and inclusive
18th - May, 2008	Salinillas (El Salvador)	Youth and development
19th - April, 2009	Lisbon (Portugal)	Education and Innovation
20th - October 2010	Buenos Aires (Argentina)	Education with social inclusion

The 15th LCE: Latin American Agreement on Education

In this meeting the topic of quality education appears as a right and an important element for development and democracy. Education must be included in development strategies of all the countries taking part in the LCE.

As many LCE countries spend their budgets on foreign debt, the compliance with this right is difficult. In this way we must not forget to strengthen the finance of education by means of additional budgets. The proposal is the debt-for-education-swap. Most of the money will be spent on primary and secondary education and research. Education is the main homogenization factor against exclusion in a continent of inequality and differences between rich and poor.

In this meeting it is proposed that OEI form a regional network for the exchange of multimedia materials of support to teachers; to encourage the efficient use of the new technologies in the school environment and especially in continual in-service training.

Proposals:
– The creation of a Latin American Space for Knowledge concerning the transformation of higher education, this played a key role. It produces, transmits

and disseminates knowledge to society, generate new ideas and form the scientific and technical personnel. Transferring in addition the research results to the productive, to solve problems and to develop Latin American countries.
- A Latin American Agreement for Education advanced as a strategic element for the promotion of an education promoting equity and social justice, looking for innovative financing mechanisms, emphasizing the foreign debt swap for investments in education.

The 16th LCE: Latin American Pace of Knowledge through Higher Education, Scientific Investigation, Technological Development and Innovation

This meeting begins with generalizing literacy as a priority in which access to basic education for all children and adults in the region is needed in this work. Education is therefore guaranteed as a fundamental right. To support it, a plan is approved to eradicate illiteracy in the region during the period 2007-2015, and to encourage reading and writing proficiency. In addition, facilitation of access for all to the technological disciplines is in focus.
Proposals:
- The creation of a Latin American Space of Knowledge, which promotes the exchange of teachers and pupils and quality of higher education.
- The Latin American Plan of Literacy and Basic education of Young and Adult Persons, 2008-2015 also focuses on how the service of foreign debt influences on the funding of the education sector, an issue already pointed out in the previous LCE. Generalization of literacy and basic education for all, including digital literacy, are concluded as both possible and necessary objectives for Latin America.

The 17th LCE: Social Cohesion and Social Policies to Achieve Inclusive Societies in Latin America

This year dedicated special attention to the importance of literacy and the preservation and diffusion of cultural identity of the indigenous population. It is highlighted that indigenous populations in the LCE countries experience grave social inequality. To remedy this situation, education is suggested as a prioritized instrument to effectively foster social cohesion.

A focus in this LCE is the *Latin American literacy Plan*; networks of educational portals; strengthening of education in Latin America; cooperation needed to reach the Millennium Development Goals; preservation and diffusion of identity and culture of the indigenous populations; educational finance; and foreign debt swap for social investment.

The meeting also highlighted the *Latin American Space of Knowledge* as an instrument of exchange and cooperation and also to tackle the network of educational portals.

Proposals:
– Program Educational Goal 2021: the education wanted for young people of the Bicentenary, promising advancement in the set targets, goals and mechanisms of regional evaluation.
– Program Pablo Neruda, developed to encourage mobility of students, researchers and teachers of postgraduate courses, in order to contribute in developing human resources highly qualified in areas considered a priority by the countries of the region.

The 18th LCE: Educational Goals 2021 – The Education Wanted for the Generation of the Bicentenary

In this LCE it was expressed a will to agree among all the countries on common educational goals, which allows development of the region's educational systems towards a more advanced position in globally. This is also recognized as a strategy to advance cohesion and social inclusion.

The final target of the goals is to achieve, during the next decade, an education that gives satisfactory answers to social demands: more pupils who study, and study longer, with an offer of recognized, equitable and inclusive quality and promoting participation in all sectors of society.

The main challenges which most of the countries of the region face are described as the absence of competitiveness of public schools, the limited number of years pupils attend school, lack of an attractive curriculum to keep pupils in school, the insufficient resources to face the demands of the pupils, the situation of the professorship, poor management of public resources and to the limited academic results obtained compared to that of richer countries.

Proposals:
– To continue with efforts to universalize literacy and basic education.
– Promote the quality of education to reduce school failure and reduce the causes which originate it.
– Promote vocational education to provide better opportunities for young people and all nations.

The 19th LCE: Education and Innovation

In this conference an agreement was reached to fight illiteracy and to extend education to foster innovation. The most immediate target is to generalize basic education and to attend to the 15 million children still out of school. This meeting raised the target that more than half of the children from 3 to 6 years-old should have access to school in 2015, and by 2021 to include all children. It is a situation that varies among the countries.[xi] The target of this LCE is to approach basic education due to the project of the *Educational Goals 2021* that tries to transform the Latin American education during the next decade.

Another goal is to generalize the basic primary and higher education, improving simultaneously its quality and to increase attendance of young people in higher secondary education, professional polytechnics and university level. A focus is also put on the connection between education and the labor market, access to life-long learning, and strengthening of the teaching profession. Another target is to extend education to all levels and access to new technologies.

The 20th LCE: Education for Social Inclusion

Education is a decisive instrument for development, the struggle against poverty, defense of fundamental rights and social cohesion. It guarantees educational inclusion across universal policies. Education is seen as promoting values that contemplates solidarity, peace, respect of human rights and democratic formation. The goals that are approved in this LCE are:
- Eradicate all illiteracy and to ensure that all people in Latin America complete basic education.
- Combat drop-out so that most young people complete 12 years of education.
- The care for the health of children as a prerequisite for their school achievement.
- To improve educational quality with the introduction of ICTs in the educational system

Proposals:
- Creation of a United Fund of Educational Cooperation.
- Creation of the Council Adviser of the Educational Goals 2021
- Design of a Distance Education project with the goal to reinforce and promote inclusive education in the region.

Analysis of the LCEs

The topics covered in these five LCEs are vast, including policies to reduce school failure and drop out (2005), the importance to acquire intercultural and bilingual education (2007), education of indigenous populations (2007), and new technologies (2009). They also introduce topics such as the importance of compensatory education policies (2005), the importance of values education (2010), and the role of NGOs to implement various projects and affirmative countervailing (2008 & 2010). Other subjects mentioned are organizational and pedagogical concerns and processes of learning (2005), life-long learning (2005), attention demanding processes and core competencies (2006), and emotions in education (2010).

The topics treated are immersed in educational reforms that the various governments have led or carried out in their respective countries. All of them raise the importance of achieving consensus for reforms and the need for adequate financial resources. The road from the planned reforms to implementation is long and many factors need to be taken into consideration.

All LCEs concern human rights and development through education. It is judged that universal literacy and basic education for all young people and adults are possible as well as necessary goals. All politicians attending these meetings undertake in the framework of government policies and strengthen national plans in their countries. This is a priority (XVI and XVII LCE).

Through all the conferences it is emphasized that ensuring free and compulsory basic education is an exercise of a human right. Education is a fundamental tool through which progress can be made in solving larger problems such as poverty and inequality (XVII LCE). It has been shown that education is necessary (though not sufficient) for economic, social and cultural development. Since the population increases its possibility of exercising their civic rights through education, this also contributes to higher levels of protection for vulnerable social groups and promoting equity in access to welfare.

Although promising initiatives have been made, the situation is not satisfactory. The LCEs evaluate the progress made by the national plans of access to education and the diversity of methods employed, according to the social and educational realities in each country, and access to education for people and institutions of remote areas of the region. One of these plans is the educational program for infants from 0 to 5 years (XIX LCE), which are met with some of the objectives of the Goals 2021 program and therefore the right to education.

Teachers have an important role in promoting human rights and there is a need for a wide and coherent focus on the issue. Recent educational reforms include demands for human rights to be included in the content of education, the modalities and scope of the initial and continuing training of teachers and their direct impact on classroom teaching practices. An element of maximum importance for teachers is technological literacy so that they can use materials to support their work and make proper use of technology in educational institutions (XV LCE).

States have the duty to promote educational policies that strengthen inclusion, social cohesion and a sense of belonging. We need to set minimum standards and improve quality. Through the promotion of educational quality and equity, better opportunities for all can be achieved. Factors that promote the right to education are to finance an increase of access to education using additional budgetary resources, more effective management of existing resources, and strengthening the dialogue between political, educational and financial actors. It is necessary to promote the convergence of new forms of financing around sustainable human development strategies related to education (LCE XV). In this environment debt swap is proposed in every LCE.

The educational policy can become an engine of economic and social development. However, there are still problems and deficiencies related to quality and equity, to make young people complete their secondary education, to continue their studies and achieve a successful job placement. Despite good intentions, this level is not yet accessible to all young people. The Committee welcomes the initiatives of the IEO to promote quality of education for their decisive impact on the reduction of failure and reducing the causes of this (XVIII LCE).

To meet the challenge of social inclusion, progress in the implementation of educational strategies should include the participation of different sectors of society, the flexibility of education systems, the increased investment in education and the development of tools to prepare young people to enter the world of work, citizenship, and of human coexistence, respect for cultural diversity, ethnic, and gender (XX LCE). It is considered necessary to prevent, correct and delete at all levels of the education system any form of discrimination, especially through the recognition of gender equality, ethnic diversity, multiculturalism and developing a safe school model in the region (XVII LCE). It is also important to reach an agreement on education that promotes social inclusion and cohesion in the region, a pact that should be met through agreements at the national and local levels. Recognition of the right to education includes values of solidarity and peace, and hence facilitating an environment where every child and youth can develop their intellectual, emotional and social characteristics.

Universal education includes provision of basic education to individuals who have not completed primary education. The processes of reducing literacy among young people and adults require flexible educational provision with a high focus on high quality and inclusion. In relation to this there is a need to coordinate Latin American political support for the development of reading and writing skills in the population. Reading is considered a tool for social inclusion and a key factor for social, cultural and economic development. Through it you can access training in new technologies which have transformed the approach to education as a generator and transmitter of knowledge. The use of new technology also requires skills in principles of equity, solidarity and respect for diversity (XVII LCE). The widespread use of ICT helps to improve the situation in the region, because they produce new knowledge relevant to the needs, circumstances and aspirations of our peoples and for its widespread application. It is unanimous the idea of strengthening the training of teachers, especially in ICT and incorporate them into the educational process of our countries at all levels.

Promotion of human rights is also related to higher education. The production of knowledge and its transfer to all areas of life of our societies is a decisive factor in raising the indices of human development as a condition for social justice (XV LCE). The importance of promoting innovation and knowledge as strategic factors in higher education policy is listed as influencing what kind of knowledge that is constructed, influencing human and societal development and social welfare. These are necessary conditions in order to increase productivity, provide better quality and accessibility of goods and services as well as increasing the international competitiveness in the region. Investments in research and higher education are needed to change the growth in the region (XVI LCE).

The public authorities shall facilitate access of all citizens to economic assets, social and cultural rights. Thus, individuals expect from society the care and aid they require to exercise those rights. At the same time, society is morally obliged to look for avenues and resources for citizens to do so. This implies that citizens also have certain duties to the society to which they belong, and must fulfill them so that the resources devoted to the attention of its members is used as intended. By accepting the rights, the state is obliged to provide the material means to perform public services. So education as a human right is a collective right rather than an individual, the holder is the individual in the community, according to two LCEs

(XVI and XX LCE). The state's role is to create framework conditions that allow the population effective access to this right.

In summary, many proposed targets have not been resolved. There are still discussions on e.g., how to combat illiteracy, suggestions on how to articulate decentralization of education, or the technological challenges facing society. A mercantilist trend is observed that defines education as a tradable service and not as a human right. The right to education is not limited to access to formal schooling, and is not limited to a certain age group. Education is then, apart from an individual guarantee, an entitlement whose highest expression is the person in the exercise of their citizenship and is not confined to a period of life but the whole course of existence of men and women.

Through the LCEs it is clear that education is recognized a necessary condition to generate development. Development is not an exclusively economic problem, but is also a process of reconciling economic growth with social development. Education is a necessary but not sufficient condition for economic, social and cultural development. Thus in the twentieth LCE it is said that "education is the key instrument for development, poverty reduction, the defense of fundamental rights and social cohesion" (p. 2). In a wider perspective, education is thus seen as an important instrument in achieving sustainable peace, development and democracy. The need to give education its profound meaning, designed to achieve the development of personality and human dignity as well as society, is a recognition of education as a permanent right, to be safeguarded in the context of convergence and the learning of all other human rights.

CONCLUSION

Through the LCEs it has been shown a desire to improve education in all Latin American countries and a tendency to gradually increase the fulfillment of human rights. However, we cannot settle for respect for human rights in a passive way. The rights require actions to be carried out, the promotion of initiatives in their defense and to encourage a process of development. To address these issues we need to take into consideration the complexity of factors present in each country and region. To ensure integration of aspirations, realities and projects it is necessary to implement contextualized local or regional solutions.

Education and training in human rights are also essential according to the LCEs. The aim is to create a culture of human rights. This has the potential of permeating the law as well as ensuring practice in everyday life including facilitating for the rights of women, children, the marginalized, and immigrants. All countries participating in the LCEs agree that education is the cornerstone on which we must build peace and personal freedom, without it, there will be no future development. The best guarantee of respect for human rights is, without doubt, the introduction of a culture and education for those rights. Although human rights are enshrined in Latin American constitutions, they are respected only when they are known and implemented.

This study has identified common themes and similar concerns about the realization of the right to education. The whole region has historical problems related to education. We should not have an exalted pedagogical optimism which asks education to solve all problems in a country. Ever since Plato and Aristotle considered education as in close relationship with the political sphere, it is pointed out how education can be a means of achieving policy objectives, including the improvement of life for all Latin American citizens.

NOTES

[i] At present the right to education is reflected in diverse international legal documents and programs on the right to education. On a global scale it is possible to divide them into two categories: binding documents, also called hard law, and not binding documents or soft law. The first category composed by covenants and conventions supposes recognition on the part of the States of their legal obligation towards them. The second category composed mostly by declarations and recommendations, provides guidelines and a normative frame, and, thus, creates moral obligations.

[ii] The 5th LCE. http://www.oei.es/vcie.htm

[iii] The 6th LCE. http://www.oei.es/vicie.htm

[iv] The 8th LCE. http://www.oei.es/viiicie.htm

[v] The 9th LCE. http://www.oei.es/ixcie.htm

[vi] The Conference of Jomtien was an important meeting in which there talked each other the place that occupies the education in the human development international politics. The consensus reached in her impelled the world campaign to promote a universal elementary education, to eradicate the illiteracy of the adults; to improve the basic educational quality and to attend to the basic needs for learning of diverse disadvantaged groups.
http://unesdoc.unesco.org/images/0012/001211/121147s.pdf.

[vii] In the World Forum of Education of Dakar there was adopted the Frame of Action of Dakar, which integrated 6 regions of action of the world, (sub-Saharan Africa, Americas, Arab Countries, Asia and the Pacific Ocean, Europe and North America and Countries of the Group E-9). There a collective commitment was evident to operate and to fulfill the targets and Education purposes for all for 2015. http://unesdoc.unesco.org/images/0012/001211/121147s.pdf.

[viii] http://www.minedu.gob.pe/educacionparatodos/InfoGen.php.

[ix] There were analyzed the results of the evaluation of 20 years of the Main Project of Education in Latin America. There appeared a pilot analysis of the possible political, social, economic and cultural stages, where the education will develop in the region in the next fifteen years. http://unesdoc.unesco.org/images/0012/001214/121485s.pdf.

[x] According to Sartori (2003) democracy is the political system where there are present the human rights (civil, political and social rights). It is a form of organization of the State; the collective decisions take for the people by means of direct or indirect participation; this gives legitimacy to the representatives. In wide sense, democracy is a form of social coexistence in which the members are free and equal. A relation seems to exist between democracy and poverty, to the effect that those countries at major democracy levels possess also a major GDP per capita, a major index of human development and a less index of poverty.

[xi] In Cuba, Argentina, Uruguay, Mexico, Chile or Ecuador the access valuations are high. In other countries as Nicaragua, El Salvador, Dominican Republic, Honduras or Guatemala, more than half of the children do not go to school. http://www.rfi.fr/actues/articles/112/article_11616.asp.

REFERENCES

Aponte-Hernández, E. (2008). Inequality, inclusion and equity in the higher education in Latin America and the Caribbean Sea: Tendencies and alternative stages in the horizon 2021. In A. L. Gazzola, A. L., & A. Didriksson (Eds.), *Tendencies of the higher education in Latin America and the Caribbean Sea* (pp. 113-154). Caracas: UNESCO/IESALC.

Bidegaray, Romero I. (2011). *Guarantee and achievement of the right to education in Latin-America. Committee of Latin-America and the Caribbean Sea for the Defense of the Women's rights.* Lima (Peru): CLADEM.

Council of Europe (1950). *Convention for the Protection of Human Rights and Fundamental Fre*edoms. Rome: Council of Europe.

Fernández Santamaría, M. R. (2003). The situation of the basic education in Latin America: Challenges for the international cooperation. *Latin-American Magazine of Education, 31,* 145-167.

Macedo, B. (2005). *Education for All, environmental education and education for sustainable development: debating aspects of the Decade of Education for Sustainable Development* (OREALC/2005/PI/H/14). Retrieved from http://unesdoc.unesco.org/images/0016/001621/162179s.pdf.

Marchesi, A., Tedesco, J. C., & Coll, C. (Eds.). (2009). *Equity and reforms in the education.* Madrid: OEI-Foundation Santillana.

Marqués Graell, P. (2011). *Quality and educational innovation in the centers.* Retrieved from http://www.peremarques.net/calida2.htm.

Martínez Usarralde, M. J. (2005). *The education in Latin America: between the quality and the equity.* Barcelona: Octaedro.

OEI. Latin-American Conferences on Education:
  The 5ᵗʰ LCE. Buenos Aires, Argentina (1995). Retrieved from http://www.oei.es/vcie.htm.
  The 6ᵗʰ LCE. Concepción, Chile (1996). Retrieved from http://www.oei.es/vicie.htm.
  The 8ᵗʰ LCE. Sintra, Portugal (1998). Retrieved from http://www.oei.es/viiicie.htm.
  The 9ᵗʰ LCE. Havana, Cuba (1999). Retrieved from http://www.oei.es/ixcie.htm.
  The 15ᵗʰ LCE. Toledo, Spain (2005). Retrieved from http://www.oei.es/xvcie.htm.
  The 16ᵗʰ LCE. Montevideo, Uruguay (2006). Retrieved from http://www.oei.es/xvicie.htm.
  The 17ᵗʰ LCE. Valparaiso, Chile (2007). Retrieved from http://www.oei.es/xviicie.htm.
  The 18ᵗʰ LCE. Salinillas, El Salvador (2008). Retrieved from http://www.oei.es/xviiicie.htm.
  The 19ᵗʰ LCE. Lisbon, Portugal (2009). Retrieved from http://www.oei.es/xixcie.htm.
  The 20ᵗʰ LCE. Buenos Aires, Argentina (2010). Retrieved from http://www.oei.es/xxcie.htm.

Pisa Tolosa, L. (2011). *Are we educated in Spain?* Retrieved from http://luispisa.blogia.com/2011/092001-somos-educados-en-espana-.php.

Ravela, P. (2007). Social inequalities and educational achievements. In SITEAL, *Social and educational tendencies in Latin-America* (pp. 108-111). Retrieved from http://www.siteal.iipe-oei.org/informetendencias/informetendencias.asp.

Sanz Fernández, F. (1997). The adults' basic education in Latin America during the nineties: From Jomtien to Dakar. *Spanish Magazine of Comparative Education, 3,* 143-176.

Sartori, G. (2003). *What is the democracy?* Mexico: Taurus.

Stramiello, C. I. (2003). The educational problems of Latin America across the Latin-American education conferences. *Spanish Magazine of Comparative Education, 9,* 193-218.

Stramiello, C. I. (2006). The right to education in the Latin-American Conferences of Education and in the Presidents' Summits (2000-2005). Tensions and expectations. In *The right to education in to world encompassed* (Vol. 1, pp. 191-200). San Sebastian: Erein.

UN (1948). *Universal Declaration of Human Right.* New York: UN General Assembly.

UN (1966a). *International Covenant on Civil and Political Rights.* New York: UN General Assembly.

UN (1966b). *International Covenant on Economic, Social and Cultural Rights.* New York: UN General Assembly.

UN (1989). *Convention on the Rights of the Child*. New York, UN General Assembly.

UNESCO (1960). *Convention against Discrimination in Education*. Paris: UNESCO General Conference.

UNESCO (2010). *I equip of the Report of Pursuit of the EPT in the World: To come to the outsiders*. Paris: UNESCO.

UNESCO and UNICEF (2007) *To Human Rights-Based Approach to Education for All*. Retrieved from http://unesdoc.unesco.org/images/0015/001548/154861E.pdf.

UNESCO. Social and Human Sciences. *Status resides about the nature and of the legal instruments and programmers*. Retrieved from http://www.unesco.org/new/es/social-and-human-sciences/themes/human-rights/advancement/networks/larno/legal-instruments/nature-and-status/.

UNICEF (2007). *The world State of the infancy: excluded and invisible*. New York/Ginebra: Unicef. Retrieved from http://www.unicef.org/spanish/sowc06/pdfs/sowc06_fullreport_sp.pdf.

Vidal Araya, L. (2007). Approach to the Educational quality notion in the Latin-American context. *Latin-American Magazine of Education*, 44 (4). Retrieved from http://www.rieoei.org/deloslectores/1959Vidal.pdf.

AFFILIATIONS

Ana Maria Montero Pedrera
Faculty of Sciences of Education
University of Seville, Spain

VEDAT SEVINCER AND HEIDI BISETH

5. TENSIONS BETWEEN NATIONAL CITIZENSHIP AND HUMAN RIGHTS

Perspectives in Greece and Turkey

INTRODUCTION

In this chapter we intend to investigate the potential role of citizenship education as a conveyor of human rights through critically examining the policy documents prescribing the values of the education systems of Greece and Turkey. We dare the assumption that citizenship education can be considered as a value package for the school system, usually including human rights, but sometimes rather conflicting with human rights perspectives. Contemporary states may experience tension when harmonizing their national values in line with human rights obligations. Through using Greece and Turkey as illustrative cases, we intend to exemplify possible tensions between citizenship education and human rights. The political aims of education are often linked to the development of a well-functioning citizenry. Therefore, citizenship education can be, in many ways, described as a mirror of desired national values to be instigated in the population in order to promote the political agenda of those in power. Although a country has ratified several human rights instruments, the underlying values of these international obligations are not necessarily in compliance with the national values promoted in citizenship education. Quite the contrary, they may be diverging. In this chapter we will present arguments supporting this assertion, starting out with background information about the study informing our discussion.

BACKGROUND INFORMATION ABOUT THE STUDY

This chapter derives from the study conducted by Sevincer (2009), seeking to comparatively evaluate the notion of citizenship education in relation to national identity formation, belonging and cosmopolitanism, and understanding citizenship policies in these two countries. The research material derives from analysis of texts consisting of legally binding documents including the constitutions of Greece and Turkey, Education Acts, decrees and legislation, and decisions by the Ministries of Education. Furthermore, national curricula are investigated as they prescribe the aims and objectives of language, history, social studies and religion, subjects constituting the major part of citizenship education in these two countries. Through

H. Biseth & H. B. Holmarsdottir (eds.), Human Rights in the Field of Comparative Education, 63–80.
© *2013 Sense Publishers. All rights reserved.*

these documents it is possible to derive the values which are considered to comprise the national civic values. While mapping these values in Greek and Turkish education policy, we attempt at the same time to unravel their competitive and conflicting nature with human rights values as presented in the human rights instruments ratified by these two countries.

The rationale for choosing these two countries is two-fold: First, their centralized governance systems make them available for policy analysis at a more or less similar level. Managerial structures as a result of this system provide similar policy units to focus on. Additionally, their characteristic social, political and cultural structures reflect insights to understand the development process of a general conceptualization of citizenship (Icduygu & Kaygusuz, 2004; Clogg, 2002). Both countries consider themselves as being part of Europe, members of international organizations and signatory parties of human rights treaties, yet at the same time, they claim to be descendants of a glorious past and with a culture which has to be protected from the threat constituted by deviating norms and values. As a result of this duality, an acute division between traditionalist and modernist ideology regulate the political context in both countries. In this value clash, the source of challenges to their enduring citizenship policies, however, is not necessarily identical. While the Greek citizenship model has been embedded in Greko-Christian tradition and values, Turkey keeps away from identifying itself with the dominant religious belief, Islam, and prefers to locate its citizenship in a secular nationalist frame.

Moreover, the relation to the historical heritage in their nation building process has different references. While Greece relates itself with the ancient Greek civilization and uses its internationally acclaimed legacy, Turkey maintains its identification based on glorification of the young Turkish Republic's history and figures. Moreover, the full membership of Greece to the European Union (EU) prepares a more binding framework for domestic policies. Regarding these similarities and differences, a Greek citizenship policy based on the Orthodox Christian and a Hellenic nationalist tradition and a Turkish citizenship policy based on a Kemalist secular nationalist ideology stand out as two frameworks which may shed light on the inquiry on a potential conflict between human rights and national citizenship.

Like many other states, Greece and Turkey have undergone tremendous societal changes as well as experiencing a global pressure to comply with international human rights regulations. This has brought together debates about the multicultural population in both countries, immigration, and ethnic conflicts at different levels, and has in turn shifted these interlinked discussions to the centre of the governments discourses and policies. This emphasis has been accelerated by a number of high profile local developments and by the increase in cultural demands of ethnic and religious minorities in both states. As a result, democratic values and human rights are now worded more loudly in policy compared to only a couple of decades ago, particularly in the area of education.

As a result of this trend, Turkey, as one of the first countries in Europe that established a *National Committee on the Decade for Human Rights Education* in

1998, has initiated human rights education classes as a pilot project in 2011 with the aim of spreading human rights values among its young people (Kaymakcan, 2002). Similarly, Greece announced in 1998 a *Human Rights Education Action Plan* in order to improve on and conduct monitoring in this area. At the same time, unrest amongst young people in Greece and ethnic minority communities in Turkey are taking place. This has contributed to increasing concerns about a possible erosion of the glorified national values within the context of citizenship education.

Researchers have conducted analyses on the changing citizenship policies separately and at different levels (see e.g., Aslan & Culha, 2008; Chelmis, 1999; Sakonidis, 2001). However, there is little information as to how citizenship education in these countries has evolved as a response to these socio-political changes and if and how citizenship education conflicts with a human rights perspective.

METHODOLOGICAL CONCERNS

Policy problems are normally characterized by conflicting values, statements in policy texts are thus difficult to detect in the contexts where legitimate power of policy is decentralized (Dryzek, 1982). Yet, in centralized structures, these texts are unobtrusive resources, rich in portraying the values in the setting and in facilitating discovery of nuances in cultural settings (Maxwell, 2004; Olssen, Codd & O'Neill, 2004).

Pinson (2007) points to the potential of educational policy documents in understanding the citizenship policy in a state. She notes that the designing and implementing education policy documents such as curriculum guidance or teaching materials are often the sites where processes of constructing the notion of citizenship and the meanings of 'being a citizen' take place. Similarly, Olssen et al. (2004) describe policy documents as the expression of political purposes, that is the statements of the courses of action that policy makers intend to follow. Thus, policy statements or documents have an enormous potential to reveal policy intentions, often in the form of values and goals, specifically in centralized systems such as Greece and Turkey.

The demand of inferential reasoning, however, stands out as a potential weakness of researching policy documents (Marshall & Rossman, 1989). It is possible to claim that documents do not provide descriptions about the reality of the social world. We do not assume that documentary accounts are accurate portrayals of the social world, but depending on the context and level of legacy, they can reveal valuable information about the underlying political intentions of society. From this perspective, even if analysing policy texts does not tell us about the implementations of the policies in question, they provide us with an insight into what is considered among policy makers to be desirable and good in education. In this sense, policy texts pose patterns of ideological goals and intentions of their creators, which make them valuable sources to understand the policies which are products of competing ideologies.

As for the policy documents in education, education laws, curriculum documents, decrees, regulations and even constitutions are the most public and concrete forms of education policy (Looney, 2001). A Foucauldian analysis of education also advocates that what is studied in schools should be understood as a significant site in which competing bodies of knowledge, identities and discourse are negotiated (McCarthy & Crichlow, 1993; Mills, 1997). These official texts carry explicit or implicit intentions and objectives of their designers (Cornbleth, 1990). In this sense, while conducting any educational research aiming to reveal competing ideologies, these documents are a strategic start.

Hence, this research focuses on the documents that reveal the notion of citizenship and the explicit values which the students are supposed to acquire as citizens. In so doing, we have limited our focus to policy documents legally binding for the educators. The documents are obtained from the Constitutions of Greece and Turkey, general education law, other legislative texts, decisions from the Ministries of Education in addition to other official texts prescribing the goals of the subjects of language, national history and religion which are the common playground of individual and state relationships on the axis of human rights and citizenship.

While analysing these documents in order to understand the citizenship policy of two states, we examined a broad range of conditions serving to promote a sense of shared national identity: the vernacular languages, fabricated rituals and traditions beside promoted vision of nation in the axis of diversity and homogenization by the state (Skinner, 1989). As a result of the intensive discussion of the parameters of citizenship policy, we ended up with two main themes: the relationship between the state and the individual, and the perception of "the other" through elevation of national language, conception of national culture, country, symbols and historical role models, national and religious ceremonies, and promoted virtues (Brown, 1999; Griffith, 2000; Hargreaves, 1998; Skinner, 1989). Through this work we have tried to unravel what kind of citizenship education is promoted in the two countries, the content of such an education, how a sense of belonging to the nation is expected to be expressed, and how and to what extent deviations from the mainstream is presented and understood, as for example visible in the attitudes towards minority languages and understanding of minority religions.

Before moving on to the discussions of these topics, we will clarify the conceptual framework we work within.

CONCEPTUAL FRAMEWORK

Historically, a citizen was simply a member or "denizen" of a city, a carrier of urban collectivity which was relatively decoupled from the demands of a state (Bennett, Grossberg, & Morris, 2005; Janoski, 1998). This city level model of citizenship was expanded in the context of the European bourgeois revolutions in the 18th and 19th Century, and the emergence of nation-states introduced a new interpretation of citizenship as a legal concept (Janoski, 1998; Purvis & Hunt,

1999). These new states recognized a larger number of inhabitants as their citizens, with a more diverse citizenry as a result. In the nation-building project, however, citizenship based on a national identity is commonly modelled around a shared history, land, language and cultural values in order to ensure social integration and make diverse people in a large territory feel politically and emotionally responsible for one another (Habermas, 1992; Purvis & Hunt, 1999; Rex, 1996; Scheilke & Schreiner, 2001). In this way, citizenship tends to be associated with and related to a person's national status, i.e. if you were to be considered a citizen of Turkey, with the rights and obligation that comes along with this status, you have to be considered Turkish, being part of the community of shared identity. Therewith some particularities were introduced to the newly gained individual citizenship liberties. First of all, the freedom of the nation was of a different, particular nature, an independence that must be defended if necessary by sacrificing the individual freedoms and rights including the right to life (Habermas, 1996). Consequently collective priorities were put above individual rights. Also, in this formulation the rights of citizenship were not unconditionally available for everyone, although it was presented as an inclusive collective membership status for the people in the nation. On the contrary, this national citizen was a territorially and culturally limited and selective term, as the nation did not include people who were left out of the sovereign national community and territory.

In this context, citizenship was problematic for both nationals who were identified as deviating from the mainstream national and cultural values, and for non-nationals. The scope of the problem was further expanded in the wake of social and political changes such as immigration, social movements, and diversification of political orientations. As a result, the status of citizenship within the nation-state, where there are already multinational entities has evolved in a new direction. Diversity and multiple identities, which were disguised by the efforts of the national homogenization project, have been worded more loudly, particularly after the atrocities of World War II, and the protection of individual and minority rights have gradually gained ground and recognition. This transition period is a 'post-national constellation', a term used by Jürgen Habermas (1996), meaning that the nation state has transferred some of its sovereignty to supranational organizations in order to protect the needs of the multiethnic and multicultural modern societies (Habermas, 1996). This process, with its legally binding conventions, has played a decisive role in a redefinition of the concept of citizenship. Herein, Paulina Tambakaki (2010) points to the central role and importance of the human rights regime. Introducing the language of human rights is, in fact, a turning point in the theory and practice of citizenship, as it accepts the rights of the individual contrary to the contractual rights and duties agreement which prevailed in nation state citizenship (Osler & Starkey, 2010).

The human rights regime presents a distinct interpretation of citizenship as a set of values granted to a human being, regardless of judicial status of the person. This cosmopolitan vision emphasizes the role of the state as the guarantor of citizens' rights, whereas the state's sovereignty can be overridden by supra-national institutions advocating for the rights of citizens unconstrained by the nation state framework (Chandler, 2003). From a legal perspective, nation states are committed to abide by the international human rights conventions they have signed and ratified. These human rights instruments are the basis for the theoretical understanding of the changing nature of citizenship (Morsink, 1999). On the other hand, some states tend to support and promote citizenship and human rights values separately, not seeing human rights as a part of or as an augmentation of citizenship itself (Habermas, 1996). A concrete reflection of this tension between two value systems is observed in schools, the platform of the cultivation of moral virtues, ideologies and attitudes. On the one hand, national citizenship within the restrictive nation state framework is built on the promotion of a common identity and loyalty towards the nation and the state (Roth & Burbules, 2007; Skeie, 2001). Hereby, citizenship education is presented as a complete package of values embedded in all school activities, explicitly or implicitly to raise citizens who are expected to internalize the national values (Banks, 2008). Embedded in a divergent value system, on the other hand, is the aim to promote a more cosmopolitan view of citizenship by using a human rights based approach (Tomaševski, 2001). The fundamental goal of human rights in education is not just to equip learners with theoretical knowledge and understanding of these values, but to create an independent citizen empowered with capabilities to act and react in accordance with international human rights perspectives. These two value systems, the nationalist focus and the human rights focus are not necessarily compatible and may at times appear as competing values (Tomaševski, 2001).

In a long leap over a serpent's nest of problems, we have come to acknowledge that we do not engage in a philosophical debate about human rights. Rather, the line of arguments presented in this chapter can be positioned partially within what Dembour (2006) would define as the natural school of thought, implying that we take human rights as proprietary rights of all human beings and the international adherence to human rights indicates a sort of consensus of this value system. One example of this alleged consensus is the universal appreciation of the Convention of the Rights of the Child (CRC) (UN, 1989). This may be seen as an illustration of how citizenship in a state is not fully working as a protector of some of the most vulnerable among us, the children. At the same time we recognize the restraints present when individuals are dependent on a state to both grant them rights as well as to protect them from violations of these rights. Hence, we write in a tradition where human rights are considered fundamental values in society and universal, yet recognize the tension that may occur when national values conflict with what is considered international human rights.

In the following sections we will discuss two dimensions of the visible tension between these two values system. Although they are not comprehensive of the topic at hand, we expect them to serve as examples of how the strive for an ideal citizenship education may prove to be at odds with other values that the country has committed to. First, a focus will be on the state-individual relationship in an attempt to unravel the strain between communitarian and liberal aspects of citizenship. Then we will explore how the domestic perspectives on "the others" in education may come in conflict with human rights aspects.

THE STATE-INDIVIDUAL RELATIONSHIP

A common pattern in the educational objective of both Greece and Turkey is a focus on educating citizens, whereas human rights instruments value education of human beings. This can be interpreted as both states using education as an instrument in developing a citizenry according to their political convictions, contrary to human rights instruments focusing on education as an inherent entitlement of every human being. This difference may signal a fundamental deviation of understanding the relationship between the state and the individual. In the national legislation of both Greece and Turkey, education is presented as an entitlement of domestic citizens. Whereas through the human rights perspective, an individual's existence in and of itself creates grounds for eligibility to education. We understand that this can be considered a rather speculative argument, but there are several aspects of the Greek and Turkish legislation which can substantiate such a claim. This will be illustrated in the following arguments.

Greek education has historically been shaped around the objective of raising ideal citizens symbolized in the Fatherland, Family and Religion-triad (Makrinioti & Solomon, 1999). Citizenship education aims at transmitting the basic components of Greek national identity by promoting national symbols and glorification of national heroes as well as promoting the role of the Greek language in the conservation of the national culture (Chelmis, 1999). One of the fundamental objectives of education has been to develop a sense of loyalty and belonging to the nation with a focus on acquisition of an in-depth knowledge of historical events in Greece, national enemies and national allies (Chelmis, 1999). Article 16 of the Greek Constitution (Greek Government, 2001) regulates education, arts, and science and dictates the core mission of compulsory education in Greece as educating for nationalism and collective values with a focus on moral, intellectual, vocational and physical training of Greeks, the development of national and religious consciousness and values, and the creation of free and responsible citizens.

The individual rights recognized by the Greek Constitution are based on two general clauses of the Constitution: Article 2 for the value of the person and Article 5 for human dignity. A human rights emphasis is made in article 5, which repeats that individual human rights apply to all residents of Greece. If these articles are to be evaluated based on the premise that the state is a positively engaged participant willing to promote and protect human rights and to respect, protect, and fulfill the rights of its people, a harmonic coexistence of national citizenship values and human rights values looks possible in Greece. Article 4, however, underlines in the fourth paragraph that political rights are granted to Greek citizens only. So it constitutes an obstacle to voting and to the ability of active participation in civil and political life of the state and society.

This makes participation in political and social rights exclusively available to national citizens who have been educated with national and religious consciousness and who fulfill their duties to protect the independence and sovereignty of the fatherland (Greek Constitution, Article 4). When comparing with the Universal Declaration of Human Rights (UDHR) (UN, 1948) a tension seems to emerge.

69

Already in Article 2 in the UDHR it is declared that individuals are considered to have their rights protected by the state "without distinction of any kind, such as race, color, sex, language, religion, political or other opinion, national or social origin, property, birth or other status" (UN, 1948). These clear universal standards set out to go above and beyond any of the contractual official citizenship relationships with the individuals and the state, and not limited to individuals with an official status as citizens.

In addition to the fundamental regulations of the Greek Constitution, the Greek Law on the structure and organisation of primary and secondary education (Law 1566/1985) (Ministry of Education and Religious Affairs, 1985) is another important legal text regulating structure and operation of the primary and secondary education in Greece. Officially decreed objectives and purposes of education in this law tend to affirm the promotion of human rights, often repeating the wording of international human rights instruments. The education in Greece, however, explicitly continues to carry on the implant of the nationalist creed in new generations and the development of their skills so as to enable them to sacrifice their individual needs and desires for national unity and sovereignty. On this basis, the first objective of education is laid down as follows:

> Students [are] to become free, responsible, democratic citizens, to defend national independence, territorial integrity of the country and democracy, be inspired by love for human life and nature and to improve the loyalty to the homeland and the original elements of the Orthodox Christian tradition. Freedom of religious conscience is inviolable. (Ministry of Education and Religious Affairs, 1985, Article 1)

Given that this is the first article in the law it is of rather high significance. Although the students are to become free and democratic citizens, they are also expected to have a specific loyalty to Greece and comply with one particular religion, Orthodox Christianity. Even if the focus of religion is on its *traditional* elements, one religion is given priority over others and loyalty is expected, indicating some of the characteristics of an ideal citizenry and the aim of education. To some extent this is problematic from a human rights perspective. The individual freedom is fundamental within a human rights paradigm, including religious freedom, and an emphasis is put on a loyalty of a more cosmopolitan nature than what is described in the Greek Education Law.

Similarly, Article 4 of the same law assigns more specific ideological roles to compulsory primary education. In particular, elementary school students are expected to gradually become familiar with ethical, religious, national, humanitarian and other values. What is more, this education is required to help pupils become free, responsible and democratic citizens, as well as citizens capable of fighting for national independence and democracy (Ministry of Education and Religious Affairs, 1985, Article 4).

Herein, a problematic relationship between individuals and the state is revisited by giving duty to feel morally attached to the state and defend national and territorial sovereignty as these are described as main characteristics of the ideal individual. If citizens do not want to, for example, take up arms to defend Greece as a way of "protecting their fatherland" they are not considered as fulfilling their civic duty. This is then contradicting the freedom of conscience and political views granted to individuals through human rights instruments. Hence, this can serve as an illustration of the tension between the values promoted through citizenship education and human rights found in international conventions.

In the Turkish Constitution (1982), which was put into force by the military government in 1980, the role of the state driven education is prescribed. Its Article 42 entitled *Education rights and duties* determines the scope of educational activities. Education and instruction is controlled by the Government, and the Turkish citizens are to be educated in the frame of Atatürk's principles of nationalism, statism, laicism, reformism, populism, republicanism, and revolution (Turkish Government – Turkish Constitution, 1982, Article 42). In the next paragraph of the Article, it is stated that ideologies contrasting with the sovereignty of the Turkish state are to be avoided and the educational objectives are designed to ensure national unity (Turkish Government, 1982, Amendment, 3/10/2001-4709/1). The characteristics and content of the so-called contrasting ideologies are, however, not defined in further detail, but since national unity is held high individual human rights have the potential of being an ideology contrasting the sovereignty of the Turkish state. Ultimate compliance to Atatürk's principles, as laid down in Article 42, blurs the state-individual relationship as this relationship is not only regulated through legislation, duties and rights, but also included a particular set of values which the citizen is expected to comply with. This opens up for a tension between national values and individual human rights, which can be expected to also be visible in the education system.

On the other hand, the Turkish Law of National Education (Law 25212/2003) (Ministry of National Education, 2003) describes the general purpose of education to include respect for human rights as well as to raise all Turkish citizens as individuals who are committed to Atatürk's principles. These principles include the Atatürk Nationalism as defined in the Constitution. The students are expected to develop traits enabling them to protect and develop the national, human, moral and cultural values of the Turkish nation. What is more, students are to love and continuously try to appraise their family, country and nation, and to be aware of their duties and responsibilities towards the Turkish Republic. Although human rights appear as part and parcel of the educational law, the individual's obligations towards the state and the sovereign nation are presented as a moral duty. This value system again blurs the picture of legal rights and obligations of the citizens, introducing an understanding of liberal rights as inferior to the expectations of the state toward its citizens.

From the above presentation it is evident that education is to serve as an institution in which national citizens are to acquire a common sense of belonging and a national culture with a loyal commitment to the development of a collective society. The ideal citizen, in accordance with the collective values of the Greek and Turkish nations, is a modern person who keeps an active role in protecting and promoting the country and nation's prosperity and independence. These ideals are worded in the Greek Education Law, illustrated through this quote:

> To develop creative and critical thinking and perception of collective effort and cooperation, to take initiative and responsible participation, to contribute decisively in the progress of society and the development of the Greek state. (Ministry of Education and Religious Affairs, 1985, Article 1)

Likewise, Turkish Education Law (Law 25212/2003) (Ministry of National Education, 2003) determines the role of the students as to increase the welfare and happiness of the Turkish citizens and Turkish society, and to support and facilitate economic, social and cultural development in national unity and integration, and finally to make the Turkish nation a constructive, creative and distinguished partner in modern civilization (Ministry of National Education, 2003, Article 4).

These objectives are potentially incompatible with some basic human rights values. It seems as if the individual freedom and empowerment, as is the focus of human rights values, are not core values in the Greek and Turkish understanding of an ideal citizen. Rather empowerment of the state and nation is emphasized at the expense of individual. Individual empowerment is rarely visible in the texts.

THE STATE'S PERSPECTIVES OF "THE OTHERS"

Perspectives on who are considered to be or not to be included in mainstream society are an important aspect of human rights perspectives. The way a state handles diversity can be described as a litmus test on their dedication towards democracy and human rights. Policies on how to deal with linguistic and religious diversity are relevant in this discussion as human rights instruments grant individual's the right to not be discriminated against and promote individual freedoms. Hence, if the education system is in compliance with their human rights obligations, these aspects should be visible in the citizenship education in school. We are now going to investigate closer how some of these aspects are treated in the policy documents of Greece and Turkey.

The confrontations of values in both countries are backed by history lessons transmitting values of ethnocentric visions of historical developments. In Greece, the persistent approach has been teaching of the glorious past of Hellenic Greek civilization and independence of Greece, which is organized around significant historical wars and great personalities (Zambeta, 2000). This has shaped the Greek history education in the 19th century, the era of national integration of the Greek social formation, and is based on the sovereignty of the nation. This approach has prevailed in the country until the democratization process of Greece which started after the last military dictatorship. This approach has been fed with the ideology of Hellenism, rivalry with Turkey and the idea of being a nation surrounded by enemies, and, hence, a strong sense of nationalism seems not only important, but as a neutralizing agent against dangerous domestic and international enemies (Aycan, 2005). The portrayal of "the others" as a threat to social cohesion, based on historical narratives is thus an important element in the teaching of history.

Therefore the current history education objectives continue to be nationalist oriented (Makriyianni & Psaltis, 2007). The general purpose of history is described as to help students to learn and appreciate the history and cultural heritage of Greece and shape national consciousness as members of the Greek nation (Ministry of Education and Religious Affairs, 2006). The narrative promoted through the textbooks promotes a picture of the ancient Greek civilization and the brave struggles for freedom of the Greeks (Makriyianni & Psaltis, 2007). Before discussing this any further, we turn our attention to the Turkish situation.

It is also observed that history teaching in Turkey takes a somewhat similar approach, yet with a more secular nationalist stand. The stories of the War of Independence, major Turkish leaders and specifically Atatürk's life and revolutions constitute the major part of history teaching. The objectives of history teaching in Turkish education are aimed:

> [To] make students understand the role of Atatürk and his principles and its contribution to the development of Turkey, acquire the motivation of guarding the secular, democratic, nationalist and westernized virtues of the Turkish republic; to make them acquire a consciousness of history, future and today, to make the students take responsibility to conserve cultural and historical heritage by teaching them basic principles and pillars of Turkish history, culture and historical events; to make students internalize the national identity, the components of the identity and necessity of preserving that identity; to make students comprehend the importance of national unity by creating a bridge between past and present; to make them learn about the civilizations throughout the history; to make them comprehend the contribution of Turkish nation to the humanity and world civilization ...; and to make them comprehend the fundamental universal values such as peace, tolerance, democracy and human rights and ensure them to be sensitive to these values. (Law 25212/2003)

The most striking point in this quote is how the individual's responsibilities towards the state are emphasized. The students have a moral duty and responsibility to conserve cultural and historical heritage and cultivating a national identity. In this frame, history teaching has a clear ideological aim of shaping the national citizens in compliance with the topics addressed in the constitution and the educational law.

Simultaneously, history teaching in both Greece and Turkey involves appreciation and elevation of national values, historical role models such as Ataturk and finally respect for the rights and dignity of others. While they express their aspiration to develop a spirit of friendship and cooperation with all peoples on earth, they continue to reinforce national myths and traditions. Hence their focus privileges a national perspective over a cosmopolitan worldview present in human rights instruments. Additionally, the emphasis on the territorial and national sovereignty and identity in history teaching leads to a tension between the universalism of an egalitarian legal community – supported by human rights – and the particularism of a cultural community connected by origin and fate (Habermas, 1996).

Educational activities connected to religion and language also pose challenges in achieving a peaceful perception of "the others". To understand this better, the status of religion in both countries needs to be highlighted. In the Turkish Constitution, the laicity of the state apparatus is presented as one of the unalterable articles (Turkish Government – Turkish Constitution, Article 4). Under the strict laicism of the Turkish Republic, religion is seen to be approached as a rival to Turkish nationalism and state ideology aligning Atatürk's principles as exemplified here:

> No protection shall be accorded to an activity, ideology and conviction contrary to Turkish national interests, the principle of the indivisibility of the existence of Turkey with its state and territory, Turkish historical and moral values or the nationalism, principles, reforms and modernism of Atatürk and that, as required by the principle of secularism, there shall be no interference whatsoever by sacred religious feelings in state affairs and politics. (Turkish Constitution – Amendment 3/10/2001-4709/1)

This statement has a potential to lead to arbitrary interpretation of what convictions and ideologies that represent a threat to the unity of Turkey and its fundamental values. Political and social movements with different identity claims have been regarded as divisive and put under pressure using the above phrase from the Constitution (Aydin & Colak, 2004). Consecutive closing of 26 political parties with the accusation of undermining the secular regime and/or indivisibility of the existence of the country since the introduction of multi-party system is one of the best illuminating examples of this practice.

Religious education is neither let aside by the state. Article 24 of the Constitution grants the state the single authority in ensuring and supervision of religious education, and ironically religious education is mandatory in both primary and secondary education under the name of *Din Kulturu ve Ahlak Bilgisi* (Religion and Moral Education).The general objectives of this state-driven compulsory subject includes getting to know Atatürk's views on Islam, major contemporary religions, the concept of secularism, love for the country in the frame of Islam and the principles of Islam from a Turkish historical context. This approach to teaching religion has at least two implications relevant to this discussion. First of all it supports the allegiance to the state by teaching students about the heroic and holy nature of an individual sacrifice for the country's sovereignty as well as solidifying the iconic national father, Atatürk. Secondly, it helps the state to ensure that values important to those who are not considered core citizens of Turkey, e.g., Alevism (a particular Muslim sect) and other Islamic congregations are prohibited from penetrating religious education. Thus, what is considered as a core religious perspective of Turkishness is protected in the national citizenship project.

The relation between the state, education and religion in Greece is different from Turkey, on the other hand. The fact that the Ministry of Education includes religion (Ministry of Education and Religious Affairs, 2001) is concrete evidence of this divergence. The second paragraph of Article 16 in the Greek Constitution draws the lines of religion teaching, implying that the major content is expected to relate to the Orthodox Christian tradition. Additionally, the framework of the religious education provided by the Constitution is specified by Law no. 1566/1985 (Ministry of Education and Religious Affairs, 1985), more specifically "to realize the deeper significance of the Orthodox Christian character and sustained commitment to universal values". In other words, it sets as the primary purpose of education to develop students who are rooted in the Orthodox Christian tradition, and at the same time respecting human rights. In the Law on Education (Ministry of Education and Religious Affairs, 1985), religion is set as a compulsory subject for all students. Circular no. 104071/G2/4.8.2008 issued by the Ministry of Education and Religious Affairs (2008), however, exempts non-Orthodox students from this subject. What is remarkable is that students, who are not part of mainstream religion, are exempted from a subject that traditionally constitutes the backbone of Greek national education as well as citizenship education. This situation makes the Greek religious education an interesting case when it comes to how diversity and freedom of religion is practiced. It is evident that religious education is constructed for the Orthodox Christian Greek citizens as presented in the Constitution and the Educational Law. This approach makes human rights education problematic. Since religious education is considered a core element in citizenship education, an exclusionary practice is taking place. Students belonging to other denominations, or none at all, are exempted from this core of citizenship education. Their deviation from mainstream society, in this case Orthodox Christianity, creates citizens perceived as lacking an essential characteristic of what is considered to be a Greek citizen. They do not belong to Orthodox Christianity, nor do they receive education about core values as Greek citizens as those themes are placed in a *religious* subject. What is more, including mainly students who are already devoted to Orthodox Christianity in the religious classes in school supports the State in preserving the status quo, and other potentially threatening perspectives are kept out of the way. We argue that the Greek State is somewhat avoiding the social reality of a multi-religious country. How to handle this diversity is not made a pivotal part of citizenship education, and creating tension when advocating for a more cosmopolitan society infused with human rights.

Another noticeable and reflective practice of the Greek and Turkish ethno-religious particularism is the compulsory Morning Prayer in Greece and the pledge of allegiance ceremony (*Andimiz*) in Turkey. A Greek Presidential Decree (201/1998, Article 5.5) makes the common prayer of students and teachers in the school yard prior to the start of the school day mandatory in Greece. The same decree even explains how this ceremony is to be carried out during rainy days. The heterodox students attend the ceremony without participating in the prayer, keeping absolute silence while their teachers and fellow students pray according to Christian Orthodox tradition. A similar compulsory ceremony is arranged in Turkish primary schools every morning. This ceremony, which is more nationalist than religious, is required to be done in both private and public primary schools according to Article 12 in the primary education legislation (Ministry of National

Education, 1973). Herein, students recite an oath called *Andimiz* in which they all, except for non-Turkish citizens say:

> I am a Turk. I am honest and I am a hard worker. My duty is to protect those younger than me and to respect my elders, to love my country and my people more than I love myself. My ideal is to progress. Hey, Great Atatürk! I solemnly promise to walk on the road you have opened, to the goal you have showed, without stopping. I offer my existence to the Turkish nation as a gift. How happy for the one who says 'I am a Turk'.[i]

The backbone of citizenship education in Turkey is to develop towards being a Turk. This also implies walking in the footsteps of Atatürk. Although the school is secular in theory, the role of Atatürk, as exemplified in the *Andimiz*, seems to be rather heroic and almost holy in nature. What is more, one of the duties of a Turkish citizen is to recite *Andimiz* in school- only those who are non-Turkish citizens are exempted from this activity. The consequence of this exemption and non-participation is that "the other" is not considered to be part of the Turkish citizenry.

Despite divergence in the practices of religious or ideological teaching in Greece and Turkey, they share similar challenges to the understanding of religious freedom presented in Article 18 of the UDHR (UN, 1948). This article states that everyone has the right to freedom of thought, conscience and religion. It applies to religious and secular beliefs including political opinions. This right also includes freedom to practice or manifest his or her religion or belief in teaching, practice, worship and observance (Osler & Starkey, 2010). In both countries, students who do not participate in the above outlined activities tend to be excluded from the definition of what constitutes a citizen. One of the complex tensions between citizenship education and human rights values in both countries stems from the fact that there is no religious or ideological neutrality, alienating even further those who are considered "the other".

Another vital component of cultural rights, and thus relevant to a state's perspectives on "the others", is the right to use your own language although it differs from the official language of the country you live in (Bruthiaux, 2008; Council of Europe, 1992; Kymlicka & Patten, 2003; UNESCO, 1996). Language is often considered to be the most conspicuous symbol of national identity. Such an important building block of the membership to a nation receives a significant focus in both countries' citizenship values. Article 42 in the Turkish Constitution, for example, dictates that no language other than Turkish may be taught as mother tongue to Turkish citizens in education. The foreign languages to be taught in educational institutions are defined by laws (Turkish Constitution, Article 42). The objective of teaching language at schools is to ensure that students gain ability to communicate with their environment in a proper way, to love and admire Turkish language, be informed about its grammar, to use it correctly and confidently, to improve the skills of listening and reading, to have a national feeling and enthusiasm, to get acquainted with Turkish culture, admiring it, loving the Turkish land, life, humanity and nature (Ministry of National Education, 2003). The situation in Greece is quite similar. The unchallengeable oneness of Greek language education is under protection of the Greek Constitution. Some objectives of language teaching are to make students appreciate the importance of language as a key expression of Greek culture, its importance for the nation, to identify the structure and characteristics of the Greek national language, to recognize and appreciate the preserved continuity of the Greek language and the richness of its interactive forms, realizing the social and geographical diversity of the Greek language, to develop skills and abilities which will contribute to harmonious and balanced development, and to carry out a life as a responsible and creative citizen.

Language uniformity is thus present in both countries and considered an instrument of uniting each nation. However, a tension is present in regards to human rights as cultural and linguistic rights for minorities are not promoted but rather seen as a threat. Although languages of immigrants are allowed to some extent in schools, it is considered rather as a means in the integration process into mainstream society rather than an individual right and a resource for society.

IN CLOSING

In this chapter we have tried to highlight tensions between citizenship education and human rights. This may appear somewhat contradictory in the outset, but through the illustrative examples of Greece and Turkey it is evident that the national values of citizenship are doomed to collide with the cosmopolitan framework provided by the human rights instruments. This tension is particularly visible in the relationship between the individual and the state and in relation to people who are not considered as members of mainstream society.

Habermas (1996) proposes a solution to this inevitable conflict, which is for states to convent into a cosmopolitan understanding of the nation as an entity based on diversity among its citizens. Accordingly, the nation state must get rid of the nationalism that had originally been the vehicle for its sovereignty (Habermas, 1996). Maybe the only possibility to implement human rights is an entire shift of attitudes on what constitutes national citizenship, where human rights function as the value basis. According to Camilleri and Falk (1992), the challenge is to rethink these concepts in order to enable a negotiation between national and cosmopolitan perspectives on the meaning of community membership. However, the problem, particularly in the context of centralized and strong nation-states such as Greece and Turkey, is to assume that human rights and national values in citizenship are negotiable and have an opportunity of coexistence. This is, in our opinion, problematic. A more desirable path to a just society is offered through cosmopolitan citizenship using human rights as a package of values. This offers a radically new model for understanding the value system of citizenship.

NOTES

[i] The statement "How happy for the one who says 'I am a Turk'" is a saying of Atatürk and considered a motto fundamental to Turkish nationalism.

BIBLIOGRAPHY

Aycan, N. (2005). The process of getting identity in Turkish society: Kemalist education. *Journal of Social Sciences, 1*(3), 136-140.

Aydin, E., & Colak, Y. (2004). Dilemmas of Turkish democracy: The encounter between Kemalist Laicism and Islamism in 1990s Turkey. In D. O. Scott (Ed.), *Democracy: Free exercise and diverse visions and religion* (pp. 202-220). Kent, Ohio: Kent State University Press.

Banks, J. A. (2008). Diversity, group identity, and citizenship education in a global age. *Educational Researcher, 37*(3), 129-139.

Bennett, T., Grossberg, L., & Morris, M. (2005). *New keywords – A revised vocabulary of culture and society.* Oxford: Blackwell.

Brown, D. (1999). Are there good and bad nationalisms? *Nations and Nationalism, 5*(2), 281-302.

Bruthiaux, P. (2008). Language rights in historical and contemporary perspective. *Journal of Multilingual and Multicultural Development, 30*(1), 73-85.

Camilleri, J., & Falk, J. (1992). *The end of sovereignty? The politics of a shrinking and fragmenting world.* Aldershot: Edward Elgar.

Chandler, D. (2003). New rights for old? Cosmopolitan citizenship and the critique of state sovereignty. *Political Studies, 51*(2), 339-356.

Chelmis, K. S. (1999). Citizenship values and political education in Greek primary school: An historical perspective. In A. Ross (Ed.), *Young citizen in Europe. Proceedings of the First Conference of the Children's Identity and Citizenship in Europe Thematic Network* (pp. 65-71). London: CiCe Publishers.

Clogg, R. (2002). *A concise history of Greece.* Cambridge: Cambridge University Press.

Cornbleth, C. (1990). *Curriculum in context.* Basingstoke: Falmer Press.

Council of Europe (1992). *The European Charter for Regional or Minority Languages.* Strasbourg: Council of Europe.

Dembour, M. B. (2006). *Who believes in human rights? Reflections on the European Convention.* Cambridge: Cambridge University Press.

Dryzek, J. (1982). Policy analysis as hermeneutic activity. *Policy Sciences, 14,* 309-329.

Greek Government (2001). *The constitution of Greece.* Athens: National Legislative Bodies.

Greek Presidential Decree (1998). No. 201/1998 (July 1) on the operation of primary education institutions.

Griffith, R. (2000). *National curriculum: National disaster? Education and citizenship.* London: Routledge.

Habermas, J. (1992). Citizenship and national identity: Some reflections of the future of Europe. *Praxis International, 12*(1), 1-19.

Habermas, J. (1996). The European nation-state: Its achievements and its limits. On the past and future of sovereignty and citizenship. In G. Balakrishnan (Ed.), *Mapping the nation* (pp. 281-316). London: Verso.

Hargreaves, D. (1998). A new partnership of stakeholders and a national strategy for research in education. In J. Rudduck & D. McIntyre (Eds.), *Challenges for educational research* (pp. 114-138). London: PCP/Sage.

Icduygu, A., & Kaygusuz, O. (2004). The politics of citizenship by drawing borders: Foreign policy and the construction of national citizenship identity in Turkey. *Middle Eastern Studies, 40*(6), 26-50.

Janoski, T. (1998), *Citizenship and civil society: A framework of rights and obligations in liberal, traditional, and social democratic regimes.* Cambridge: Cambridge University Press.

Kaymakcan, R. (2002). *Religious education in modern Turkey in the context of freedom of religion or belief.* Oslo Coalition on Freedom of Religion or Belief. Retrieved from: http://folk.uio.no/leirvik/OsloCoalition/RecepKaymakcan.htm.

Kymlicka, W., & Patten, A. (2003). Introduction: Language rights and political theory: Context, issues and approaches. In W. Kymlicka & A. Patten (Eds.), *Language rights and political theory* (pp. 1-51). Oxford: Oxford University Press.

Looney, A. (2001). Curriculum as policy: Some implications of contemporary policy studies for the analysis of curriculum policy, with particular reference to post-primary curriculum policy in the Republic of Ireland. *The Curriculum Journal, 12*(2), 149-162.

Makrinioti, D., & Solomon, J. (1999). The discourse of citizenship education in Greece: National identity and social diversity. In J. V. Torney-Purta, J. Schwille, & J.-A. Amadeo (Eds.), *Civic education across countries: twenty-four national studies from the IEA Civic Education Project* (pp. 285-311). Amsterdam: IEA.

Makriyianni, C., & Psaltis, C. (2007). History teaching and reconciliation. *Cyprus Review, 19*, 43-69.

Marshall, C., & Rossmann, G. B. (1989). *Designing qualitative research.* Newbury Park, CA: Sage.

Maxwell, J. A. (2004). *Qualitative research design: An interactive approach.* Beverly Hills, CA: Sage.

McCarthy, C., & Crichlow, W. (1993). Introduction. In C. McCarthy & W. Crichlow (Eds.), *Race, identity and representation in education* (pp. xiii-xxix). New York: Routledge.

Mills, S. (1997). *Discourse.* Abingdon: Routledge.

Ministry of Education and Religious Affairs (Greece) (1985). *Law 1566/1985 Structure and Operation of Primary and Secondary Education.*

Ministry of Education and Religious Affairs (Greece) (2006). *The Curriculum of Primary Education guidance.*

Ministry of Education and Religious Affairs (Greece) (2008). *Circular 104071/G2/4.8.2008 issued on the status of non-Orthodox student in religion classes.*

Ministry of National Education (Turkey) (1973). *Principal Law (no: 1739) Organization and Operation of Primary Schools.*

Ministry of National Education (Turkey) (2003). *Law 25212/2003 Primary Education Aims and Structures.*

Morsink, J. (1999). *The universal declaration of human rights: Origins, drafting, and intent.* Philadelphia: University of Pennsylvania Press.

Olssen, M., Codd, J., & O'Neill, A. M. (2004). *Education policy: Globalization, citizenship and democracy.* Thousand Oaks: Sage.

Osler, A., & Starkey, H. (2010). *Teachers and human rights education.* Stoke-on-Trent: Trentham.

Pinson, H. (2007). Inclusive curriculum? Challenges to the role of citizenship. Education in a Jewish and democratic state. *Curriculum Inquiry, 34*(4), 303-328.

Purvis, T., & Hunt, A. (1999). Citizenship versus identity: Transformations in the discourses and practices of citizenship. *Social and Legal Studies, 8*, 457-482.

Rex, J. (1996). National identity in the democratic multi-cultural state. *Sociological Research Online, 1*, 2.

Roth, K., & Burbules, N. C. (2007). Introduction. In K. Roth & N. C. Burbules (Eds.), *Changing notions of citizenship education in contemporary nation-states* (pp. 1-9). Rotterdam: Sense Publishers.

Sakonidis, H. (2001). Social and civilization conflicts in the classroom teaching math: The case of the minority schools in Thrace. In E. Tressou & S. Mitakidou (Eds.), *Education of linguistic minorities* (pp. 410-420). Thessaloniki: Paratiritis.

Scheilke, C., & Schreiner, P. (Eds.) (2001). *Towards religious competence: Diversity as a challenge for education in Europe.* Lit Verlag: Münster.

Sevincer, V. (2009). *Changing notion of citizenship in Greece and Turkey: A comparative analysis of citizenship policies through education.* Unpublished dissertation. University of Oslo, Oslo, Norway.

Skeie, G. (2001). Citizenship, identity, politics and religious education. In H. Brock, H. Günter, C. T. Scheilke, & P. Schreiner (Eds.), *Towards religious competence: Diversity as a challenge for education in Europe* (pp. 237-252). Lit Verlag: Münster.

Skinner, Q. (1989). The state. In T. Ball, J. Farr & R. L. Hanson (Eds.), *Political innovation and conceptual change.* Cambridge: Cambridge University Press.

Tambakaki, P. (2010). *Human rights, or citizenship?* Abingdon: Birkbeck Law Press.
Tomaševski, K. (2001). Human rights in education as prerequisite for human rights education. *Right to Education Primers, No. 4*. Gothenburg: Lund University.
Turkish Government (1982). *The Constitution of the Republic of Turkey*.
UN (1948). *Universal Declaration of Human Rights*. New York: UN.
UN (1989). *Convention on the Rights of the Child*. New York: UN.
UNESCO (1996). *Universal Declaration of Linguistic Rights. Barcelona: World Conference on Linguistic Rights*. Retrieved from http://www.unesco.org/cpp/uk/declarations/linguistic.pdf.
Zambeta, E. (2000). Religion and national identity in Greek education. *Intercultural Education, 11*(2), 145-155.

AFFILIATIONS

Vedat Sevincer
Department of Educational Research
University of Oslo, Norway

Heidi Biseth
Faculty of Teacher Education
Buskerud University College, Norway

CATARINA TOMÁS AND MARIANA DIAS

6. INTERPRETING CHILDREN'S RIGHTS

A new Challenge for Education[i]

INTRODUCTION

We live in a time where social contradictions, disparities and inequalities are more visible and increasingly acute. While time and space are contracting in the virtual domain, territorial boundaries remain fixed and there is lingering intolerance shown towards others in the context of everyday life. There is a continual search for common global values, which is reflected in the concerns and actions of a large range of associations, movements, initiatives and struggles in many sectors of society, including the children's rights sector. However, the effectiveness of these struggles is limited in their impact on reducing social inequalities in the world, which Sorj (2004) refers to as the paradox of democracy. It's important to understand the gap between legal frameworks and social practices, between "law in books" and "law in action" (Santos, 1993).

This gap is even greater when we refer to childhood because there is consensus when it comes to children's rights but the intensity of their promotion is rather weak. The importance of the issue of children's rights has been formally acknowledged across the world, a development that has been reflected in legislative changes in many countries in recent years. In spite of this and the development of the discourse related to the promotion of children's rights within social and political institutions, we are still, however, very far from an ideal situation in terms of respect for these rights.

Reflecting on Western modernity from its roots (i.e. structures and concepts) to its development and on current practices towards transnational options, a distant and unrealised goal remains. In this chapter we refer to it as the assurance of children's rights. For this purpose, it is important to observe the impact of these discrepancies on different groups within society, such as children.

This chapter examines the life circumstances of children in Portugal and addresses the issue in two parts. The first attempts to describe the circumstances of southern European countries. These countries have certain characteristics that distinguish them from their European counterparts: a late transition to the democratic system, a semi-peripheral position in the global economy and a distinct social model. In the second part we analyse how these circumstances have been

H. Biseth & H. B. Holmarsdottir (eds.), Human Rights in the Field of Comparative Education, 81–95.
© *2013 Sense Publishers. All rights reserved.*

expressed regarding the implementation of international children's rights provisions in Portugal. In our discussion we pay particular attention to issues of equity and children's educational participation. We contend that despite the advances in promoting children's rights, following the democratic transition in 1974, Portuguese development in this area is marred by a contradiction between policy rhetoric, law implementation and change in social practices.

CHILDREN'S RIGHTS IN A GLOBALIZED WORLD

It is generally recognised that profound changes have occurred in recent decades. The destabilisation of the economic foundations of the Keynesian state (based upon mass production, low price energy) and the development of globalisation led to the emergence of a new political and economic agenda, in the neoliberal mould. In relation to the impact of globalisation, it has been argued that it has placed a variety of constraints on State intervention: difficulty in maintaining clearly-defined national frontiers, given the increased mobility of finances and production; the need to give priority to the foreign competitiveness of the economy, as opposed to regulating market excesses (Blackmore, 1999); the absence of legal instruments to exercise effective fiscal control over the activities of ever more powerful economic agents. Alongside these changes has come an increased scepticism about the capacity of the State to pursue inclusive social policies designed to make viable a more equitable and participatory society.

The logical outcome of this scenario has been increasing pressure to cut back and privatise services provided by the State, the quest for alternatives to direct public provision (contracting out, partnerships) and the gradual opening up of the public sector to the dictates of the market (competition, cost reduction) (Dias, 2006, 2008).

The effects of globalisation, including the effects of regulation emanating from the aforementioned agencies within the field of children's education, have led to a process of policy imposition (Cortesão & Stoer, 2001). In central Europe during the 1990's several changes in childhood policy were influenced by economic consultancies. For example, consultants from Harvard University, the World Bank, the IMF and the EU adopted terms and concepts such as privatization, efficiency and individualization, which later influenced the description of protection and education for small children in countries like Poland, Hungary or Bulgaria (Tomás, 2011). Thus, it can be argued that some agencies have attempted to adopt the role of the State, especially in the case of semi-peripheral countries such as Portugal. Under the influence of neo-liberal perspectives and the constraints imposed by the process of globalisation, the role of the nation State has been modified and limited and become more competitive in two senses of the word: firstly by cutting down its running costs and secondly in giving primacy to the economic dimensions of its activity (Dias, 2008).

Diverse forms of social groups have emerged around various organisational interests and objectives. Indeed, we have witnessed the transformation of principles in relation to civil and legal standards, as in the case of children's rights. These have been marked by different kinds of logic and reasoning, but particularly by the market logic, which presupposes a set of negotiations, commitments and resource management economics. Financial, budgetary and policy choices do not always coincide, and do not always prioritise children's rights. Institutions such as UNICEF have advocated the need for states to allocate financial resources to meet policy objectives and implement laws to fulfil children's rights (Rozga, 2001). However, Portugal has a long tradition of attempting to reform education and welfare, two systems of major importance for children, without changing the financial support.

Using Soares' (2002) terminology, most discourses on childhood are decorative and rhetoric: 'decorative', as it is politically correct to refer to the discourse on children's rights as appropriate and desirable in the language of progressive politics; 'rhetoric', because many of those who speak this decorative language of progressive politics consider it neither relevant nor attainable in children's daily lives.

How can we characterize the effect of globalisation on child rights? Overall, the implementation of children's rights has progressed at a very slow pace, anaemic in its impact on the everyday lives of children. In addition, we are seeing a sliding devaluation of the rights of the child and an inability to maintain such rights guaranteed and enshrined in the State. It seems there is an inevitability about the postponement of this interminable institutionalization to secure children's rights (Archard, 1993; Hammarberg, 1990; Sgritta, 1997; Tomás, 2011).

Several authors have engaged in the debate on globalisation and childhood. Until now, research has focused mainly on the impact of globalisation processes on children, particularly on economic and political actions (Cornia & Jolly, 1987; Frønes, 1994; Lee, 2001; Qvortrup, 2005; Ruddick, 2003; Stephens, 1995); aspects of the physical well-being of children and women (UNICEF, 2001, 2003, 2005); the impact of supranational agencies (Kaufman & Rizzini, 2002; Rizzini, 2004); aspects related to the economy, changes in the family, transnational migration and cultural aspects (Prout, 2005); globalisation, poverty and children's rights, the relationship between childhood, labour and globalisation (Bourdillon, 2004; Liebel, 2000); the global network of adoption, trafficking for forced labour or sexual tourism (Fonseca, 2002); and finally the issues of child refugees or children in armed conflicts (Hammad, 1999). A majority of researchers share the view that children and childhood in general are affected by globalisation in various ways and that children are active contributors and recipients in the globalisation processes. However, the impact of the globalisation process on childhood warrants a more detailed analysis at the national level. Portugal, as a semiperipheral society (Santos, 1991, 1993), presents a unique set of specificities in this regard.

SOCIO-DEMOGRAPHIC CHARACTERISTICS: A SNAPSHOT OF CHILDHOOD DIVERSITY IN PORTUGAL

In the past century Portuguese society has undergone considerable changes that have transformed its social, economic and cultural structure. During the thirty-seven years since the revolution (April 25th, 1974), Portugal has endured several complex and turbulent processes, which have impacted on a wide variety of social sectors. These sectors themselves are not exempt from their own contradictions and complexities, including the Carnation Revolution, decolonization, the change to socialism, the transition to democracy, the intervention of the International Monetary Fund, European Union integration and the current economic crisis.

From a socio-demographic perspective, the most important challenges in recent decades for Portuguese society have been, firstly, the emergence of an ageing population (the ageing index in 1960 was 27.3%, rising to 102.2% in 2001) and secondly, a low fertility rate (Pordata, 2011). The shift towards an ageing population has been very sudden and sharp. Birth and fertility rates have declined to the lowest in Europe and the mortality rate has remained at similar levels, but the child mortality rate has dropped dramatically to what is now one of the best levels worldwide. Table 1 below summarizes some of the main socio-demographic characteristics of children in Portugal in the last four decades.

Table 1. Socio demographic characteristics of children in Portugal

Indicators	Data
Number of children (0-14 years)	1960: 2.59 millions 2005: 1.64 millions
Total fertility rate	1960: 3 children per woman of fertile age 2008: 1.37
Portuguese children as a percentage of the total national population (2005)	15, 6%. Less than the retired population aged over 65: 17.1%
Age of women at birth of first child	1960: 25.0 2008: 28.4
Child mortality rate	1960: 77.5 % 2008: 3.3%

Source: INE (2001, 2006, 2009) and UNICEF (2007)

In Portugal, many of the social changes occurred later than in most European countries. Significant changes were concentrated within a relatively short period of time and its impact was, therefore, more intense. One of the most significant changes in Portuguese society, as can be seen from Table 1, was the decrease in birth and fertility rates. Portuguese society has lost children dramatically. The negative impacts of this loss are however less severe due to the increase of immigrant children living in the country (in 2006 represented 2% of the total child population).

Life expectancy at birth increased considerably (from 2006-2008, the age for women was 81.7 years and for men, 75.5); however the size of households has declined in the same period, reaching a current average of three persons per household (Pordata, 2011). The number of marriages has decreased and in 2008 (43,228) the figure was much lower than in 1960 (69,457) and there has been an increase in non-Catholic marriages (1960: 9.3%; 2008: 55.6%). The number of divorces increased between 1996 and 2008 and it continues to grow (749 in 1960; 26,110 in 2008) and the number of unmarried Portuguese also rose (Pordata, 2011).

All these factors have an impact on the way childhood is understood, as well as going a long way in explaining the diversity and complexity of the living conditions of children in contemporary Portuguese families (Sarmento, 2008).

At the economic level, Portugal also experienced important changes: the service sector has become the dominant contributor to the Portuguese economy, agriculture became almost residual and the working population moved to urban and coastal areas. Simultaneously, other changes were noticeable such as job insecurity, low wages and labour market flexibility. Portugal also became one of the countries with the highest rate of full-time working women in Europe in addition to severe wage inequalities between men and women (Almeida, André & Lalanda, 2002; Santos, 1993; Sarmento, 2008). All these changes came about without economic measures and compensatory mechanisms, for example, a policy on work-life balance, adequate infrastructure and family support systems (including access to and the cost of services) including nurseries, kindergartens, nursing homes, community services and benefits such as flexible work solutions for families with young children (extended period for maternity/paternity leave or flexible timetable). These changes had significant repercussions on family and reproduction levels (Almeida et al., 2002; Guerreiro, Lobo, & Lobo, 2009). They also influenced our understanding about the place of children within the family (Cunha, 2007) and investment in their development, especially in the field of education. Besides similarities with other southern countries, Portugal has certain specificities as a semiperipheral society,[ii] namely a weak welfare state. Some authors have even expressed that one cannot truly speak of a welfare state in Portugal (Santos, 1991), given the nature of the development of social security structures.

One factor, however, that continues to characterize Portuguese society is the low number of childless couples. Fewer women in Portugal are childless when compared to other European countries: in 2003 22.5% of couples had no children (INE, 2007). "In Europe, nearly one in eight households (12%) is caring for a child under the age of six. In Spain, Cyprus and Portugal such households make up more than 15% of total households. Only Bulgaria, Germany and Finland have less than 10% of households with at least one child under the age of six" (OECD, 2009, p. 12). Another important fact is that young couples often continue to benefit from the support of their parents, particularly in the provision of care to their children and in financial support. Grandparents continue to play a central role in the socialising and leisure activities of children in Portugal.

THE CHILDHOOD SITUATION IN PORTUGAL: THE GAME OF MIRRORS

We refer to the contradictions that emerge in the case of Portugal as 'the game of mirrors'. Portugal is a country where social indicators on childhood express the situation of transition in which the country is currently in. For example, child mortality rates are among the lowest in the world, but the chance of children carrying out prolonged schooling is the lowest in the EU; the protection policies of

Portuguese children improved in the last decades, but even a decade ago Portugal was one of the western countries where child labor exploitation most occurred (Tomás, Fernandes, & Sarmento, 2011).

These contradictions are a legacy of the failure of the welfare state (Mozzicafredo, 1997; Santos, 1993; Silva, 2002) and its specific features within a European context. In particular, these include features such as discontinuity, fragmentation and segmentation of social sectors and social policies, lack of partnership and integration of its respective operations. There is a lack of cohesive and integrated approaches (Rodrigues, 2000). We do not intend, however, to oversimplify the complex nature of the problem. The data and analysis provide insight into the circumstances of children in Portugal.

From a methodological point of view, our work is based upon statistic and documentary analysis. We collected data from national (INE) and international statistics (Eurostat, Eurydice) relevant to the analysis of children life conditions since the transition to democracy in Portugal (1974). These data include aspects relating to the following fields: demography (e.g. birth and mortality rate); education (pre-school frequency, school success dropout, school failure); social justice (poverty levels, inequality of income distribution). These data are discussed within a theoretical framework based upon sociological and public policies analyses. Previous research by the authors in this field was also taken into account (Dias, 2008; Tomás, 2008, 2011).

The data analysis on Portuguese children is characterized by a set of pictures that reflect and overlap. While progress has been made in a number of areas of social life, one can identify obstacles, setbacks and contradictions in other fields. Portuguese society is characterized by strong social inequalities. According to the latest figures from Eurostat, the rate of risk of poverty (after social transfers) is estimated for the European Union (EU 25) at about 16% (2006). Nowadays Portugal stands at 18% (REAPN, 2008; ESF, 2009; OECD, 2009).

The comfort indicators of the population have evolved significantly in the last three decades, but not for all children, due to the increase of social inequality. This is a paradoxical situation, probably not particular to Portuguese society, but with greater relevance in our society and with serious implications for childhood. In fact, today children are generally in a better situation than 50 years ago in the world (UNICEF, 2001) also in Portugal, but there are children living in the most deprived situations as a result of the increase in social inequalities. An important indicator on this issue is that child poverty in Portugal is higher than the poverty of the population in general. As a social group, children are the most vulnerable to poverty in Portugal: one in five Portuguese children is exposed to poverty. Portugal is one of eight European countries where there are high levels of child poverty (REAPN, 2008).

> In most European countries the child poverty rate is higher than the overall poverty rate (the only exceptions in 2006 were Denmark, Germany, Cyprus and Finland). In a number of countries, [including Portugal], the child poverty rate is higher than the pensioner poverty rate. So even before the recession, child poverty in most European countries was getting worse and, if

we consider generational equity is a test of the UN Charter on the Right of a Child not to live in poverty, then there are many countries in Europe that need to look to their laurels. (Bradshaw, 2009, p. 30)

However, it should be acknowledged that contrary to the situation in many European countries, the risk profile in Portugal covers children living in homes where both parents have jobs. This is a reflection of a number of social factors such as low levels of education of parents, the disparity between the wages of individuals whose parents are graduates and those whose parents have not completed secondary education (OECD, 2010). These problems are further aggravated by factors such as migration and multiculturalism, the changing family structure, the dilution of informal mechanisms of social control, the institutionalization of children's everyday lives, urbanization and metro-politanisation that increase the complexity of modern childhood experiences.

CHILDREN AND FAMILY SUPPORT SERVICES

The experience of childhood poverty has been exacerbated by the delay in introducing childhood educational programmes, social welfare support for children and adequate provision of support to families in educating children between 0 to 3 years old (OECD, 2009).

This lack of support is visible when we analyze public spending on childhood in OECD countries: Mexico has the lowest level of public expenditure on children while Norway has the highest. Portugal's expenditure is eighth from the bottom (OECD, 2009).

When we expand our analysis outside the EU-29, the problems attendant on the risk of poverty for Portuguese children become clearer. In a comparison of the EU-29, including late accession countries, Portugal is ranked in 21st place when considering childhood disadvantage.

Reference should also be made to our longstanding tradition of inadequate education and social services for children, which does little to promote equal opportunities in this area. In this sense, some authors consider that the State should have a strategic role in preschool education including the group of 0-3 years old (Dias, 2008).The reluctance of the State to play a strategic role in this area is aligned with the inadequate provision of family policies to address the growing involvement of women in the labour market (Portugal, 2000) or the coordination between them. Despite the creation of governmental structures that recognize the specific situation of Portuguese women following the transition to democracy (Commission for Women's Rights) [Comissão para a Condição Feminina], governmental support to the effective exercise of maternity/paternity has been scant. The social movements that protect and promote women's rights have low expression in Portugal. Thus, the creation of a network of institutions for early childhood education (0-6 years) was very late in Portugal, which results in short supply of pre-school childcare services and very high costs for families, because there are not public socio educational services for children from 0 to 3 years old, the network of public kindergartens (for the age group 3-6 years) is insufficient for the demands, and private kindergartens are too expensive for families. According to the Childhood Decides report (OECD, 2009), Portugal is one of the OECD countries with most limited public investment channels for children up to five years old. As a consequence, children's life quality in Portugal is far below the average of the core European countries (DEB, 2000).

Even in the course of compulsory education the problem of disconnection between school and family schedules has only recently begun to be seriously considered. Leisure time activities have begun to be implemented in schools very recently and a lot of problems remain to be solved in this field (space, human resources, supervision, adequacy to flexible parent work schedules).

Through the policy of compulsory education, the Portuguese State has indeed created conditions that lead to the need to support families and children. Leisure time activities, which have recently been introduced in schools on a full-time basis and which are still to be fully implemented, have thus far not been favourably received.

ACCESS TO AND SUCCESS IN COMPULSORY EDUCATION

Portugal was one of the first countries in Europe to introduce compulsory primary education, in 1834. However, its development has been slow. Upon the establishment of the Republic (1910), approximately three quarters of Portugal's population were unable to read or write. In the past decades, the great challenge for Portugal has been to increase the literacy rates of the Portuguese population, as can be seen in Figure 1, with a concerted effort in the second half of the period, characterized by the attainment of the goal of widespread coverage of the population.

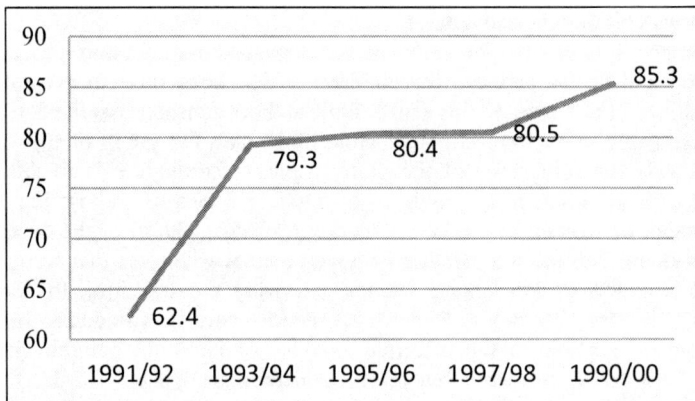

Source: Dias (2008)

Figure 1. Compulsory rate of schooling of 9 years (%), Continental Portugal[iii]

In spite of the significant evolution in literacy rates in Portugal we are still a long way from catching up with European levels of education. Furthermore, even among the young population, school dropout is relatively high (see Figure 4), showing that the patterns of qualification in Portugal are unlikely to change significantly in the near future.

Figure 2 illustrates the school dropout rates in EU-27 countries and Portugal is clearly above the average. The analysis of Figure 2 shows us that in 2010, within the set of EU-27 countries, only Malta had higher school dropout and training rates than Portugal (36.9% versus 28.7%). Spain had almost identical results to Portugal (28.4%). The fourth country with a higher result was Italy, although very different from those observed in Malta, Portugal and Spain.

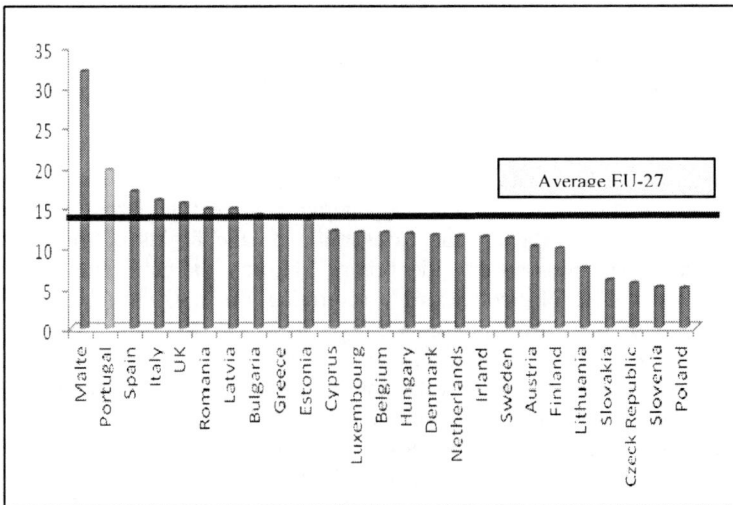

Source: Observatory of Inequalities, 2010 [Observatório das Desigualdades]

Figure 2. Early leavers from education[iv] in EU-27 countries (2010)

Portugal shows a degree of school dropout and training rates (28.7%) above those found in the EU-27 (14.9%). This trend is even more pronounced in men and in the autonomous regions (Azores and Madeira). The table also shows that Portugal is far from reaching the universalization of secondary education that is now considered the minimum education degree for inclusion in knowledge based economies (Dias, 2008). Similar problems emerge with regard to national investment in education.

Portugal is above the European average and equal to the percentages of France or Latvia (both 5.8%). However, the analytical reading of this indicator involves some ambiguity. Consideration of Portugal's positive stand in this context demonstrates the limitations of analysis based solely on GDP. Indeed, when additional resources other than financial are considered, we conclude that Portugal invests much less in its education system when compared to other countries with high education levels and schooling growth rates (Martins, 2005).

CHILDHOOD IN DANGER/SOCIAL RISK

The social indicators of Portuguese children presented in this paper express a paradoxical reality: the global situation of Portuguese children has improved significantly in recent decades; however the development of this improvement has been uneven and the effects on social inequalities are, in some cases, clearly unsatisfactory (Sarmento, 2008; Tomás, 2011). As a consequence, certain groups of children in Portugal are in particularly vulnerable situations. Successive governments have tried to respond, on varying degree, by creating services and special programmes. These responses include:

– The setting up of Commissions for the Protection of Minors (Decree Law No 189/91, of 17 May),[v] which began to address the identification of children at risk. This law required that the new legal system be organized on a partner-communitarian base with collective social responsibility. This law was drafted in a period when there was other legislation to protect the family and children and young people, namely the Convention on the Rights of the Child, the European Convention on the Adoption of Children, the publication of Decree-Law No. 190/92 of September 3, reforming the law on foster care, and resolution of the European Council No. 30/92 of 18 August that created a project to support families and children.
– Measures were taken to protect the lowest income individuals and families with the creation of the Guaranteed Minimum Income (1996).
– A programme for the elimination of Child Labour [PEETI] was drawn up. This established measures to prevent school dropout and to promote the school and social reintegration of children in labour exploitation situations. More recently, this programme was reorganized in order to create conditions for the completion of compulsory schooling and to integrate responses in the social, educational and training fields (1998).

Despite these initiatives there are still groups of children living in very difficult circumstances in Portugal, as is clear from Table 2.

Even children who are not victims of social exclusion face other problems. The provision of accessible and quality education services is not yet guaranteed for all. Real efforts to widen the availability of kindergarten for children in Portugal have only occurred in the past decade, and universal preschool education is still far from guaranteed. There continues to be problems with compulsory schooling and failure rates in secondary education are very high. In addition, certain groups of children, particularly those with special educational needs or those from ethnic minority groups, remain at a disadvantage at all levels of education.

Table 2. Children at risk in Portugal[vi]

Children's situations	Data
Institutionalized (2008)	3.910 children (less than 470 in 2007, representing a decrease of 3%).
In danger	− Statistics provided by Commissions for the Protection of Minors: 2000: 1623 signalled children ; 2008: 33.394 signalled children; − Main institutions that have been identified children in danger: schools (23,2%) and police (17,8%); − Portuguese children victims of family violence or violent death with unknown causes: 3.7 per 100,000 (higher in developed countries).

Source: Tomás et al., 2011

CONCLUSIONS

The last two decades of the twentieth century saw considerable development in the rights of the child and the establishment of social justice for children. In Portugal, while there has been significant advancement in policy, there is a disparity in the progression from policy to practice. On the one hand, conventions and international treaties reinforce and legitimize changes; on the other hand, these same documents have little impact on the experiences of children living in poverty, and the mere ratification of such agreements does not mean that children's rights are assured.

According to Santos (1993), this discrepancy between policy and practice is particularly high in the Portuguese context and is endemic to our society. The specificity of the Portuguese case could be explained by the following factors: the continuation of an authoritarian culture which has slowed the development of active citizenship; the weakness of social movements that defend the rights of those most in need; the presence of strong pressure groups that "privatize" the state; and a justice system which is slow, ineffectual, corporate, and still dominated by a culture that does not punish lax underperformance.

In these circumstances, it can be concluded that Portugal demonstrates similar patterns to those of core European countries in respect of its legislative approach to the protection of children's rights. However, it remains far from achieving the levels of child welfare that one finds in most European countries.

Children's rights are not yet a political priority in Portugal. Strictly, we can only speak about a number of measures, namely concerning provision and protection rights. However, even those rights, are not concerted and coordinated in a national policy level. It is a policy of low intensity, because the implementation of children's rights led to a very slow, heterogeneous and anaemic process in its impact on children's lives. Portugal has weak political and social intervention concerning childhood, characterized by an incipient and also weak network between the multiple organisms that work with childhood, weak human and financial resources, and also little visibility of social activity in the children's rights area (associations, NGO, lobbies) (Fernandes & Tomás, 2010).

Portuguese efforts to protect children need to penetrate all spheres of civil society, including social, political and educational, attesting to the country's commitment to children. Children's rights cannot, however, be safeguarded through policies targeted only at children. The persistence of very low levels of education in Portugal and the intergenerational transmission of poverty and life chances warrant a greater effort in fostering lifelong learning for all.

NOTES

[i]   This study was conducted as a part of a larger research project entitled "Local strategies for school improvement in deprived areas: Challenging private and public programmes" (PTDC/CPE-CED/114789/2009), funded by *Fundação para a Ciência e Tecnologia*, Portugal.

[ii] Besides the similarities with other countries within the European Union, Portugal has specificities as a semiperipheral country, namely the absence of a strong, organized civil society based on social movements and citizen organizations; an authoritarian culture; a gap between the formal definition of citizens' rights and the actual access to these rights; the weakness of social movements. For details see Santos (1991, 1993) and Santos and Rodríguez-Garavito (2005).

[iii] Without autonomous regions, Madeira and Azores.

[iv] Percentage of the population aged 18-24 with at most lower secondary education and not in further education or training.

[v]   In 1999, there was a Reform of the Juridical system of Child Protection – with the legal division between child victims of neglect or harm, protected by *the Protection Law of Children and Young people in Danger* (Law No. 147/99, of1 of September) and children in conflict with the law, who had committed actions qualified as crimes protected by the *Tutelar Educative Law* – Law No. 169/99, of 14 of September).

[vi] It is to be noted that data will be analysed taking into account increased evidence of the social problems of Portuguese children. The documented increase in the number of children in social danger/ at risk that have been identified does not reflect a real increase. A greater awareness of the actors and social institutions and the advanced legal framework that protects children has led to a higher level of reporting of such risks.

REFERENCES

Almeida, A., André, I., & Lalanda, P. (2002). Novos padrões e outros cenários para a fecundidade em Portugal [New standards and other scenarios for fertility in Portugal], *Análise Social*, Vol. XXXVII, 163, 371-409.

Archard, D. (1993). *Children: Rights and childhood*. London: Routledge.

Blackmore, J. (1999). Localization/globalization and the midwife state, *Journal of Education Policy*, *14*(1), 33-54.

Bourdillon, M. (2004). Children in development. *Progress in Development Studies*, *4*(2), 99-113.

Bradshaw, J. (2009). Social inclusion and child poverty. In *Changing childhood in a changing Europe. An ESF interdisciplinary workshop report* (pp. 29-36). France: ESF.

Commissions for the Protection of Minors (1991). *Decree-Law 189 of 17 May 1991*.

Cornia, A., & Jolly, R. (1987). *The impact of the world recession on children*. Oxford: Pergamon Press.

Cortesão, L., & Stoer, S. (2001). Cartografando a transnacionalização do campo educativo: O caso português [Mapping the transnationalization of the educational field: The Portuguese case]. In B. Santos (Ed.), *Globalização, fatalidade ou Utopia?* (pp. 369-406). Porto: Edições Afrontamento.

Cunha, V. (2007). *O lugar dos filhos: Ideias, práticas e significados* [The place of children: Ideas, practices and meanings]. Lisboa: ICS.

DEB (2000). *A educação pré-escolar e os cuidados para a infância em Portugal. Estudo da OCDE* [The pre-school education and care for children in Portugal. OECD study]. Lisboa: Departamento da Educação Básica.

Dias, M. (2006). *Educação e formação: Prioridades e estratégias 2007-2013* [Education and training: Priorities and strategies 2007-2013]. Lisboa: CIED.

Dias, M. (2008). *Poder e participação na escola pública (1986-2004)* [Power and participation in public school (1986-2004)]. Lisboa: Colibri/IPL.

ESF (2009). *Changing childhood in a changing Europe. An ESF interdisciplinary workshop report.* France: ESF.

Fernandes, N., & Tomás, C. (2010). Report of Portugal. In H. Brozaitis (Ed.), *Institutional framework and measures that Portugal developed about policies in the area of the Children's Rights and Well-being.* Lithuania: Public Policy and Management Institute.

Fonseca, C. (2002). The politics of adoption: Child rights in the Brazilian setting. *Law and Policy, 24,* 199-228.

Frønes, I. (1994). Dimension of childhood. In J. Qvortrup, M. Bardy, G. Sgritta, & H. Wintersberger (Eds.), *Childhood matters, social theory, practice and politics* (pp. 145-164). Aldershot: Avebury.

GEPE/ME (2009). *Educação em números – Portugal 2009* [Education in numbers – Portugal 2009]. Lisboa: GEPE/ME.

Guerreiro, M., Lobo, Torres, A., & Lobo, C. (2009). Changing families: Configurations, values and recomposition processes. In M. Guerreiro, A. Torres, & C. Lobo (Eds.), *Welfare and everyday life* (pp. 7-35). Oeiras: Celta Editora.

Hammad, S. (1999). The CRC: 'Words on paper' or a reality for children? *The International Journal of Children's Rights, 7,* 215-237.

Hammarberg, T. (1990). The UN Convention on the rights of the child – and how to make it work. *Human Rights Quarterly, 12,* 97-105.

INE (2001). Recenseamentos Gerais da População [General Census of Population]. Lisboa: INE.

INE (2006). Recenseamentos Gerais da População [General Census of Population]. Lisboa: INE.

INE (2007). Recenseamentos Gerais da População [General Census of Population]. Lisboa: INE.

INE (2009). Recenseamentos Gerais da População [General Census of Population]. Lisboa: INE.

INE (2009). *50 Anos de Estatísticas da Educação* [50 years of Statistics of Education]. Lisboa: GEPE/ME / INE, I.P.

Kaufman, N., & Rizzini, I. (2002). *Globalization and children. Exploring potentials for enhancing opportunities in the lives of children and youth.* New York: Kluwer Academic/Plenum Publishers.

Lee, N. (2001). *Childhood and society. Growing up in an age of uncertainty.* Maidenhead: Open University Press.

Liebel, M. (2000). *La outra infancia, niñez trabajadora y acción social* [The other childhood, working children and social action]. Lima: IFEJANT.

Martins, S. (2005). Portugal, um lugar de fronteira na Europa: Uma leitura de indicadores socioeducacionais [Portugal, a place border in Europe: A reading of social and educational indicators]. *Sociologia, 49,* 141-161.

Mozzicafreddo, J. (1997). *Estado-providência e cidadania em Portugal* [Welfare state and citizenship in Portugal]. Oeiras: Celta Editora.

Observatório das Desigualdades (2010). *Observatory of inequalities.* Lisboa: CIES-IUL.

OECD (2009). *Doing better for children.* Paris: OECD.

OECD (2010). *Going for growth.* Paris: OECD.

Pordata (2011). *Base de dados Portugal Contemporâneo* [Data base contemporary Portugal]. Lisboa: Fundação Francisco Manuel dos Santos http://www.pordata.pt/.

Portugal, S. (2000). Retórica e acção governativa na área das políticas de família desde 1974 [Rhetoric and government action in the area of family policies since 1974]. *Revista Crítica de Ciências Sociais, 56,* 81-92.

Prout, A. (2005). *The future of childhood*. New York/London: Routledge Falmer.

Qvortrup, J. (2005). Macro-análise da infância [Macro analysis of childhood]. In P. Christensen & A. James (Eds.), *Investigando com crianças. Perspectivas e práticas* (pp. 73-96). Porto: Escola Superior de Educação de Paula Frassinetti.

REAPN (2008). *Indicadores sobre a pobreza. Portugal e União Europeia* [Indicators on poverty. Portugal and European Union]. Porto: REAPN.

Rizzini,I. (2004). Infância e globalização. Análise das transformações económicas, políticas e sociais [Childhood and globalization. Analysis of the economic, political and social changes]. *Sociologia, Problemas e Práticas, 44*, 11-26.

Rodrigues, E. (2000). O estado-providência e os processos de exclusão social: Considerações teóricas e estatísticas em torno do caso português [The welfare state and the processes of social exclusion: Theoretical considerations and statistics about the Portuguese case]. *Sociologia, 10*.

Rozga, D. (2001). *Applying a human rights based approach to programming: Experiences of UNICEF*. London. Paper prepared for the Workshop on Human Rights, Assets and Livelihood Security, and Sustainable Development, London, UK, 19-20 June 2001.

Ruddick, S. (2003).The politics of aging: Globalization and the restructuring of youth and childhood. *Antipode, 35*, 334-362.

Santos, B. (1991). State, wage relations and social welfare in the semiperiphery: The case of Portugal. *Oficina do CES, 23*, 1-53.

Santos, B. (org.) (1993), *Portugal, Um retrato singular* [Portugal. A singular portrait]. Porto: Edições Afrontamento.

Santos, B., & Rodríguez-Garavito, C. (Eds.) (2005). *Law and globalization from below: Towards a cosmopolitan legality*. Cambridge: Cambridge University Press.

Sarmento, M. (2008). Os olhares da sociedade portuguesa sobre a criança [The perspectives of Portuguese society over the child]. In *A educação de infância – Propostas de reflexão para um Debate Nacional sobre Educação*. Lisboa: CNE.

Sgritta, G. (1997). Inconsistencies: Childhood on the economic and political agenda. *Childhood, 4*(4), 375-404.

Silva, P. (2002). O modelo de welfare da Europa do Sul: Reflexões sobre a utilidade do conceito [The model of welfare in Southern Europe: Reflections on the usefulness of the concept]. *Sociologia, 38*, 25-59.

Soares, N. (2002). *Os Direitos das crianças nas encruzilhadas da protecção e da participação* [Children's rights in the crossroads of protection and participation]. http://cedic.iec.uminho.pt/Textos_de_Trabalho/menu_base_text_trab.htm.

Sorj, B. (2004). *A democracia inesperada. Cidadania, direitos humanos e desigualdade social* [Democracy unexpected. Citizenship, human rights and social inequality]. Rio de Janeiro: Jorge Zahar Editor.

Stephens, S. (1995). *Children and politics of culture*. New Jersey: Princeton University Press.

Tomás, C. (2008). Childhood and rights: Reflections on the UN Convention on the Rights of the Child. *Childhood's Today, 2*(2), 1-14.

Tomás, C. (2011). *"Há muitos mundos no mundo". Cosmopolitismo, participação e direitos das crianças* ["There are many worlds in the world". Cosmopolitism, participation and rights of children]. Porto: Edições Afrontamento.

Tomás, C., Fernandes, N., & Sarmento, M. (2011). Jogos de imagens e espelhos: Um olhar sociológico sobre a infância e as crianças em Portugal [Games images and mirrors: A sociological perspective on childhood and children in Portugal]. In V. Müller (Ed.). *Crianças dos países de língua portuguesa: Histórias, culturas e direitos* (pp. 194-227). Maringá: EDUEM.

UNICEF (2001). *The State of the World's Children 2002*. New York: United Nations Children's Fund.

UNICEF (2003). *The State of the World's Children 2004*. New York: United Nations Children's Fund.

UNICEF (2005). *The State of the World's Children 2006*. New York: United Nations Children's Fund.

UNICEF (2007). *The State of the World's Children 2008*. New York: United Nations Children's Fund.

AFFILIATIONS

Catarina Tomás
Institute Polytechnic of Lisbon and Research Centre for the Social Sciences (CICS)
University of Minho, Portugal

Mariana Dias
Institute Polytechnic of Lisbon, Portugal

SUSAN J. COUREY AND PAM LEPAGE

7. CULTURALLY RESPONSIVE PEDAGOGY AND HUMAN RIGHTS

Identifying Global Values in the Classroom

INTRODUCTION

In a most surprising way, it has come to our attention that our graduate students, who are diligently studying to become special education teachers, had a limited understanding of human rights, but a significant interest in learning about the topic. We teach at a California State University in one of this nation's most liberal cities. Our students perceive themselves as politically active, tolerant, and liberal but we are not sure how carefully they reflect on, and research, the foundation of their beliefs. Here is what happened in class one evening last semester that made us realize that we may not be providing opportunity for our students to think in a more critical way about global issues. In an introductory special education class, we were discussing how teachers could be more culturally responsive. We had already discussed "White privilege" (Sleeter, 2000) in the United States with dominant versus sub-dominant cultures (Willie, 1996), before we asked the class to think of shared values across cultural and geographical divides, as well as across boundaries created by socio-economic status. While we waited for the class to respond, we asked, "What about human rights, doesn't every culture value human rights?" In an abrupt and frenzied-like diatribe, students shouted out responses like, "...the United States doesn't value human rights, look at Abu Ghraib" and "What about what our military is doing around the world?" "Why isn't the United States doing more in Rwanda?" Calmly, we asked for a show of hands for who knew about the history of Human Rights. With no show of hands, we asked our students to explain what they actually knew about the history of human rights beyond what they learned from the media. In response, the class continued to condemn the United States record on human rights with overly generalized, media-like rhetoric and without substantive facts or theoretical perspectives.

At that moment we realized several things about our students' education. First, these graduate students were probably never asked to think deeply about the theory and politics behind human rights. Most of these students grew up in the United States and took for granted their own human rights. Of course they know more about civil rights because the rights of individuals with disabilities were established through civil rights legislation and that is all part of our curriculum. Through the

H. Biseth & H. B. Holmarsdottir (eds.), Human Rights in the Field of Comparative Education, 97–108.
© *2013 Sense Publishers. All rights reserved.*

ever-present media in many young people's lives, human rights abuses around the world are reported almost on a daily basis (genocide, torture, rape, and inscription). Media reports condemn the United States for not rushing in and protecting the human rights of subdominant cultures, tribes, and individuals dominated by dictatorships. We asked students why they were so quickly incited toward anger. There seemed to be an underlying, not conscious, hegemonic instinct that was responsible, in part, for the anger. It was ironic that we had just finished discussing White privilege in the US and how dominant cultures doled out civil rights and yet the students were unwittingly presenting themselves as angry citizens of what they seemed to perceive as the world's hegemony. To be passionate about injustice is admirable, but to be incited toward anger by the media without fully understanding human rights violations as well as their role as change agents, and the role of other countries around the world was allowing oneself to be educated and indoctrinated by the media. We wanted our students to think globally and to develop the attitudinal and ethical dispositions necessary for promotion of global civility and international understanding (Reimers, 2009). As special educators, we decided we all needed to develop better ways to view our work through a Human Rights Education (HRE) perspective (Osler & Starkey, 2010) and incorporate it into our curriculum so that our students could think critically and become prepared to teach the global citizens of tomorrow.

In our special education teacher preparation program, we not only cover content and pedagogy in the curriculum but we focus on the rights of individuals with disabilities and the federal legislation that protects those rights. However, we rarely venture out into the global environment beyond U.S. federal legislation. We suddenly realized that we were not providing opportunity for our students to think of themselves as agents of change capable of creating a multicultural democracy that recognizes all people have equal moral worth (Osler, 2005). The teachers we prepare must not only think of themselves as agents of change, they need to define their role within their own classrooms, their schools and their communities as a human rights activist. We must start to introduce our teachers to human rights education and they must continue to develop their understanding and classroom activities that help their students to see themselves in a global community. Then, through continued scholarship and by attending conferences and workshops, our teachers can truly have an impact on building a global civil society.

SPECIAL EDUCATION TEACHERS AS HUMAN RIGHTS ACTIVISTS

How do we know our pre-service teachers are capable and willing to think and reflect critically on their roles as globally competent and culturally responsive educators? These special education teachers are graduate students who passionately enter the field fully aware that they will face many challenges and receive low wages compared to professionals in other fields who require the same amount of education. In the first semester of training to be a special education teacher, these graduate students are asked to write a philosophy statement that explains what they hope to accomplish. Here are some of the passionate things students wrote in their philosophy statements:

... my classroom becomes a caring school community where children will be the positive force supporting each other on their social and academic journey in this world.

... Just as it is important for me as an educator to understand each student as a learner, it is my role to help my students reflect on their learning styles, so that they may advocate for their own needs in any classroom setting.

... The earthquake [China 2008] helped me recognize these realities. As a professional teacher, I strongly believe that all individuals, including those with labels of disability have a right to develop their optimal potential and become productive members of society.

General education teachers see themselves as having an important role in upholding the American ideal of equal opportunity firmly grounded in free education. Most of them believe strongly in social justice. These teachers enter the United States' public school system that strives to inculcate the ideals of equality and freedom in the individual; Universal education for all citizens is a cornerstone in the US democracy.

Our students, however, enter special education, which has been a source of moral, ethical, and legal debate. In fact, the very existence of special education services to meet the educational needs of individual students with disabilities is a result of litigation that parallels the civil rights movement in the US during the 1960's. As our students progress in their special education studies, they become keenly aware of the need to protect the rights of individuals with disabilities and their parents because their classroom practices are defined and guarded by US Federal Legislation (e.g., IDEA 2004). So, by taking on the role of a special education teacher, our students become de facto defenders of the educational rights of children with disabilities and they are passionate about that role (LePage, Nielsen, & Fearn, 2008). In essence, they are already human rights defenders but they have not been provided with the opportunity or rhetoric to view themselves through this human rights perspective. Further, they have not been provided with adequate opportunities to think of themselves and their practice in a more global role. We realized that our efforts to infuse our curriculum with culturally responsive practices that include examining "culturally relevant and responsive anti-bias curricula and pedagogy" (Chen, Nimmo, & Fraser, 2009, p. 101), is not enough. We need to take our students beyond the walls of the classroom, out onto the global stage so that they have the opportunity to think about "global citizenship" as it relates to national and local educational issues (Myers & Zaman, 2009).

So we embarked on a journey to design a program that would educate our graduate students about the issues surrounding global citizenship, education and human rights. It was our hope to provide students with the historical and theoretical perspectives that influenced the emergence of human rights after World War II and education as a fundamental human right. Moreover, we wanted to create an arena that provided our students and the community with the opportunity to discuss local and national issues that pertain to human rights and education. Finally, we did not want to just talk about the issues, but we wanted to seek out and share active ways to help our students develop a democratic moral perspective of human rights in the classroom, community, country and world (Osler, 2005). In this way, as our students moved into their own classrooms, they could teach and be active role models for global thinking for their students and their communities.

Here we present our developing program in three segments. We use the term 'developing' because we hope to continually make changes that are responsive to changing local, national and world conditions. The first segment is concerned with defining human rights and connecting them to culturally relevant pedagogy, and the problems inherent in the realization of that concept. Second, we discuss how to develop culturally responsive classroom practices that promote the ideals of cultural democracy and empowerment. Finally, we present specific ways for teachers to bring human rights and democracy into their classrooms and local communities.

WHY CONNECT HUMAN RIGHTS AND CULTURALLY RESPONSIVE PEDAGOGY?

The United Nations' (UN) 1948 Universal Declaration of Human Rights (UN, 1948), as well as the UN's 1989 Convention on the Rights of the Child (UN, 1989), and the UN's International Covenant on Economic, Social, and Cultural Rights (UN, 1966) all declare education as a fundamental human right. Most recently, in September 2000, the United Nations outlined specific goals for educational improvement in the United Nations Millennium Declaration. This declaration commits all 189 member states to expand and improve early childhood care and education, to ensure that all children have access to a free and compulsory primary education of good quality, to achieve a 50% reduction in adult illiteracy (especially among women), to achieve gender equality in primary and secondary education, and to improve all aspects of education (Lindahl, 2006; UNESCO, 2000). Despite the declarations and covenants, the realization of education as a universal fundamental human right has not been accomplished. Consequently, it is our hope that by incorporating human rights education into our teacher preparation program, we could empower our students to view themselves in a more global arena. We want to inspire them to become agents of change by being more than culturally competent; we want them to help their students to understand the importance of human rights in a global community.

Students can read about protections that have been afforded to individuals in a society throughout history for thousands of years. There is evidence all the way back through Babylonian, and Greek and Roman documents that human beings have made references to varied ideals about human rights (Ishay, 2004). Much of the rhetoric revolves around the concept of natural law or universal truths as a basis for rights, which rely on enlightenment or divine intervention for interpretation.

Natural rights are inherently controversial because they have been viewed as a result of Western religions and ethical principals disguised as universal values and designed to further Western expansion and imperialism (Myers & Zaman, 2009; Pagden, 2003). Universal truths are also not easily agreed upon and are often less universal and more culturally or religiously defined. The desire to define human rights seems to have existed in theoretical discussions but has not been universally realized because there has been no universal definition or guarantor of those rights. Unlike legal rights, which are defined by nation states and rely on the power of the state to guarantee and prevent violations (Ingram, 2008), human rights were not defined or guaranteed by a universal international body until after World War II. In response to the horrors of the war and to prevent future abominations, the Allied powers in 1945 began to form the UN, an international organization dedicated to preserving peace and human rights. Three years later, the General Assembly of the UN ratified the Universal Declaration of Human Rights (UDHR) (UN, 1948).

The dichotomy between legal rights and natural rights and the tension it created was dissipated by the UDHR. The preamble of the UDHR made way for the foundation of a universal understanding of human rights including: "recognition of the inherent dignity and of the equal and inalienable rights of all members of the human family and the foundation of freedom, justice and peace in the world" (UN, 1948, p. 3). Hence, human rights exist whether or not they are underwritten or overridden by any state, local or international organization; they are inherent to individual human beings. Our Global Neighborhood (The Commission on Global Governance, 1995), a document written by an international team and published by the UN, discusses the creation of the UDHR and how the diverse members of the Universal Rights Commission affirmed a universal conception of the person and the legitimacy of international law unencumbered by Western bias. The person is an autonomous human being with intrinsic human rights. Further, the document states that global citizenship is based on a strong commitment to principals of equity and democracy grounded in civil society. The realization of human rights is dependent on international law supported by a legal, political, and cultural world order (Pagden, 2003). As the commission laid out these definitions and conditions, a blueprint for a more just and equitable world was being drawn. Over the last half-decade, a conglomerate of public and private organizations, nation states, and individuals have used this blueprint to judge the progress of the realization of human rights. Our students must become more fully aware of the creation of this UDHR so that they and their students can take part in this project for building a better future.

What we found was that most of our students did not know about the history of human rights, either before or after World War II or the history of the UN, how the UN functioned, or how the United States was involved with the UN, or what countries the US government did or did not support with financial aide and why. This type of content was important to our students since many of them wanted to know more about the experiences of new immigrants who were entering the US. Trends in immigration and birth rates indicate that soon there will be no majority racial or ethnic group in the United States – no one group that makes up more than

101

50% of the total population. The growth in minority populations is projected to continue and eventually transform the demographics of the country. The nation's Hispanic and Asian populations are projected to triple over the next fifty years, but the non-Hispanic white population would drop to about 50% by 2050 (Center for Public Education, 2007). US immigrants are no longer just coming from Mexico, but also Central and South America and Africa. Our immigrant population is no longer mainly European, but comes from China and other South East Asian countries, the Middle East and India. Our students wanted to know more about the children from other countries as well as children born to foreign-born parents.

While the stage was set for the realization of human rights around the world well over a half of a century ago, these rights existed only in so far as individuals benefited from the realization of their rights. While there are many reasons why human rights are not being realized, one of the most basic reasons, and one that is even relevant in the US, especially around issues of disability, is that in order for an individual to realize human rights, he or she must know about them (Osler & Starkey, 2010). Though human rights are intrinsic to the individual human being, they are not intrinsically understood or realized. Human rights are the international instruments for holding governments accountable for providing equal access to educational and employment opportunities, justice, goods and services for all members of a multicultural democracy (Osler & Starkey, 2010). As such, it is through education that we can inform young children in classrooms, and their parents in communities, and relatives beyond the local community.

So, we realized that by using global human rights as a foundation for culturally relevant pedagogy, or at least connecting the two concepts, we were 1) helping US students learn important content about their country's history and its connection with the rest of the world, 2) helping teachers better understand children who were born abroad or whose families were born abroad, 3) providing teachers a chance to discuss moral issues associated with their country's political decision-making and with people in need, and 4) providing interesting ideas for culturally relevant pedagogy that moved beyond what many of these students had heard in other classes (although often not implemented in classrooms).

MORE THAN CULTURALLY RESPONSIVE PEDAGOGY

In order for teachers to think globally and act locally, they must first reflect on their teaching practice in two ways. We found that first teachers must examine their own sociocultural identities (Villegas & Lucas, 2002). They need to explore and reflect on the various social and cultural groups to which they belong by choice or by default, including race, ethnicity, social class, language, religion, and gender groups. Through a critical self-analysis, teachers can recognize the nature and scope of their attachments to those groups and how membership in them has defined their personal and family histories (Villegas & Lucas, 2002). Second, teachers must try to shift their view of diversity from something that exists in others to the relationships that develop between teachers and students (Chen, Nimmo, & Fraser, 2009). In this way, teachers are more prepared to identify bias and create a classroom environment that fosters a most sophisticated understanding and appreciation of other cultures. In the past few years, multiculturalism in the classroom included sharing foods from around the world and a few key phrases from various languages. Today culturally competent teachers must be more than tolerant of other cultures; they must embrace them and ensure that elements of all cultures represented in the classroom are acknowledged, valued, and integrated into the curriculum. Further, teachers must work harder to reach out to parents from other cultures and make them a valued asset to the school (Gerena, 2011).

Three useful strategies that teachers can use to earnestly reflect on their assumptions and biases are teacher research, self-study, and portfolios (Berry, 2009; Gilles, Wilson, & Elias, 2010). Teacher research allows teachers to not only reflect on their teaching, but to systematically inquire into their attitudes and assumptions. Often, we observe, reflect and then come to conclusions about students, colleagues, parents, as well as classroom contexts and behaviors, but when those conclusions are put under the microscope, we find the assumptions we use to make sense of our reflections are often flawed. So, we need to check our beliefs and assumptions and revise our thinking based on evidence from systematic self-study and teacher research. Teacher educators can also use portfolios as a means to help teachers reflect. Teacher education programs have students put educational materials together and then critically reflect on the learning they have acquired over time, once again looking at evidence to exam their own development process (Killeavy & Maloney, 2010; McIntyre & Dangel, 2009).

In determining ways to incorporate culturally relevant practices in the classroom, Chen et al. (2009) present James A. Banks' *Transformation Approach* that requires structural changes to the traditional curriculum to enable students to consider concepts, events, and themes from the perspective of diverse ethnic and cultural groups. In addition, they discuss the importance of an anti-bias approach to curriculum design and classroom management that fosters cultural democracy and empowerment. Chen et al. (2009) propose the following four objectives for designing curriculum and instruction:

1) To nurture the construction of a knowledgeable, confident identity as an individual and as a member of multiple cultural groups; 2) to promote comfortable, empathetic interactions with people from diverse backgrounds; 3) to foster each child's ability to critically think about bias and injustice; and 4) to cultivate each child's ability to stand up for herself or himself, and for others, in the face of bias and injustice. (p. 101)

In this way, all students learn to be secure about their identities and more fully participate in their home culture and the classroom culture, whether they are members of the dominant or non-dominant local culture. Teachers who design classrooms with these goals in mind are modeling the moral and ethical imperative underlying human rights, preserving the autonomy and dignity of every individual. Culturally responsive classrooms enable students to think globally, critically, and freely about their place in the school, community, nation and world. In classrooms that appreciate diversity, students from transnational households do not have to navigate two cultural identities, the nationality of their country of origin and the new United States identity cultivated in traditional classrooms (Myers & Zaman, 2009). A longitudinal research study of 5,000 children of immigrants reports that after four years of high school, adolescents were more likely to identify with the nationality of their home country than with being a U.S. citizen (Portes & Rumbaut, 2001 in Myers & Zaman, 2009 p. 2598). Cultural and political integration is difficult for children and adolescents without guidance to bridge the two identities. Students with non-dominant cultural backgrounds are less likely to achieve academically at the level of their peers from the dominant culture, and more likely to develop critical views of state and national governmental policies (Myers & Zaman, 2009). However, by developing a sense of global citizenship with the ability to live in different cultures and move across different societies fluently, students can be more open to new and different cultures. They learn that their well-being is connected to the well-being of the class and community. Students learn to depend on each other, treat each other as equals, and try to understand each other's beliefs, customs, values, and behaviors so that they can collectively tackle problems facing their classroom, community and world (Zhao, 2009).

GETTING STARTED IN THE CULTURALLY RESPONSIVE CLASSROOM

In our experience working with special education teachers, we found that most teachers, when given the opportunity to reflect on their personal philosophy and practice, truly believe that the dignity and autonomy of every individual must be protected and that education is a universal right, in fact the cornerstone of democracy. However, even after a lesson on human rights and the culturally responsible classroom, without an explicit activity that focuses on implementation, they most likely will go back to school the next day and do exactly what they did the day before because they do not know how to start setting up a culturally responsive classroom with a global focus. They find it especially difficult when they are not well supported in their beliefs or practices by the school or other teachers. We acknowledge that it is hard for a number of reasons and we explain that developing into a culturally responsible teacher is a process that begins with baby steps, and progresses with risk taking, self-reflection, education, practice, and patience.

Why is it hard to make change? Our major focus in this section of the paper has been on making changes in teacher dispositions and classroom and community practices. For our teachers, making structural changes to the existing curriculum in local schools is very difficult. Teachers are working with a standards-based curricula designed to strengthen the science and mathematics knowledge of our nation's youth. As special education teachers, they are more outrageously charged with closing the achievement gap between students with disabilities and their typically developing peers.

We will discuss two areas of education where teachers can take action toward developing culturally responsive classrooms with a global focus. First, teachers can consider what goes on in their classroom, what curriculum is presented, its content, and how the classroom is managed. Second, teachers can also consider how their classrooms are situated in the community. In this way, teachers can focus on making minor changes in the curriculum and their classroom management that will have noticeable effects on the culture in their classrooms. In turn, involvement in the community will enable a teacher to create a classroom climate where parents feel welcome and are not intimidated to participate.

Culturally responsive teaching is not about adding more content to the existing curriculum; it is about developing a mind-set that values content and character development. Vellegas and Lucas (2002) propose six characteristics, which lay out the essential dispositions, knowledge, and skills for teaching in a culturally diverse society. By recognizing competence and making changes in the following areas, teachers can make progress towards cultural competence:

(a) Becoming culturally conscious; recognizing that there are multiple ways of perceiving reality and that these ways are influenced by one's location in the social order; (b) developing affirming views of students from diverse backgrounds, seeing resources for learning in all students rather than viewing differences as problems to be overcome; (c) seeing himself or herself as both responsible for and capable of bringing about educational change that will make schools more responsive to all students; (d) understanding how learners construct knowledge and being capable of promoting learners' knowledge construction; (e) knowing about the lives of his or her students; and (f) using his or her knowledge about students' lives to design instruction that builds on what they already know while stretching them beyond the familiar. (pp. 21-29)

These six qualities constitute the central themes or strands that give conceptual coherence to the type of teacher education seen as necessary for preparing culturally responsive teachers (Vellegas & Lucas, 2002). Rather than making curricula changes in schools, Vellegas and Lucas propose making changes in the teachers' approach to the curriculum. In this way, cultural diversity and competency is an asset and serves to motivate immigrant students and students from subdominant cultures who strive to navigate cultural identities to engage in classroom activities (Reimers, 2009).

Teachers are often presented with a curriculum chosen by a committee at their school. While new teachers can work to get on that committee to make change, change is nonetheless slow. However, there are ways for teachers to administer an existing curriculum and address the appropriate content standards while also incorporating global education and human rights. For example, Lucas (2009) discusses how to incorporate human rights education in the social studies classroom at the elementary and middle school level. In her discussion, Lucas explains that elementary students are not too young to learn about some harsh realities involved in the struggle for human rights because they are exposed to the same media coverage of human rights abuses and global tragedies as graduate students. An informed classroom discussion can help young students think about and process the complex issues that surround global tragedies like the devastating earthquake and tsunami in Japan, the earthquake in Haiti or the devastation of New Orleans by Katrina. Flowers et al.'s (2000) research suggests that by the age of ten, attitudes about human dignity and equality are already firmly established. Elementary students need to understand that human rights are an intrinsic human value and that governments and ordinary citizens have a responsibility for making the kinds of changes that benefit all people. Lucas provides suggestions on how to use the book, *A Life Like Mine: How Children Live Around the World* (Kindersley, 2002). Developed by UNICEF, the book focuses on the daily lives and chores of eighteen different children around the world. With pictures and narratives that center on the real-life situations that students everywhere can relate to, it serves as a springboard for classroom activities and discussions. Lucas provides concrete suggestions for using the book at different levels and she includes an in-depth plan to create a UN simulation.

Teachers who work at developing culturally competent classrooms and work to involve the community in the schooling of their children begin to shape changes in educational thinking and practices. Reimers (2009) describe these changes in educational thinking as a blending of the endeavour toward academic excellence and the development of character education. He describes culturally responsive education with a global focus as education that includes academic excellence, character development, global awareness, problem solving ability, technological proficiency, and civic competency (Reimers, 2009).

Finally, Reimers (2009) suggests that when a teacher designs a culturally competent classroom with a focus on global competence, they are better able to tap the resources in their culturally diverse communities. He believes that teacher-led movements can advance global education better than political advocates because they do not rely on "bureaucratic instruments of control" but rely on non-threatening grassroots efforts that can originate in the local community (Reimers, 2009, p. 6). Mary Cowhey learned firsthand that grassroots organizing not only lead to parent empowerment but also to increased student achievement (Cowhey, 2010). Cowhey described how her effort to empower low-income parents led to the development of a thriving organization of low-income families of color who collectively worked to improve the academic achievement of their children.

In her article, *Learning to Roar*, Cowhey (2010) includes a list of grassroots organizing principles to create a successful organization of parents. She includes useful suggestions like using small cozy places for meetings and avoiding institutional spaces where people are less likely to feel comfortable. She suggests starting small but working to create a critical mass; parents need to see that other parents like themselves will be at the meeting. This is especially true for parents of special needs children who often need the support of other parents, not only for themselves, but also for their children who sometimes have trouble socializing with other kids. Cowhey includes lessons they learned as they created a thriving organization of low-income families of color.

In this chapter, we presented some new ideas for developing classrooms of special education teachers who support culturally responsive teaching by emphasizing a global perspective. It is our hope that readers are inspired by our passion and seek to add to this developing field of teacher preparation and global awareness.

REFERENCES

Berry, A. (2009). Exploring vision in self study. *Studying Teacher Education, 5*(2), 159-162.

Center for Public Education (2007). *Practical information and analysis about public education.* Retrieved from http://www.centerforpubliceducation.org/You-May-Also-Be-Interested-In-landing-page-level/Organizing-a-School-YMABI/The-United-States-of-education-The-changing-demographics-of-the-United-States-and-their-schools.html.

Chen, D. W., Nimmo, J., & Fraser, H. (2009). Becoming a culturally responsive early childhood educator: A tool to support reflection by teachers embarking on the anti-bias journey. *Multicultural Perspectives, 11*(2), 101-106.

Commission on Global Governance, The (1995). *Our global neighborhood.* Oxford University Press.

Cowhey, M. (2010). Learning to roar. *The Education Digest,* January 2010.

DK & UNICEF (2002). *A life like mine: How children live around the world.* New York: DK Publishing.

Flowers, N., Bernbaum, M., Rudelius-Palmer, K., & Tolman, J. (2000). *The human rights education handbook: Effective practices for learning, action, and change.* Minneapolis, MN: The Human Rights Resource Center and the Stanley Foundation.

Gerena, L. (2011). Parental voice and involvement in cultural context: Understanding rationales, values, and motivational constructs in a dual immersion setting. *Urban Education, 46*(3), 342-370.

Gilles, C., Wilson, J., & Elias, M., (2010). Sustaining teachers' growth and renewal through action research, induction programs, and collaboration. *Teacher Education Quarterly, 37*(1), 91-108.

IDEA (2004). Individuals with Disabilities Education Improvement Act of 2004, PL 108-446, 20U.S.C. §§ 1400 et seq.

Ingram, J. D. (2008). What is a "right to have rights"? Three images of the politics of human rights. *American Political Science Review, 102*(4), 401-416.

Ishay, M. R. (2004). *The history of human rights: From ancient times to the globalization era.* Berkeley: University of California Press.

Kindersley, D. (2002). *A life like mine.* DK and UNICEF.

Killeavy, M., & Moloney, A. (2010). Reflection in a social space: Can blogging support reflective practice for beginning teachers? *Teaching and Teacher Education: An International Journal of Research and Studies. 26*(4), 1070-1076.

LePage, P., Nielsen, S., & Fearn, E. (2008). Charting the dispositional knowledge of teachers in special education. *Teacher Education and Special Education, 31,* 77-92.

Lindahl, R. (2006). The right to education in a globalized world. *Journal of Studies in International Education, 10*(1), 5-26.

Lucas, A. G. (2009). Teaching about human rights in the elementary classroom using the book *A life like mine: How children live around the world. The Social Studies,* March/April.

McIntyre, C., & Dangel, J. R. (2009). Teacher candidate portfolios: Routine or reflective practice action? *Action in Teacher Education, 31*(2), 74-85.

Myers, J. P., & Zaman, H. A. (2009). Negotiating the global and national: Immigrant and dominant – Culture adolescents' vocabularies of citizenship in a transnational world. *Teachers College Record, 111* (11), 2589-2625.

Osler, A. (2005). *Teachers, human rights, and diversity.* Stoke on Trent, UK, and Sterling, USA: Trentham Books.

Osler, A., & Starkey, H. (2010). *Teachers and human rights education.* Stoke on Trent, UK and Sterling, USA: Trentham Books.

Pagden, A. (2003). Human rights, natural rights, and Europe's imperial legacy. *Political Theory, 31*(2).

Reimers, F. M. (2009). Leading for global competency. *Teaching for the 21st Century, 67*(1).

Sleeter, C. (2000). Diversity vs. White privilege. *Rethinking School Online, 15*(2).

UN (1948). UN Universal Declaration of Human Rights. Retrieved from http://www.ohchr.org/en/udhr/pages/introduction.aspx.

UN (1966). International Covenant on Economic, Social and Cultural Rights. Retrieved from http://www2.ohchr.org/english/law/cescr.htm.

UN (1989). Convention on the Rights of the Child (CRC). Retrieved from http://www.ohchr.org/english/law/crc.htm.

UNESCO (2000). The Dakar Framework of Action. Education for All: Meeting our Collective Commitments. Paris: UNESCO. Retrieved from http://2.unesco.org/wef/en_conf/dakfram.shtm.

Villegas, A., & Lucas, T. (2002). Preparing culturally responsive teachers: Rethinking the curriculum. *Journal of Teacher Education, 53*(1).

Villegas, A., & Lucas, T. (2005). Preparing culturally responsive teachers: Rethinking the curriculum. *Journal of Teacher Education, 56* (1).

Willie, C. V. (1996). Robin M. Williams, Jr. lecture, 1995-dominant and subdominant people of power: A new way of conceptualizing minority and majority populations. *Sociological Forum, 11*(1).

Zhao, Y. (2009). Needed: Global villagers. *Educational Leadership, 67*(1), 60-65.

AFFILIATIONS

Susan J. Courey
Department of Special Education
San Francisco State University, USA

Pam LePage
Department of Special Education
San Francisco State University, USA

MINA AFKIR

8. MOROCCAN CHILDREN'S RIGHTS IN AN EDUCATIONAL SPACE

INTRODUCTION

Since its ratification of the UN Convention on the Rights of the Child in July 1993, the Moroccan government has made great efforts to show its clear commitment and strong will to improve the Moroccan child's situation. At the legal level, legislation was introduced or amended to better children's conditions. In the new Labor Code of 2003, for instance, the minimum age for children's employment was raised from 12 to 15 years, restrictions were made on the maximum hours of work, and employers were prohibited from making children work in dangerous jobs that involve among others heavy machines and toxic material. In the Penal Code, which was amended in December 2003, child sexual abuse, child pornography, child prostitution, and child sex tourism are considered crimes and are severely punished. At the institutional level, Morocco created different structures to promote children's rights. For example, it created the Child Parliament in a bid to acknowledge children's rights to express their opinions and to provide a platform for them to talk about their problems. Becoming bound by international law to the Convention on the Rights of the Child, the Moroccan government also created the National Observatory of the Rights of the Child to monitor the application of the convention.

In the field of education, Morocco has also tried to improve its educational policy reflecting its strong will to make changes in the status of children's educational rights. At the institutional level, a Supreme Council for Education was created to assess the national education system and the reform programs that Morocco has been engaged in since the implementation of the National Charter for Education and Training in 2000. In addition to this, vital reforms have been implemented, such as the extension of the length of basic education from five years to nine years, the increase in providing education in rural and impoverished areas, the expansion of non-formal education programs to educate those who drop out early from school to enter the labor market, and the increase of primary school enrolment in an attempt to achieve an enrolment rate of 100%. For instance, the Gross Enrolment Ratio (GER) increased from 65% in 1991 to 108% in 2009 (UNESCO Institute for Statistics, 2009).

In spite of all these endeavors that reflect Morocco's belief that education is a right and not a privilege, the language situation in which children live sometimes

H. Biseth & H. B. Holmarsdottir (eds.), Human Rights in the Field of Comparative Education, 109–123.

threatens their educational attainment. In Morocco, the official language is Arabic as stated in the country's constitution.[i] Arabic, which belongs to the Semitic language family, was introduced in Morocco in the seventh century AD with the Arab-Islamic conquests. The arabization of the Amazigh people, the indigenous inhabitants of Morocco, was at the beginning necessary in order to establish the beliefs and practices of the new religion. As Ennaji (2005) stated, "the remarkable relation between Arabic and Islam [...] made this spread and dominance of Arabic unavoidable. In fact, to understand the Qur'an, one has to be literate in Arabic" (p. 10). Today, in addition to the Amazigh language,[ii] which has managed to survive in spite of centuries of stigmatization and marginalization (El Kirat, 2009), two varieties of Arabic are on the Moroccan linguistic market, namely Standard Arabic, which is a modern version of Classical Arabic, and Moroccan Arabic, which is referred to as Darija by Moroccan people.

The two varieties of Arabic stand in a diglossic relationship. Ferguson (1972)[iii] defined diglossia as

> a relatively stable language situation in which, in addition to the primary dialects of the language [...], there is a very divergent, highly codified (often grammatically more complex) superposed variety, the vehicle of a large and respected body of written literature, either of an earlier period or in another speech community, which is learned largely by formal education and is used for most written and formal spoken purposes but is not used by any sector of the community for ordinary conversation. (pp. 244-245)

In Morocco, Moroccan Arabic, which the child hears and speaks at home, and Standard Arabic, which he/she reads and writes at school, are both referred to as Arabic. However, they are different lexically, phonologically, morphologically, and syntactically. Furthermore, they do not have the same status, and they fulfill different communicative functions in the Moroccan society. Standard Arabic, which is the 'high' variety,[iv] is a written language that is codified and standardized. It has no native speakers; it is no one's mother tongue, and it is learned at school. Although illiterate people cannot read or write Standard Arabic, because they have never been to school, many of them can understand some of it and would follow television and radio programs broadcast in it. Moroccan Arabic, the 'low' variety, is the mother tongue of a large proportion of the Moroccan population. It is mainly used for oral communication, and it has officially and theoretically no place in the school space because it has no writing system, and it is neither codified nor standardized. This entails that for the Moroccan child, there is a mismatch between the language of everyday interaction and the language of the school. The aim of this chapter is to offer insights into how the acquisition of literacy interacts with this language situation in which Moroccan children live. It will show how shifting from Moroccan Arabic to Standard Arabic when making the transition to school makes some Moroccan children enter the educational space with a risk of failure.

METHODS

The Sample

The children who participated in the study were 52 first graders who were drawn from two distinct social groups, 26 (13 males and 13 females) from a middle-class group and 26 (13 males and 13 females) from a working-class group. Middle-class children's age ranged from 6 years 3 months to 7 years while working-class children's age ranged from 7 years 3 months to 7 years 11 months. In Morocco, children from the two socioeconomic backgrounds do not generally mix in primary schools. The primary schools attended by working-class children are sponsored by the Ministry of Education and are free, and the primary schools that serve middle-class children are private. Moreover, middle-class children start primary schooling at six while working-class children enter public schools at seven. One similarity between the two types of schools, however, is that they both follow the national curriculum prescribed by the Ministry of Education.

Instruments

The children were visited in their primary schools[v] and were administered a battery of literacy tests after six months of schooling in Grade 1. The literacy measures, which included a word decoding test, a vocabulary test, and a narrative production task, were used in order to see how the students' literacy acquisition interacts with the diglossic language situation in which they live. Decoding and vocabulary are areas where interference between the two languages is likely to occur because the two languages exhibit phonetic and lexical differences. The narrative production task was employed because the children would need all their language skills to produce a connected piece of discourse. The children's achievement at this stage of their literacy development is highly predictive of subsequent literacy. If the children's diglossic situation is found to impede and hence slow down their acquisition of early basic reading skills such as decoding and vocabulary, this means that diglossia should be added to the other cognitive and social factors that hinder Moroccan children's literacy acquisition.

After many weeks of classroom observation in different primary schools, the tests were constructed by the author based on children's textbooks. All the tests were evaluated by eight experienced teachers to determine their appropriateness and their level of difficulty. Items that were described as inappropriate were replaced with others. The tests were also all pilot-tested on six working-class children and six middle-class children qualified as poor, average, and good readers by the grades they got in the first semester.

The tests were presented in a fixed order for all children, and they were all administered individually during one session. All the instructions were oral and in Moroccan Arabic. During classroom observations, the author noticed that teachers, in most cases if not all, would read instructions in Standard Arabic and then translate them to Moroccan Arabic. Teachers did not translate only when the instruction in an exercise was so frequent in children's textbooks that it had become routinized.

The Word Decoding Test

In the word decoding test, the children were asked to read a list of 40 items that increased in difficulty. Classroom observations in many first grade classrooms, an examination of the textbooks used by children in their first year of schooling, and discussions with the teachers that were observed made it clear that what constitutes a difficult word for a Moroccan child is not necessarily a long word. Difficult words are words that are not frequent in classroom interaction and textbooks, words that are difficult to pronounce, and words that incorporate letters that have difficult configurations. One of the basic characteristics of the Arabic writing system is that the same letter has different shapes depending on whether it is at the beginning, middle, or end of the word and sometimes also depending on the neighboring letter that occurs before it when it is at the end of a word. For example, the letter 'غ' 'ɣ', the voiced uvular fricative in Arabic, takes four different forms because, in addition to its shapes at the beginning 'غـ' and in the middle of a word 'ـغـ', it has two configurations 'ـغ' and 'غ' when it occurs at the end of a word depending on the adjacent letter.

The Vocabulary Test

In the vocabulary test, the children were presented with a colored picture and were asked to name it. All the pictures were pre-tested on six working-class children (poor, average, and good readers) and six middle-class children (poor, average, and good readers), and the ones that were not clear were replaced with others. The total number of pictures was 34. The words that name the pictures differed in their degree of difficulty. They were selected from 100 words that had been randomly picked by the author from children's reading textbooks and then graded in terms of difficulty by five experienced primary school teachers.

The Narrative Production Task

In the narrative production task, the children were shown a set of picture prompts and were asked to build an oral story out of them. This task was more demanding than the decoding and vocabulary tests because the children were required to produce a connected piece of text where they made use of all their skills. The children were allowed as much time as they needed to look at the pictures. The narration task was meant to test children's school language and their way of producing a text in school settings.

RESULTS AND DISCUSSION

The main finding of the study is that for the Moroccan children the borders between Moroccan Arabic, the home language, and Standard Arabic, the language of literacy, were sometimes blurred. The children's performance in the literacy tests revealed that their mother tongue sometimes interfered with their literacy acquisition, creating a state of confusion and hampering their achievement in Standard Arabic.

Word Decoding

The children's performance in the word decoding test has shown that in some cases their poor decoding was due to the linguistic habits they had brought with them from the home to the school. A common mistake in children's answers, as the following misdecoded words show, was to shorten long vowels or to replace short ones with their long counterparts (consonants with a dot under them are emphatic consonants. In Arabic, emphasis is a secondary articulation that involves the retraction of the dorsum of the tongue).

Standard Arabic	Children's misdecoding	English
1. fu: • atun	fu • atun	Towel
2. sari:datum	sari̱datun	Pullover
3. risa:latun	risa̱latun	Letter
4. na:fidatun	nafi:datun	Window
5. sama̱katun	sama:katun	Fish
6. nami̱run	nami:run	Tiger
7. mi?ðanatun	mi?ða:natun	Minaret
8. bulbu̱l	bulbu:lun	Nightingale
9. ku̱ratun	ku:ratun	Ball
10. xu̱ðru:fun	xu:ðru:fun	spinning top
11. minda̱datun	minda:datun	Desk
12. ʕina̱bun	ʕina:bun	Grapes

Moroccan Arabic, the children's mother tongue, has no long vowels. When Moroccan children start schooling, they find themselves confronted with a new phonetic aspect that they have to master. From an articulatory point of view, their vocal tract is not used to lengthen vowels. Second, the long vowels represented in the Standard Arabic script are a source of confusion for beginning readers (Afkir, 2001). Standard Arabic has four long vowels: 'و', which stands for 'u:', 'ي' and 'ى', which stand for 'i:' (the first one is used in the middle of a word and the second one at the end of it), and 'ا', which stands for 'a:'. The fact that Moroccan Arabic does not have long vowels and the fact that they are used in conjunction with diacritics for short vowels make them hard to learn. Another source of difficulty is that these symbols, which stand for long vowels, stand also for consonants. For example, 'و' (the labio-velar 'w'), which stands for the vowel 'u:', is also a consonant in Standard Arabic as in the word 'وردة' (pronounced phonetically as warda) 'flower'.

Decoding skills are very important because they are highly predictive of reading proficiency (Öney & Durgunoğlu, 1997; Snow, 1993; Wagner, 1993); a good word decoder is a fluent reader. This is so because decoding and comprehension skills interact (Paris, 2005). As Perfetti (2010) stated, "there is a strong causal relation between decoding and comprehension in that fluent or automatic decoding allows more processing resources to be available for comprehension" (p. 294). A child with low decoding abilities is a child with a poor level of comprehension. When words are read slowly and inaccurately, this negatively affects and impedes the comprehension process. Decoding vowels accurately is even more pertinent in a language like Standard Arabic, where short vowels are not alphabetic letters but diacritic marks that are placed above or below letters. A word like 'k-t-b' 'كتب', without diacritics or strokes for vowels, can be read as 'kataba' 'he wrote', 'kutiba' 'was written', and 'kutubun' 'books' depending on the context of the sentence. This is why decoding incorrectly a vowel may greatly affect comprehension. The middle-class children outperformed the sample of working-class children in the sentence comprehension test because they decoded better. Although the decoding test has shown that children from both socioeconomic backgrounds suffered from problems of interference[vi], middle-class children achieved higher than working-class children in this test for other reasons. They mastered well the Standard Arabic script, where many letters look quite similar, where many letters have dots, where there is gemination[vii] and they also most likely had better blending skills.

Vocabulary

The children's performance in the vocabulary test reflected more the extent to which diglossia may hinder their literacy acquisition. In the vocabulary test, both middle-class and working-class children received average scores. In the working-class group, 52.18% of the pictures were named correctly compared to 52.06% in the other group (t-test, p=.98). Although the working-class group's score was only slightly better, it is important to point out that both groups struggled with common words.

One of the factors that may account for first graders' average scores in the vocabulary test is the diglossic situation in which they live. One important source of vocabulary learning is adult-child conversations (Tabors, Beals, & Weizman, 2001). Fernald and Weisleder (2011) noted that "speech directed to the young child in an engaging way is essential for the optimal development of vocabulary knowledge" (p. 3). Research (Beals & Tabors, 1995; Weizman & Snow, 2001) has shown that there is a link between children's performance on vocabulary tests and their exposure to sophisticated vocabulary through social interaction in the home context. Beals and Tabors (1995) found such a link in a study they conducted with American kindergarten children. The children who took part in their study were tape recorded with their mothers in different home conversational contexts when they were 3 and 4 years-old, and they were administered the Peabody Picture Vocabulary Test (Dunn & Dunn, 1981) when they were 5 years-old. One of the aims of the study was to find out how exposure to rare vocabulary in these home conversational contexts was related to children's performance in the vocabulary test. The results of a correlational analysis have shown that there are associations between exposure to rare words through social interaction at age 3 and 4 and performance on the vocabulary test at age 5. Children's achievement in the vocabulary test was predicted by the vocabulary they were exposed to in adult-child conversations. Weizman and Snow (2001), in a study of 53 working-class mothers and their 5 year-old children, also found correlations between maternal use of sophisticated words in home talk and vocabulary outcomes at age five.

For Moroccan children, they cannot benefit from social interaction in the home environment to foster their vocabulary learning, because they are deprived of opportunities to be exposed to new vocabulary items that they have not heard before or to rare lexical items that are triggered by specific topics in their homes. For them, conversations with their caregivers cannot support their vocabulary acquisition in the language of instruction as these conversations are conducted in Moroccan Arabic and reading and writing are done in Standard Arabic. Moreover and more interestingly, Moroccan children do not have a chance to hear again in naturally occurring interaction the vocabulary items they have already been exposed to in the school setting. The learning of vocabulary items is gradual; one way a word is fully acquired as part of one's vocabulary stock is by encountering it in other contexts. For the Moroccan school child, this could happen in the school context where the same word may be used in different reading materials or by the teacher in different learning situations but unfortunately not in the home context, where the language of everyday interaction is different from the language of literacy. Even when parents are literate and may from time to time ask the child about the equivalent of a Standard Arabic word in Moroccan Arabic or vice versa, this still remains a very insignificant contribution to children's vocabulary development, because it cannot have the same effect as in cases where the language a child reads and writes is the same as the language he/she hears and speaks in the home context.

One category of mistakes that show that Moroccan children would have performed better in the vocabulary test if their vocabulary acquisition were supported by the language of the home is provided in the following example.

Standard Arabic	Children's answers	English
1. miknasatun	miknisatun	broom
2. miḍrabun	miḍra:bun	racket
3. mi•ha:tun	miḍra:bun	saucepan
4. samakatun	mi•hatun	fish
5. maɣsilun	maɣɣa:silun	sink
6. ?ibri:qun	barqun	coffee pot
7. xuðru:fun	xurfun	spinning top
6. θuʕba:nun	taʕbun	snake

In this group of lexical items, children supplied answers that were quite close to what they had been asked for. For instance, in items 1, 2, 3, and 4, to name the four pictures they were shown by the author, they provided the right words in Standard Arabic, but with mispronounced vowels. In items 5, 6, 7, and 8, they modified the words that name the prompt pictures by adding, deleting, or changing a sound or more than one sound. Mistakes like these indicate that the children's mastery of a given vocabulary item was not fully developed. They still needed to encounter it in other contexts so that it would become part of their vocabulary stock. The common feature of all these vocabulary items (broom, racket, saucepan, fish, sink, coffee pot, spinning top, snake) is that they are very common everyday words, which means that if the language of literacy for these children were Moroccan Arabic, they would have been exposed to these lexical items many times through social interaction in their family discourse, and they would have made less errors when naming the pictures that represent them in the test. Maamouri (1998) pointed out that Arab children face many challenges when they start school; one of these is "[the] important lexical differences even in commonplace everyday words and functional terms" (p. 47). All this suggests that to shift from one language to another in order to acquire literacy puts Moroccan children at a disadvantage because they struggle even with the easiest words in the lexicon let alone more demanding levels such as morphology and syntax.

In addition to the fact that the diglossic situation in which children live makes it difficult for them to benefit from social interaction in the home context to expand and promote their vocabulary knowledge, it also causes them problems with regard to interference that prevent them from doing well in vocabulary tests. One category of mistakes that reflect the extent to which diglossia can have a negative impact on children's efficient vocabulary learning involves children's recourse to Moroccan Arabic to fill in their lexical gaps. For some picture prompts, the children replaced a given vocabulary item in Standard Arabic with its counterpart in Moroccan Arabic, and they very frequently incorporated some changes on this word to make it sound like words in Standard Arabic as illustrated in the following answers.

Standard Arabic	Children's answers	Moroccan Arabic	English
1. miknasatun	ʃa ••abatun	ʃə••aba	broom
2. miknasatun	ʃa••a:batun	ʃə••aba	broom
3. θuʕba:nun	hinʃun	hnəʃ	serpent
4. sari:datun	trikkun	trikku	sweater
5. ʃawkatun	furʃi: •atun	fərʃi•a	fork
6. ʃawkatun	furʃi•un	fərʃi•a	fork
7. ʕaӡalatun	rweydatun	rwida	tire
8. difdiʕatun	ӡranatun	ӡrana	toad
9. xuðru:fun	•rumbiyyatun	•rumbiyya	spinning top
10. zirrun	•adfatun	•ədfa	button
11. zirrun	ʕuqdatun	ʕuqda	button
12. sikki:nun	mu:sun	mu:s	knife
13. sari:run	musiyyatun	namusiyya	bed
14. fusta:nun	kiswatun	kəswa	dress

The vocabulary items children produced to name the prompt pictures in column 2 belong to Moroccan Arabic, but they modified them to make them appropriate for the school context. For instance, they replaced all the schwas (the central vowel schwa 'ə' is one of the basic characteristics of Moroccan Arabic as opposed to Standard Arabic) with non-central vowels, and they added to all of them the suffixes '+un' or '+tun', which indicate the masculine singular and the feminine singular in Standard Arabic respectively and which do not exist in Moroccan Arabic. The children's recourse to Moroccan Arabic as a strategy to avoid keeping silent would probably decrease their chances to make more efforts to acquire the vocabulary of the school language. They knew that for each picture they could not name there is a lexical item that could be easily retrieved from their stock of Moroccan Arabic vocabulary.

This negative transfer at the lexical level, which I have explained as a strategy Moroccan children employ to avoid silence or embarrassment in the face of unknown words, may also be interpreted as a case of confusion. First, Moroccan Arabic and Standard Arabic are linguistically related. Although they are lexically, phonologically, morphologically, and syntactically different, they both represent some kind of Arabic. For instance, at the lexical level, while some words are completely different, others are quite similar. The word for 'fire' is 'naːr' in Standard Arabic and 'ʕafya' in Moroccan Arabic whereas the word for 'apple' is 'tuffaːha' in Standard Arabic and 'təffaha' in Moroccan Arabic. The fact that there is some linguistic relatedness between the low variety and the high variety of Arabic creates some kind of confusion for children, who would borrow from their mother tongue without really being aware that they are mixing two different codes. As Maamouri (1998) stated, "the intermingling of *fushas*[viii] and *colloquials* in the Arab region and the lack of clear-cut linguistic marking barriers aggravate the insecurity of the young learners who seem confused by what constitutes *fusha* in the Arabic forms which surround them and what does not" (p. 42). In addition to this, teachers' language behavior in classrooms may be considered as another source of confusion for beginning readers. Since their first day at school, Moroccan children, like all the other children in the Arab world, realize that their teacher is using a language that is different from the one employed outside school. However, the fact that the teachers themselves shift from one variety of Arabic to another in a non-systematic way in their classroom talk makes it difficult for learners to recognize the real borders between the two. They would simply adopt the discourse habits of their teachers by mixing Moroccan Arabic and Standard Arabic because for them this is a language behavior that is acceptable in the school setting since it is practiced by their teachers.

The Narrative Production Task

In addition to word decoding and vocabulary, the children's performance in the narrative production task also revealed how the borders between Moroccan Arabic and Standard Arabic were not clear-cut for them and how this could have a negative impact on their literacy outcomes. The mean length of the stories orally generated by the sample of working-class children is 22.37 words per story (range: between 8 words and 41 words) compared to 20.87 words (range: between 6 words and 38 words) in the middle-class group. However, it is important to note that although children from both socioeconomic backgrounds produced oral stories that were similar in length, middle-class children's performance was better because they did not rely on Moroccan Arabic as much as children in the other group (Test: t-test, df: 48, p= .009).

One strategy that characterizes the stories produced by children from both socioeconomic backgrounds is their use of Moroccan Arabic or Moroccan Arabic with some modifications. The length measure is not always a revealing one; a story produced by a child may be long simply because he resorted to Moroccan Arabic. While some children would keep silent, skip a picture, or say 'maʕrəftʃ' in Moroccan Arabic 'I don't know' when they found it difficult to process the information presented in a given picture, others resorted to another strategy, which consisted of shifting from the language of the school to the language of the home. The following story produced by a working-class girl is an illustration of this (words in Moroccan Arabic are underlined).

The child: 7 years 11 months, working-class, female

Arabic:

dahaba Karim wa wa·aːha. innahu fi: alkuːṛati. wa wa wa innahu al alma al .. allaṛaf innahu ʒat innahu daru lih iddawaː? .. waʔinnahu .. innahu naʕsun fəssbi·aṛ.

English:

Karim went and and he fell. He was in football. And and and he the the amb (the child tried to produce the Standard Arabic word 'ambulance', but he was not able to do so) the the police car it came. They gave him medicines … and he is … he is asleep in hospital.

The story constructed by the child is quite complete. All the pictures were incorporated by her, which indicates that she tried to adjust to the requirements of her audience while accomplishing the task. Although she was aware that the author knew the story, she behaved as if the latter did not and included as many details as she could. This ability to assume that one's reader or one's listener does not share the same information, even in cases where he does, is one of the basic requirements of becoming literate. In school settings, even shared meanings should be lexicalized, and the child who is aware of this could handle school tasks more easily. However, to accomplish the task, the child used both Standard Arabic and Moroccan Arabic. The words 'ʒat' 'it came', 'daru lih' 'they gave him', and 'fəssbi·aṛ' 'in hospital' were given in Moroccan Arabic. The words '·aːha' 'he fell', 'allaṛaf' 'police car' and 'naʕsun' 'asleep' were also drawn from Moroccan Arabic, but they were modified by the child to make them sound more like words in Standard Arabic.

Standard Arabic	Moroccan Arabic	Children's answers	English
aqaʕa	aḥ	aːḥa	'he fell'
sayyaːratu ʃʃurʕati	laṛaf	allaṛaf	'the police car'
naːʔimun	naʕǝs	naʕsun	'the police car'

In this group of words, for the Moroccan Arabic verb 'ˑaḥ' 'he fell', the child added the suffix '+a' 'ˑaːḥa' to make it sound like a Standard Arabic verb in the perfect form, and she also lengthened the short vowel 'a'(ˑaːḥa) because there is a verb pattern like this in Standard Arabic. For the Moroccan Arabic word 'laṛaf' 'the police car', the child added 'al' (al+laṛaf), the definite article in Standard Arabic. Finally, for the word 'naʕǝs' 'asleep', the child omitted the schwa, which is a highly frequent vowel in Moroccan Arabic, and added the suffix '+un' (naʕs+un), which is a nominative suffix for verbal adjectives in Standard Arabic.

The child's recourse to such words or to purely Moroccan Arabic words probably resulted from her inability to produce discourse in the language of the school. Most of the words the child took from Moroccan Arabic were generated after repetitions or a pause, which indicates that she resorted to them because she was unable to come up with their equivalents in Standard Arabic. The vocabulary of the home language is more easily retrieved from memory and its syntax is more accessible, which facilitates language production. It is a strategy that relieves the burden of information processing and hence helps children increase the length of their stories.

CONCLUSION

As the findings of the study have shown, the children's performance in the literacy tests administered to them in first grade was affected by the diglossic language situation in which they live. In the decoding test, their answers revealed that their home language has a vowel system that is different from that of Standard Arabic, which made them mix up the two languages. In the vocabulary test, the borders between the two languages were also blurred. The children fell back on the lexicon of Moroccan Arabic to avoid silence and embarrassment in the face of unknown words, but the fact that they incorporated some changes on the 'borrowed' words to make them sound like Standard Arabic ones can be attributed to the confusion the two related languages create in their minds. The same holds true for the narrative production task, where the subjects relied heavily on the language of the home, which is considered as inappropriate in the school context.

The problems that the Moroccan children face because of diglossia make some of them enter the educational space with the risk of failure. In Moroccan primary schools, decoding skills are considered as the most important component of reading in first grade, as can be inferred from the curriculum where a great deal of time is devoted to sounding out letters and words. Since decoding is the skill that is targeted at this stage of children's literacy development, this means that a child who struggles to decode is a child who is making a slow start in his/her process of becoming literate. Poor decoding skills also discourage children from reading a lot both in and out of school because they find it difficult to read. More interestingly, Wagner (1993) found that for the Moroccan first graders who participated in his study "early word decoding skills at the single word level explained an additional 14% of the variance of year 5 reading achievement" (p. 100). Concerning the vocabulary results, the children's low vocabulary knowledge will probably impede their reading comprehension because a child's vocabulary size indexes his world knowledge, which is very crucial in the task of comprehension (Snow, 1993). Dickinson, Cote, and Smith (1993) also stated that vocabulary is seen as associated not only with reading comprehension, which is simply one component of literacy, but with academic success in general.

The implication of these findings is the fact that Moroccan children start their schooling in a language that is different from their mother tongue, which threatens one of their basic human rights, i.e. their right to education. The Moroccan government has been implementing educational reforms since its independence in 1956, but the issue of diglossia has never been at the center of educational debates. In the last reform, which gave birth to the National Charter of Education and Training (2000), the language question was given consideration, but the languages that were mentioned were Standard Arabic, Amazigh, and foreign languages. Moroccan Arabic was not mentioned as if it did not create any problem for children's beginning literacy. Decision makers and education experts should be aware of these problems. Moving from the home to the school is a big step in the life of a child and making the child feel secure and comfortable in this new environment should be an important concern in terms of education. Furthermore, we can question whether or not access to education is real if the language of instruction is not understood.

For an education policy grounded in a diglossic speech community to guarantee children's rights, it should see mother tongue education as legitimate and hence offer new possibilities to remake the local educational space regardless of questions of politics and ideology. Mother tongue education is essential especially for early literacy. Children's mother tongue can be used at the beginning of their literacy acquisition to bridge their transition from home to school. Fifty eight years ago, UNESCO (1953) advocated the use of a child's mother tongue for literacy acquisition, stating that:

> Psychologically, it is the medium of meaningful signs that in his mind works automatically for expression and understanding. Sociologically, it is a means of identification among the members of the community to which he belongs. Educationally, he learns more quickly through it than through an unfamiliar medium. (p. 11)

This is still of great relevance today. It is obvious that by being introduced to literacy in their mother tongue, children can easily make sense of the signs they decode because they correspond to familiar forms they have already encountered in their daily life and will hence learn quickly. What is, however, more interesting is that children can rely on all their previously acquired linguistic skills (syntactic, semantic, and lexical) to understand and to produce language, which will make the learning experience more meaningful to them and the educational space more secure. To use the mother tongue as a medium of instruction for early literacy will certainly not constitute a threat to Standard Arabic, the lingua franca of Arab speakers, and will not devalue it because "dual loyalty" is a characteristic of Arabic diglossia (Salhi, 2001). In Morocco, Moroccan Arabic has no longer a devalued status. This language, which was considered as a low variety that has no prestige because it is limited to oral communication, is today invading the space of Standard Arabic. It is employed frequently in the media, at school (although the language of literacy is theoretically Standard Arabic), and even in mosques, where the dominant and exclusive language was Standard Arabic. Although Moroccan Arabic has been experiencing a kind of valorization this last decade because there is more awareness of its importance as a carrier of local culture and heritage and as one of the resources that index Moroccans' identity (Afkir, 2009), Standard Arabic is still held in higher esteem and derives its value from being the language of religion. What is ultimately important is that children's right to education involves more than physical access. Thus, Morrow (2007) reminds us that one cannot refer to access as 'meaningful' education on the basis only of enrolment, as access stands for more than whether or not children are enrolled in school. Education becomes meaningful when it provides children with 'epistemic access' – that is, access to learning and content knowledge (Morrow, 2007). Having access to learning and content knowledge in a language that children are familiar with provides them with a realistic right to education.

NOTES

[i] Amazigh, which has been marginalized for hundreds of years, became an official language after the reform of the Moroccan constitution in July 2011.

[ii] Amazigh, which is the language of the first inhabitants of Morocco, belongs to the Hamito-Semitic language family. It is an autonomous language, and it has only remote genetic relations with Arabic. The Amazigh language has been referred to as Berber before. 'Berber', a derogatory word initially used by the Greeks to refer to people who did not speak Classical Greek, does not exist in the verbal repertoire of Moroccans whatever their ethnic group is, and it is mainly employed by foreigners. Today, the word Amazigh is the one adopted by Moroccan researchers to refer to the Berber language.

[iii] Ferguson's article was first published in 1959 in the journal *Word, 15*, pp. 325-340. It was Charles Ferguson who introduced the term 'diglossia' into the English-language literature to describe the situation found in places like the Arabic-speaking world, Greece, German-speaking Switzerland and the Island of Haiti.

[iv] 'High' and 'low' are terms employed by Ferguson (1959) to describe the varieties that stand in a diglossic relationship. Since then, the terms have been used by linguists because they reflect the kind of attitudes that most speakers in diglossic speech communities hold towards the two varieties. In Morocco, for many speakers, Moroccan Arabic is not considered as a language because for them the real language is Standard Arabic, which they consider as more beautiful and purer.

[v] The author obtained written permission from the Ministry of Education that allowed her to visit the schools and administer the tests.

[vi] 'Interference' is a term that was originally introduced by Uriel Weinreich in his book *Languages in contact: Findings and problems* (1953, 1968) to explain the influence of L1 on the acquisition of L2. It refers to the negative transfer of patterns from the mother tongue to the target language.

[vii] 'Gemination' refers to consonant length in Standard Arabic and Moroccan Arabic. Phonetically, geminates are pronounced for a longer period of time than short consonants. In the Standard Arabic writing system, gemination is represented by a diacritic (called shadda in Standard Arabic) that is written above a consonant. This diacritic looks like the letter 'w' in the Latin writing system.

[viii] In the Arab diglossic speech communities, Standard Arabic, the high variety, is called 'fusha' and the low varieties such as Moroccan Arabic, Tunisian Arabic, and Syrian Arabic are called 'colloquials'.

REFERENCES

Afkir, M. (2001). *Language socialization and the acquisition of literacy in Morocco*. Unpublished PhD thesis, Mohammed V University, Rabat, Morocco (with joint supervision at Harvard Graduate School of Education).

Afkir, M. (2009). *Moroccan Arabic-French code-switching: What value for French in today's Moroccan society?* Paper presented at the International Symposium on Bilingualism, Utrecht, The Netherlands.

Beals, D., & Tabors, P. (1995). Arboretum, bureaucratic and carbohydrates: Preschoolers' exposure to rare vocabulary at home. *First Language, 15*, 57-76.

Dickinson, D. K., Cote, L., & Smith, M. (1993). Learning vocabulary in preschool: Social and discourse contexts affecting vocabulary growth. In C. Daiute (Ed.), *The development of literacy through social interaction* (pp. 67-78). San Francisco, CA: Jossey-Bass.

Dunn, L. M., & Dunn, L. M. (1981). *Peabody picture vocabulary test–revised*. Circle Pines, MN: American Guidance Service.

El Kirat, Y. (2009). Issues in the representation of Amazigh language and identity in North Africa. *Langues et Littératures, 19*, 179-196.

Ennaji, M. (2005). *Multilingualism, cultural identity, and education in Morocco*. New York: Springer.

Ferguson, C. (1972). Diglossia. In P. P. Giglioli (Ed.), *Language and social context* (pp.232-251). Harmondsworth, Middlesex: Penguin Books.

Fernald, A., & Weisleder, A. (2011). Early language experience is vital to developing fluency in understanding. In S. B. Neuman & D. K. Dickinson (Eds.), *Handbook of early literacy research* (pp. 3-19). New York, NY: Guilford Press.

Labor Code (amended version). (2003). Morocco.

Maamouri, M. (1998). *Language, education, and human development: Arabic diglossia and its impact on the quality of education in the Arab region*. Paper presented at the Mediterranean Development Forum, Marrakech, Morocco.

Morrow, W.E. (2007) *Learning to teach in South Africa*. Cape Town: HSRC Press.

National Charter for Education and Training (2000). Morocco.

Öney, B., & Durgunoğlu, A. (1997). Beginning to read in Turkish: A phonologically transparent orthography. *Applied Psycholinguistics, 18*, 1-15.

Paris, S. G. (2005). Reinterpreting the development of reading skills. *Reading Research Quarterly, 40*(2), 184-202.

Penal Code (amended version). (2003). Morocco.

Perfetti, C. (2010). Decoding, vocabulary, and comprehension: The golden triangle of reading skill. In M. G. McKeown & L. Kucan (Eds.), *Bringing reading research to life* (pp. 291-303). New York, NY: Guilford Press.

Salhi, R. (2001). *Mother tongue education: A legitimate or subversive claim?* Paper presented at AIMS conference, Tangier, Morocco.

Snow, C. E. (1993). Families as social contexts for literacy development. In C. Daiute (Ed.), *The development of literacy through social interaction* (pp.11-24). San Francisco, CA: Jossey-Bass.

Tabors, P. O., Beals, D. E., & Weizman, Z. O. (2001). 'You know what oxygen is?': Learning new words at home. In D. K. Dickinson & P. O. Tabors (Eds.), *Beginning literacy with language: Young children learning at home and school* (pp. 93-110). Baltimore: Paul H. Brookes.

UNESCO (1953). The use of vernacular languages in education. Paris, France: UNESCO.

UNESCO Institute for Statistics (2009). Morocco report. Paris: UNESCO.

Wagner, D. (1993). *Literacy, culture, and development: Becoming literate in Morocco.* Cambridge: Cambridge University Press.

Weizman, Z. & Snow, C. E. (2001). Lexical input as related to children's vocabulary acquisition: Effects of sophisticated exposure and support for meaning. *Developmental Psychology, 37*(2), 265-79.

AFFILIATIONS

Mina Afkir
Faculty of Letters and Humanities
Hassan II University
Casablanca, Morocco

KAREN CARLISLE AND JOANNE HUGHES

9. THE ROLE OF INTER-SCHOOL COLLABORATION IN PROMOTING INTER-GROUP RELATIONS

The Northern Ireland Perspective

INTRODUCTION

The relationship between education and diversity has been brought into sharp focus in Britain and beyond, where research has pointed to a dynamic between social fragmentation and separate schooling for different ethnic/faith groups. Sir Herman Ouseley (2001), in a review of race relations in Bradford, argued that 'virtual apartheid' between schools has led to polarisation, racial tension and a failure to prepare children adequately for life in a multi-ethnic society. The Cantle Review Team (The Cantle Report, 2001) highlighted how distinct ethnic and religious groups can live in very close proximity to one another without ever developing cultural or social bonds. Although the nature of proposed action varies, there is a consistent emphasis on enhancing inter-group contact between members of separate faith communities. Theory emanating primarily from the discipline of social psychology provides a strong rationale for this approach, and there is now a considerable body of internationally generated evidence that endorses the value of inter-group contact in ameliorating prejudice and promoting mutual understanding. There are also considerable challenges to the practical application of this approach and key among these are the discrepancies that exist between receptiveness towards contact and the effectiveness of contact in different contexts (Dixon, Durrheim, & Tredoux, 2005). Furthermore Cantle suggests that schools are seen as central in the drive to create more cohesive communities (The Cantle Report, 2001), with some commentators advocating structural change to ensure that separate schools are 'open to all' (Berkeley, 2008) and others arguing for interventions to promote collaborative inter-school engagement (The Cantle Report, 2001). Indeed, the promotion of collaborative working is not limited to education. In recent years social policy in the UK and Europe has emphasised the need for collaboration to meet the educational, health and social needs of individuals, families and communities (Anning, Cotttell, Frost, Green, & Robinson, 2006; Frost, 2005; Pollit, 2003). Supporters have argued that effective collaborative activity has the potential to increase efficiency of services, bring together complementary services and foster innovation (Lowndes & Skelcher, 1998). Despite positive policy rhetoric and purported benefits it is interesting that

H. Biseth & H. B. Holmarsdottir (eds.), Human Rights in the Field of Comparative Education, 125–145.
© *2013 Sense Publishers. All rights reserved.*

the practical outworking of collaborative activity is often undermined and challenged by a range of factors. Logistical and operational issues that infuse the collaborative and partnership process can make it difficult to ensure that collaboration works effectively (Atkinson, Wilkin, Stott, Doherty, & Kinder, 2002). In addition and perhaps more fundamentally, organisational culture and value systems have a similar potential to present significant challenges for effective collaborative working (Higham & Yeomans, 2010). The education system in Northern Ireland provides a context for exploring inter-school collaboration within a diverse and divided society. The majority of children in Northern Ireland are educated in schools segregated by religious affiliation. Thus, many schools engaged in collaboration have to contend with challenges of relationship and trust building between groups of individuals who would not normally come into contact with each other. This chapter, based on the findings of a large scale survey and interviews conducted by the authors in 2009, will examine attitudes and experiences of cross-sectoral collaboration in Northern Ireland schools and the potential for collaborative activity to promote inter-group relations.

INTER-SCHOOL COLLABORATION

In recent years education policies in the UK have focused on schools working together to help raise standards, increase subject choice and improve student performance (Department for Education and Skills (DfES), 2005; Department of Education for Northern Ireland (DENI), 2007). Collaboration between schools has also been instigated within a context of greater economic rationalisation (Thorpe & Williams, 2002). Northern Ireland presents a distinctive context for the examination of collaboration. Not only has there been an increasing emphasis on collaboration between public bodies (including schools) to ensure that services are delivered as effectively and efficiently as possible, (Office of First Minister and Deputy First Minister (OFMDFM), 2006; DENI, 2006) but collaboration has been recognised as a key mechanism to ensure that children have access to a more broadly based curriculum (DENI, 2007).

Research suggests that schools become involved in different types of collaborations relating to, for example, shared expertise, geographic location or to break down cultural barriers. The focus can vary in terms of the extent and depth of the relationship between schools (Atkinson Springate, Johnson, & Halsey, 2007). McMeeking, Lines, Blenkinsop, & Schagen (2004) pointed to inter-personal factors such as the commitment and drive of key individuals as important in giving the status necessary for the establishment of collaborative activities. External factors such as availability of funding and local authority initiatives to fulfil specific requirements can also provide the motivation for inter-school collaboration, for example funding packages for collegiate and school clusters to enhance economic viability of small rural schools (Thorpe & Williams, 2002). Other drivers for collaborative working include mutuality of interests and parity of esteem between partners (Peters 1996; Atkinson et al., 2007).

Whilst evidence of the positive impact of collaboration on school improvement is limited (see Muijs, 2008), some commentators have argued that engagement in collaborative learning communities can impact positively for all participants. For schools there are economic advantages such as pooling of resources and funding (Hanford,Houck, Iler & Morgan, 1997). They also benefit from sharing of good practice and increased professional development for teachers which in turn can improve pupil attainment and raise standards (Aiston, Rudd & O'Donnell, 2002). The exchange of ideas and shared professional development can lessen feelings of isolation amongst teaching staff and improve confidence and morale (Aiston et al., 2002). The educational experience of pupils working within a learning community can be enhanced through an increased interaction with pupils from other schools and the greater choice afforded to them can also increase attainment (Atkinson et al., 2007; DfES, 2007).

Despite the endorsement of collaborative work at policy level and perceived benefits for the school community, working in this way at both operational and strategic levels remains a challenge. Difficulties such as alignment of timetables, distance between collaborating schools and lack of funding can impact on the process of sustainable school collaboration (Donnelly & Gallagher, 2008). Furthermore, the Northern Ireland Education and Training Inspectorate, Chief Inspectors report 2006-2008 (Education Training Inspectorate (ETI), 2009) recognised that attention should be paid to operational issues associated with inter-school collaboration:

> The operational outworking of curricular collaboration presents particular challenges for schools and colleges. It is important that the relevant policy-makers listen carefully to the practical difficulties. (p. 8)

The fostering of effective collaboration is further complicated given that schools are expected both to compete in the education market place and to collaborate (Connolly & James, 2006). This is exacerbated by factors such as academically selective schools and changes in local demography resulting in falling enrolments, all which promote competition between schools. Others have also pointed to problems of establishing trust between partners and differences in school ethos, values and culture between collaborating schools as potential inhibitors of effective collaboration (McMeeking, Lines, Blenkinsop & Schagen, 2004; Muijs, 2008).

The literature on collaboration emphasises its complexity and, in contrast to the optimistic policy rhetoric, tends to focus upon the difficulties and limitations of collaborative working. Moreover, given the complexity of collaboration between schools, Atkinson et al. (2007) argued that,

> [there is a] dearth of good empirical evidence relating to school collaboration. Research that has been conducted tended to be focused on evaluations of particular initiatives rather than the processes involved in inter-school collaboration per se. (p. 102)

Our study, in an attempt to contribute to the literature on school collaboration sought to explore process issues relating to school collaboration in Northern

Ireland. Our aim was to arrive at an understanding of the factors that enable, enhance and inhibit schools in a deeply divided educational context to work together in a spirit of cooperation to deliver both educational outcomes for pupils and enhanced inter-group relations. The following section considers the policy impetus for curricular collaboration within a system of religiously separate education in Northern Ireland, all of which provides an interesting dimension for exploring inter-school collaboration.

THE NORTHERN IRELAND CONTEXT

Northern Ireland is a society in transition from a prolonged conflict spanning more than thirty years and resulting in the deaths of more than 3,600 people (Fitzduff & O'Hagan, 2009). Although the causes of the conflict are complex and manifold, one considerable aspect has been a history of hostile relations between Catholics and Protestants. These ostensibly 'religious' categories used to define the two main communities also align with distinctive political persuasions and cultural traditions. In general, most Protestants desire the maintenance of a Union with Britain, and most Catholics aspire to a united Ireland. Throughout its history, Northern Ireland has been a segregated society within which every aspect of life such as housing, education, work and recreation has been affected by socio-political divisions. In 1998, following the paramilitary ceasefires and a protracted series of talks between the main political parties in Northern Ireland and the British and Irish Governments, a peace agreement was reached between the main Unionist and Nationalist politicians. The Good Friday Agreement heralded the beginning of a new more peaceful era in the politics of Northern Ireland. Despite political agreement and subsequent devolved government, the relationship between the two main communities continues to be strained (Police Service Northern Ireland (PSNI), 2009). Whilst the reasons for the continued unrest are complex, the separate school system in Northern Ireland has been the site for a range of policy and structural interventions aimed at reconciliation between the two communities.

The education system in Northern Ireland is divided into parallel systems for Protestants and Catholics with relatively few planned religiously mixed schools and even fewer with an informally mixed religious enrolment. Around 94% of pupils attend either predominantly Protestant (State Controlled[i]) or predominantly Catholic (Maintained[ii]) schools. Approximately 5% of pupils in Maintained schools are non-Catholic and less than 10% of pupils in Controlled schools are Catholic. Integrated schools account for around 5% of the pupil population and have more mixed enrolments.

Although educationalists are divided on the causal relationship between the separate education system and the perpetuation of division and conflict (Gallagher et al., 2010), there is a consensus that education can contribute to promoting inter-group relations (The Cantle Report, 2001). Reflecting this perspective, the Department of Education has supported a range of initiatives to promote cross-sectoral school collaboration and contact between Protestant and Catholic children in Northern Ireland (for example, Schools Community Relations Programme and the 2007 Education Order which mainstreamed Personal Development and Mutual Understanding (PDMU) in the primary sector and Local and Global Citizenship (LGC) in post primary schools). Despite the efforts of the Department of Education, findings from a recent review of education in Northern Ireland argued that the current educational structure "based almost entirely on institutional independence, and its preservation, within a competitive system is.to a greater or lesser extent, at a cost to learners' experiences and opportunities" (DENI, 2006 p27). The review highlighted the inefficiencies of current separate school structures in the context of falling numbers of school children, an oversupply of school places and concerns about growing levels of community segregation, stressing the need for greater rationalization, complemented by incentives that encourage schools to work together.

> Our argument ... is three fold: first, the educational case-access for pupils to the full range of the curriculum, to high quality teaching and to modern facilities; second, the social case–societal well-being by promoting a culture of tolerance, mutual understanding and inter-relationship through significant, purposeful and regular engagement and interaction in learning: the economic case – through cost effective provision that gives good value for money. (DENI, 2006 p. 26)

The Department of Education Northern Ireland Order (DENI, 2007) provided the broad legislative framework for greater collaboration and paved the way for the Entitlement Framework which requires that by September 2013 all schools must "provide all pupils with access to a minimum number of courses (target 24 curricular subjects) at Key Stage 4 (pupils aged 15-16 years) and a minimum number of courses at post-16 (target 27 curricular subjects)" (DENI, 2009 Section 2). Guidance from the Department of Education suggested that schools should consider a number of approaches to fulfilling the stated 24/27 courses including "co-operation and collaboration with neighbouring schools, Further Education Colleges or other providers; shared appointments of staff; and/or distance learning using ICT" (DENI, 2005, Section 1.4). However, despite the potential for curricular collaboration to promote inter-group relations and bring together pupils and teachers who would not normally come into contact with each other, there is no statutory obligation within the Entitlement Framework for cross-sectoral school collaboration.

Within the wider policy framework of the Entitlement Framework and calls for more cost effectiveness in schools, a non-statutory initiative called the Sharing Education Programme (SEP) was introduced in 2007. Funded by an international charity and guided by reconciliation principles, the emphasis of SEP is on creating opportunities for schools in the Protestant (Controlled) and Catholic (Maintained) sectors to work together on a sustained basis. Collaborating schools are encouraged to devise projects that reflect other shared educational priorities with the hope that through working together on mutually advantageous activities, better relations will be an outcome. Phase 1 of the Programme (SEP1) supported twelve school partnerships comprising almost 60 schools and over 2,500 pupils. Phase 2 of the

SEP Programme is currently underway and similarly involves twelve partnerships (70 schools in total) and over 4,000 pupils in the first year. The Programme is deliberately non-prescriptive and partnerships are asked only to ensure that collaborative activity involves 'sustainable, high quality engagement by young people from different cultural traditions and backgrounds' (Sharing Education Programme, 2010, Section 1.1).

METHODS

In order to ascertain the extent of and attitudes towards inter-school collaborative activity, the authors used a combination of quantitative and qualitative methods which according to Cohen and Manion (1994), can "map out, or explain more full, the richness and complexity of human behaviour by studying it from one or more standpoint" (p. 233). Quantitative data was collected using an online survey sent to head teachers in all schools in Northern Ireland in 2009. The survey was completed by 460 head teachers (41% of all schools in Northern Ireland[iii]), 49% of the respondents were from Protestant schools (Controlled), 38% from Catholic (Maintained) schools, 8% from Voluntary Grammar schools[iv] and 5% from religiously mixed (Integrated) schools. The survey included items on the nature and extent of previous and current collaborative activities and factors which could enhance or potentially inhibit collaboration. In addition head teachers' were asked about their attitudes towards cross-sectoral collaboration, trust and identity when engaged in collaborative activities and perceptions of the policy and social climate for collaboration. The survey was followed up with 20 semi-structured interviews with head teachers, representing the different school sectors and geographic areas in Northern Ireland. The semi-structured interviews explored in more detail head teachers' perceptions and experiences of collaboration including the context for collaboration; how schools worked together in the planning, delivery and evaluation of their activities; the challenges and supports for working collaboratively; learning gained through their participation in collaboration and the contribution of cross-sectoral collaboration to improving community relations in Northern Ireland.

THE EXPERIENCE OF INTER-SCHOOL COLLABORATION IN
NORTHERN IRELAND SCHOOLS

The majority of respondents indicated they were involved in collaborative activities (91%). Over 60% of collaborative networks reported by schools were comprised of schools from both the Protestant (Controlled) and Catholic (Maintained) sectors, which suggest that a significant proportion of schools in Northern Ireland are engaged in cross-sectoral collaboration. Many schools cited their rationale for becoming involved in collaboration was linked to curriculum provision and extending curricular choice (ranked 1st for post primary schools). Establishing links with schools from other communities (i.e. cross-sectoral collaboration) was also revealed as a common reason for becoming involved in collaboration (ranked 1st for primary schools; 2nd for post primary schools).

Reflections from head teachers indicated that it was important they were engaged in meaningful and mutually beneficial collaborative activities. Within the Northern Ireland context, collaborative activities were, in the main, based around the school curriculum. The following comments from head teachers in Catholic and Protestant schools illustrate the value of curricular collaboration, driven by the Entitlement Framework, to offer greater subject choice and meet the educational needs of pupils.

> You can offer children extra courses and they couldn't have done health and social care here ... grammar schools traditionally do academic courses ... the secondary schools are rich in vocational course but could do with more academic ... (Catholic Voluntary Grammar School)

> Our 6th formers have really benefited, it has widened their choices. Certainly for us collaboration on an educational level is about widening choice and giving our kids more opportunities because we don't have the staff or facilities to offer those courses. (Protestant School)

Interestingly, some head teachers hinted that their participation in collaboration was not simply motivated by the desire to increase subject choice and enhanced educational experience for pupils. Wider policy issues such as school budgets which are largely determined by pupil numbers and marketing of their school were cited as factors when considering the level of collaboration.

> And in terms of [my school's] future I would see that maybe almost immediately we could offer one subject in the local area learning community and maybe we don't have a post-16 but we can still be part of the post-16 arrangement and we could maybe offer 2 subjects and who knows where that could go – it's about complementing each other ... (Integrated School)

> ... the principal of the grammar school and myself were talking a long time before the community started and he said, 'I'm either going to have to make teachers redundant or send them out to be retrained' and I said to him "... [wait] because we don't have the academic subjects to the same extent so we are not far from each other. Can we not work with each other?" Then we got involved in the learning community and the four schools in [the community] were brought together to work together. (Integrated School)

Engagement in cross-sectoral collaboration to create opportunities for pupils to mix and to improve community relations were less of a priority for head teachers in post primary schools. However some head teachers referred to an 'additional' benefit of cross-sectoral collaboration in terms of bringing together pupils from different communities, who may not have an opportunity to come in contact with each other.

... because our system is segregated how are our children going to get to know each other if they don't meet each other ... But are we giving them enough opportunities to meet? I don't think we are under the present system so I think the more that we do this collaboration and as we grow and develop the courses I think that it only can be good for the education of our children. (Protestant school)

The most frequent collaborative activity for post primary pupils was mixed classes. For primary school pupils, joint school trips were cited as the most frequent activity. A significant feature of more established collaborative networks was that collaborative activity was regular, sustained and embedded within current practice.

Well our collaboration with [partner school] is an integral part of the school now and not an add-on and if it was it would not have lasted the length of time that it has done. The planning is done jointly in September and the schemes and programmes that the teachers devise are schemes and programmes that they would have done anyway on their own. It gives them the added dimension to it that you are working alongside another school. (Catholic school)

In terms of collaboration between teachers, school staff participated in joint activities at various levels including both formal and informal contact. Interviews with head teachers, suggested that it was important they were involved in strategic planning and management of collaborative activities and that this work was supported through informal networking between teaching staff.

We then produced the strategic plan which looks at what we intend to do over the next three years and from the strategic plan 2 documents came into being, one was our action plan and the other is service level agreement – so quite a bit of planning has taken place and we have a number of subgroups. Curriculum sub-groups, we have a pastoral sub-group, we have a timetable's subgroup and various others who feedback into the main meeting. (Catholic school)

There would be informal contact if maybe two teachers are sharing a particular course and they would be doing part of the courses in one school and part in another and times when they bring the groups together and obviously there has to be a lot of planning there. So we are finding more and more that teachers from a number of schools are getting together just to plan the courses themselves. (Catholic school)

Huxham (1996) argues that collaboration can be viewed as a way of working 'in association with others for some mutual benefit' (p. 7), a sentiment clearly echoed by head teachers involved in this study. Moreover, previous research has emphasised that effective organisational collaboration involves the development of a clear sense of purpose alongside mechanisms to enable staff to work together to develop and sustain shared activities (Tett, Crowther, & O'Hara, 2003). Our research would also support this view, not only was it important for those involved that there was a clear sense of purpose, i.e. enhanced educational choice and experience for pupils, but that the collaborative activities were part of normal school practice and not viewed as an add on. Whilst initial optimistic rhetoric from head teachers indicated that the collaborative experience was positive and beneficial, further exploration revealed the complexity of collaborative arrangements and factors which could support or constrain the work. The following sections explore the enabling and inhibiting factors associated with school collaboration.

ENABLING FACTORS FOR CROSS-SECTORAL COLLABORATION

Head teachers were selected from a pre-determined list in order to explain what the enabling factors for school collaboration consist of. Respondents were asked "what are the main reasons why collaboration may not work effectively?" and they could select as many reasons as appropriate. Table 1 shows that the most commonly cited facilitators of collaboration included the relationship between school leaders and funding. The least commonly cited reason was the political environment. Interview data also suggested that key inter-personal and operational factors enabled collaborative work. Furthermore, the wider policy and social context within which schools were operating could support the ongoing development of collaborative relations.

Table 1. Key enabling factors for school collaboration

Enabling Factors for collaboration	*% of respondents(n)*
Relationship between school leaders	85(367)
Availability of funding	84(365)
Commitment of other staff	76(319)
Proximity	69(309)
External bodies	27(107)
Political environment	17(73)
Other	6(36)

Inter-personal relationships

Reflecting the survey data, interviewees viewed inter-personal factors such as, positive working relationships between school leaders and school staff as crucial when schools were working collaboratively. Previous relationships between school staff and existing positive working relationships facilitated more effective collaboration. Many head teachers commented on the importance of building up good working relationships, sharing of ideas and good practice.

> I know Sue well and on a professional level we like each other and get on and there is a good professional rapport there. (Catholic School)

> … that is important but I think that [working relationship] is built up over years it's not something that just happens and I knew Sam when he was in [another school] and when he moved … that relationship continued. I think it is the friendship as well in that you know you are going to be warmly greeted and you share ideas and even if it's something you need like a policy document I would share with him and he would share with me. (Protestant School)

> We are sharing ideas and if I have an idea I want to put in place I'll talk to one of the other principals and find out how they would approach it and that sharing of ideas is very good. (Protestant School)

Interviews also revealed that the vision of head teachers committed to collaborative working was significant, not only in driving the collaboration forward but in providing leadership to the school staff and garnering their commitment to deliver collaborative activities. Strategies such as keeping staff informed of collaborative work and hosting joint training were all employed by school leadership teams as a means to ensuring their staff 'bought into' the work.

> I suppose you build the project on trust as well and working together and wanting this to succeed and that's where teachers met each other too. Once teachers met each other out on those [training] days and got to know each other and all of a sudden the friendships that have been built up in the staff have been brilliant, the staff of both [school name] and ourselves and [school name] and both lots of us. (Catholic School)

This comment from a head teacher illustrates the potential of joint training days, not only was it a useful tool for bringing staff on board with collaborative school activities but also for developing meaningful relationships between the staff, all of which contributes to a whole school commitment to collaboration.

Operational Supports

Survey data, coupled with comments from head teachers revealed a number of operational issues essential for the ongoing process of relationship building between collaborating schools. Predictably, factors such as the availability of funding, the geographical location of schools and the alignment of school policies were all key supports for effective collaboration.

Funding was identified as a vital enabling factor of collaborative working. Availability of funding facilitated the depth and sustainability of collaborative activity and head teachers reported that funding allowed them to pay for substitute teacher costs additional materials and more importantly transport to move pupils between schools.

> Funding is important, you know it is, there is no point about it ... We couldn't pay for the sub-cover [substitute teacher costs] that is needed to lend the additional support that is necessary. (Catholic School)

Linked to the support provided through funding were the logistical and operational supports required for effective collaboration. Logistics such as, the geographic location of schools impacted on the kinds of collaborative activity teachers and children could engage in. Those schools collaborating with other local schools frequently stated that being in close proximity to their partner school facilitated the planning and delivery of collaborative activity.

Other supports related to operational aspects of collaboration were raised during interviews. Head teachers reported that collaboration involved a significant investment of time in relation to the planning and delivery of collaborative activities. Consideration of issues such as alignment of timetables, planning for joint classes and the creation of joint policies were all essential for more effective collaboration.

> We have four documents in place at the moment – the first is the remit and rationale and ... we then produced the strategic plan which looks at what we intend to do over the next three years and from the strategic plan two documents came into being, one was our action plan and the other is service level agreement ... so quite a bit of planning has taken place and we have a number of subgroups. Curriculum sub groups, we have a pastoral sub group, we have a timetable's subgroup and various others who feedback into the main meeting ... we wanted to look at the whole pastoral side even when it comes down to the nitty gritty of discipline what is acceptable in one school might not be acceptable in another school even down to the wearing of uniform. We needed to approach that and identify what are the issues around pupils moving from one school to another. (Protestant School)

As the comment above indicates, those schools committed to collaboration worked together to create joint strategies and frameworks as part of the development and sustainability of their collaborative activity.

Policy and Social Context

Although external factors such as political environment and external organisations were ranked lower in survey returns than more practical and inter-personal issues, the wider context within which schools were operating was frequently alluded to in interviews. Policy frameworks such as the Entitlement Framework provided a context for cross-sectoral collaboration, thus head teachers viewed their collaborative work as supported by the Department of Education.

> I think it is supporting it and they have contrived it in a way and done it to make schools work together and the entitlement framework is the best thing for the youngsters and by … the 24/27 [subjects schools are required to offer] they are making schools work together, some schools are forced to do it and some are embracing it. (Protestant School)

An interesting point raised during interviews revealed the importance of the wider school community support when engaged in cross-sectoral collaboration. A number of head teachers reflected on the building of trust within the school community to ensure that they supported cross-sectoral collaboration and the interplay between community and schools to ascertain the level of preparedness for cross-sectoral collaboration.

> …there is trust between the principals and the teachers involved in the first instance…there's gotta be… an element of trust within the parent body in both schools, that this venture is not going to damage the identity or beliefs of either. (Catholic School)

> Often we find that it is the parents that we have to get on board rather than the children, they would still have a hankering to the past but once we can convince them and once they get the feedback from the children about their experiences then it's good. (Protestant School)

As interviews were further scrutinized it became apparent that the ongoing political peace process impacted on community support for collaboration with schools normally associated with the other main religious group.

> I sense that in recent years it's got easier because at least the overt activity of paramilitaries isn't there to the extent that it was … maybe it's part of the peace dividend –I don't sense the same degree of resistance to this sort of work as I would have done some years back. (Catholic School)

This comment, from a head teacher in a Catholic school, acknowledges that the changes in the political landscape and Northern Ireland peace process may be an enabling factor for cross-sectoral collaboration. The comment also alludes to a greater acceptance of collaboration between Catholic and Protestant schools, which may be as a result of the peace process.

INHIBITING FACTORS FOR CROSS-SECTORAL COLLABORATION

Table 2 shows the survey responses to reasons why collaboration may not work effectively. Conversely many of the inhibiting factors cited by head teachers such as lack of funding, operational issues and policy environment were contrary to the supporting factors raised in the previous section. Interview data also indicated that key constraints were linked to operational factors and the wider context that schools were operating in. As interviews were further analysed however, it became evident that other more fundamental concerns around the social and political division within Northern Ireland could impact negatively on cross-sectoral school collaboration.

Table 2. Key reasons why collaboration may not work effectively

Key reasons why collaboration may not work effectively	% of respondents (n)
Lack of funding	83 (382)
Additional workload	71(326)
Competition between schools	53 (243)
Inconsistent discipline/pastoral policies	36 (165)
Proximity of schools	32 (147)
Dilution of school ethos	21(96)
Disputes between pupils from different schools	20 (92)
Anxiety that it might generate sectarianism	19 (87)
Unsupportive policy environment	19 (87)
Lack of independence in decision making	11 (50)
Other	9 (41)

Operational Constrains of Cross-Sectoral Collaboration

Head teachers cited a number of logistical issues hindering the process of relationship building between schools. Constraints such as the distance between partner schools, organisation of transport to and additional work load for teachers were all presented as obstacles to effective collaboration. However on reflection of the importance of the availability of funding these factors appeared to present much less of a problem. Indeed, whilst the availability of funding clearly facilitated the progress of collaboration, comments from head teachers raised fears around current funding arrangements and their continuation in the long term. Concerns were raised about schools' long term commitment to cross-sectoral collaboration if funding was to be removed. Where collaborative networks were reliant on funding head teachers questioned the sustainability of the work.

> In some sense there is a truth in that some projects do run out when the money does and then you have to ask the question was it worth doing in the first place. (Protestant School)

Constraints associated with school budgets were also viewed as impacting on their ability to engage in cross-sectoral collaboration. The continued emphasis on marketization of schools and school budgets largely determined by pupil numbers alongside the culture of schools competing for an ever decreasing number of pupils could create tensions between schools. The following comment illustrates one of the dilemmas for head teachers in terms of developing collaboration:

> But it does come back to the funding issue and if schools are in competition then maybe there isn't enough of that sharing that they'll say 'Ok I'll try that but I want to safeguard my school and my staff'. So I think that until they look at the funding ... because since the education order came in 1989 we have basically been touting for business ... (Protestant School)

Head teachers expressed their reservations in terms of the value of working collaboratively within this apparent contradiction whereby schools are expected to compete within an educational marketplace whilst engaged in collaboration with each other.

Policy Environment

Linked to funding were the policy environment and the ways in which it inhibited collaboration. Whilst the Entitlement Framework advocated schools working together, there was an element of cynicism from some head teachers who felt that current education policy, whereby school funding which is largely based on pupil numbers, worked against the principles of collaboration.

> ... it is much more easy to collaborate when you are not competing for pupils which in terms means funding. (Integrated School)

> I think they need to look at ... [a] system of funding districts rather than schools and then you don't have the problem of trying to safeguard jobs. To me it is a major problem. (Protestant School)

The comments from head teachers, above, suggests that when they were in direct competition with each other the development of long term relationships between schools was difficult.

Social and Political Division in Northern Ireland

Moving onto the wider context of Northern Ireland, it is interesting to note that approximately one fifth of head teachers felt that anxieties around sectarian incidents (20% of head teachers) could potentially influence the development of collaborative relations, specifically with schools outside their own sector. As interviews were further examined it became apparent that head teachers viewed this as an issue. Head teachers working in areas which had a history of violence raised apprehensions about the potential for sectarian incidents to affect their ability to engage in collaborative activities.

… if something happens within the community you may well feel that it wouldn't be advantageous to run the project the next day. Something that happened to an individual or a family – outside incidents and it might seem insensitive. (Protestant School)

And I think that when there is heightened tension like marches and incidents in [the local area] – those sorts of things we brace ourselves because we know there are probably going to be some fall out. Even if it's just some stupid wee lad throwing a brick, something like that which is just mindless vandalism could have some quite serious knock on effects. (Catholic School)

When probed further on potential inhibitors associated with cross-sectoral collaboration, 41% of head teachers conceded that external issues, related to wider political sensitivities, could impact on cross-sectoral collaboration. Interviews indicated that anxieties were not simply limited to political differences. Indeed concerns were raised in terms of socio-cultural differences when engaged in collaborative activities.

The major challenge … is standing back and recognising that there are cultural differences here and respecting that in the other group. (Catholic School)

When considering how best to address social and political differences in cross-sectoral collaboration, the nature of collaborative activity influenced the approach adopted. Some contexts were more conducive to addressing difference than others, for example, the nature of the subject/topic in curricular collaboration. In other contexts, efforts were made to locate the activity within a more shared environment simply to generate contact between the two groups.

As part of the … project what we did was [that] we had three schools involved, a Catholic School, an Integrated School and ourselves [Protestant School] and part of the project was to take the youngsters to Belgium to see the Battlefields. Part of the problem with our history is that people are very ignorant about what happened and when those youngsters got together and saw what happened during the First World War and the enormity of it and the fact that the Irish from both traditions were fighting and dying together. There was a great realisation of the bigger picture and that maybe in this country we have fewer differences than maybe people try to portray. As part of that experience, when the children came back we organised a joint remembrance service. To have a remembrance service in a Catholic School would be unheard of. The youngsters from the three schools organised the programme and delivered the programme together and a lot of that was down to their experiences. They stood up and talked about their experiences and seeing what actually had happened and about their experiences of meeting people from other cultures. (Protestant School)

> What we've been trying to do is try to encourage as many youngsters to take part in cross-cultural activities, for example, we have a Saturday school and that is between us and [a Catholic School] and that allows youngsters to go out and do horse riding and play golf and all those nice things that you do on a Saturday morning and it gets the kids together. (Protestant School)

Our findings indicated that the majority of post primary schools opted to underplay cultural or religious differences and took a more neutral stance. In fact, survey responses suggested that many head teachers (85%) felt that collaboration should be more focused on what children have in common rather than on potentially divisive aspects. Whilst the focusing on commonalities can create a context for relationship building, there is a danger that if cultural and religious differences are not discussed, relationships may not progress beyond the superficial. The following comment from head teachers reflects some of the issues in terms of moving towards tackling some of the more contentious issues within a collaborative context.

> It is something that you work towards and I can remember many years ago working with a year 8 class and we were talking about lilies being laid at Easter time and we were talking about should they be there or should they not … and we talked about the symbolism of the lily as a symbol of hope and one child … said "I think that they should be there as a symbol of hope that the Good Friday agreement will work instead of sending us back a number of years". Now for an 11 year old child to say something like that you are really moving forward. In that way you could eventually introduce more symbols. (Integrated School)

The incident described by the head teacher is one example of how more contentious issues can be dealt with and unfold in the classroom. This approach was adopted in a mixed class in an integrated school where children are mixing on a daily basis; therefore the context was more conducive to addressing difference.

CONCLUSIONS

The aim of this chapter was to explore the experience of collaboration between schools located in a divided society. The chapter presents one approach to enhancing inter-group relations in a divided society via inter-school collaboration. Thus the findings are not only relevant to Northern Ireland but in other post-conflict situations. Evidence from the online survey and interviews with teachers revealed that the majority of schools in Northern Ireland were predisposed to building collaborative networks with schools within their locality. It was also clear that head teachers were keen to engage in a wide range of collaborative activities as a vehicle for promoting and enhancing curricular choice for their pupils. Although the majority of schools did not engage in collaboration primarily to build relationships between Catholics and Protestants, there was only limited evidence that teachers avoided contact with schools from other sectors.

The data showed a range of practical and logistical factors such as funding, timetabling and transport as key enablers for collaboration. Research has highlighted the availability of funding as a primary driver for school collaboration, whether through a government initiative (Woods et al., 2006) or through external funding bodies (Knox, 2010). Alongside operational aspects of working with other schools, head teachers regarded relationships between staff and the level of commitment to collaborative working equally important for sustaining collaboration. Similarly, other researchers have pointed to the energy and commitment of key staff driving the collaborative work (Ribchester & Edwards, 1998; Sharpe Higham, Yeomans, & Mills, 2002). Equally, the data revealed a number of constraining variables. The sustainability of collaboration when funding is withdrawn was called into question by head teachers, which has resonance in the literature on school collaboration (for example, Rudd et al., 2004; Powell Smith & Reakes, 2004). Furthermore, evidence both from this study and the literature suggests that the marketization of education which encourages competition between schools may undermine attempts to establish collaborative relationships (Connolly & James, 2006).

Unsurprisingly, given the religious, political and social divisions which pervade all aspects of life in Northern Ireland, the findings highlighted some of the unique challenges that exist when schools in a divided society attempt to engage in collaboration. The evidence highlights the complexity of the contact experience and the impact of the wider community context on the extent and type of collaborative activity (see Connolly, 2000; Dixon et al., 2005). Concerns were related to the wider community context that the schools were operating in and ensuring their school community supported the collaborative endeavours (See also Gallagher & Carlisle, 2010). In general, head teachers reported that communities were much more accepting of cross-sectoral collaboration than they may have been in the past, citing current political settlement as a critical factor in promoting collaborative activity. According to Turner (2005) working in collaboration can broaden perspectives and challenge preconceptions that may exist. Indeed, many of the head teachers interviewed cited a variety of approaches and discussed the potential for cross-sectoral collaboration to tackle identity issues. However, given that most of the collaborative activity was curricular, relationship building was not always prioritised and there could be a danger that issues related to difference may not be adequately addressed and the development of meaningful relations between Catholics and Protestants unlikely (Donnelly, 2004).

More positively the evidence demonstrates the potential of collaborative networks for encouraging teachers to promote interaction between groups that may not otherwise engage with each other. It has been argued that providing divided groups with super-ordinate and shared goals can be particularly effective in persuading such groups to engage in inter-group contact when they might not otherwise do so (Sheriff, 1966). The data here offer further support to this analysis. It was clear that most of the contact within cross-sectoral school collaboration was driven by legislative changes in education, namely the Entitlement Framework and many of the teachers explained that they would not be involved in collaboration had they not been required to work with other schools to extend curricular choice. Hence the 'super-ordinate' curricular goal encouraged collaboration across school sectors (Dovidio, Gaertner, & Kawakami, 2003).

Finally the findings highlight the challenge for policy makers both in Northern Ireland and other societies affected by conflict in respect of the potential of cross-sectoral school collaboration as a mechanism to enhance inter-group relations. Under the auspices of the Entitlement Framework, the Department of Education supports school collaboration as a mechanism for schools to fulfil the 24/27 subject choices. Despite encouraging collaboration, schools are under no statutory obligation to engage with institutions outside of their own sector to promote inter-group relations. The data from head teacher interviews show that a 'hands off' approach to identity issues and relationship building is likely to offer only limited scope for improving inter-group relations. Yet, there is danger that where groups meet but are not supported to develop an understanding of the "other" then this may have the potential to exacerbate rather than ameliorate inter-group tensions (Liechty & Clegg, 2001; Donnelly & Gallagher, 2008).

NOTES

[i] Controlled schools are managed by the state through education and library boards.
[ii] Catholic Maintained schools are owned and managed by trustees and the responsibility of the Council for Catholic Maintained Schools.
[iii] Total number of schools in Northern Ireland 2007/2008: 1137 schools (Department of Education, 2008).
[iv] Voluntary Grammar schools are academically selective schools. This selective sector requires primary school pupils to take a 'transfer test' in which only a set percentage of pupils can obtain the highest grades and gain entry. Approximately half of Voluntary Grammar schools are under Catholic management and half are managed by the Protestant churches.

REFERENCES

Aiston, S., Rudd, P., & O'Donnell, L. (2002). *School partnerships in action: A case study of West Sussex specialist schools*. Report No. 36. Slough: NFER.

Anning, A., Cotttell, D., Frost, N., Green, J., & Robinson, M. (2006). *Developing interprofessional teamwork for integrated children's services*. Berkshire: Open University Press.

Atkinson, M., Springate, I., Johnson, F., & Halsey, K. (2007). *Inter-school collaboration: A literature review*. Slough: NFER.

Atkinson, M., Wilkin, A., Stott, A., Doherty, P., & Kinder, K. (2002). *Multi-agency working: A detailed study*. Slough: National Foundation for Education Research.

Berkeley, R. (2008) *Right to divide: Faith schools and community cohesion, A Runnymede Trust summary report*. London: Runnymede Trust

Carlisle, K., Murphy, Gallagher, T., & Beggs, J. (2007). Collaborative research into collaborative teaching in post-conflict Northern Ireland. In S. M. Ritchie (Ed), *Research collaboration: Relationships and praxis* (pp. 59-172). Rotterdam: Sense Publishers.

Cohen, L., & Manion, L. (1994). *Research methods in education*. London: Routeledge & Kegan Paul.

Connolly, P. (2000) What now for the contact hypothesis? Towards a new research agenda, race. *Ethnicity and Education, 3*(2), 169-193.

Connolly, M., & James, C. (2006). Collaboration for school improvement: A resource dependency and institutional framework of analysis. *Educational Management Administration & Leadership, 34*(1), 69-87.

Department for Education and Skills (2007). *Teachernet case studies: Raising confidence and aspirations.* Retrieved from www.teachernet.gov.uk/casestudies/casestudy.cfm?id=465.

Department of Education Northern Ireland (2005). *Entitlement framework-initial guidance,* Curricular Number: DE 2005/18. Retrieved from http://www.deni.gov.uk/2005_18-entitlement_framework-initial_guidance.pdf.

Department for Education and Skills (2005). *Local collaboration for school improvement and better service delivery.* Nottingham: Department for Education and Skills.

Department of Education Northern Ireland (2006). *Report of the independent strategic review of education.* Belfast: HMSO.

Department of Education Northern Ireland (2007). *The education (curriculum minimum content) order (Northern Ireland).* Belfast: HMSO.

Department of Education Northern Ireland (2008). *Entitlement framework support: Guidance on arrangements for 2008/09 school year.* Circular Number: DE 2008/12. Retrieved from http://www.vlor.be/webEUNEC/02members_bestanden/DE%20circular%202008%20-%2012.pdf.

Department of Education Northern Ireland (2009). *Delivering the entitlement framework by 2013: Guidance on entitlement framework support arrangements for schools and area learning communities.* Curricular Number: DE 2009/08.

Dixon, J. A., Durrheim, K., & Tredoux, C. (2005). Beyond the optimal strategy: A 'reality check' for the contact hypothesis. *American Psychologist, 60*, 697-711.

Donnelly, C., & Gallagher, A. (2008). *School collaboration in Northern Ireland: Opportunities for reconciliation.* Retrieved from http://www.schoolsworkingtogether.co.uk/webpages/news/School-Collaboration-in-NI.pdf.

Donnelly, C. (2004). Constructing the ethos of tolerance and respect in an integrated school: The role of teachers, *British Educational Research Journal, 30*(2), 263-278.

Dovidio, J., Gaertner, S., & Kawakami (2003). Intergroup contact: The past, the Present and the Future, *Group Processes and Intergroup Relations, 6*(1), 5-21.

Education Training Inspectorate (2009). Chief Inspector's Report 2006-2008. Bangor: Department of Education Northern Ireland.

Fitzduff, M., & O'Hagan, L. (2009). *The Northern Ireland troubles: INCORE background paper.* Retrieved from http://cain.ulst.ac.uk/othelem/incorepaper09.htm.

Frost, N. (2005) *Professionalism, partnership and joined-up thinking: A research review of front-line working with children and families.* Devon: Research in Practice.

Gallagher, T., Stewart, A., Walker, R., Baker, M., & Lockhart, J. (2010). *Sharing education through schools working together, Shared space,* Issue 10. Belfast: Community Relations Council.

Gallagher, T., & Carlisle, K. (2010). Breaking through silence: Tackling controversial barriers through inter-professional engagement. In H. Daniels, A. Edwards, Y. Engestrom, T. Gallagher, & S. R. Ludvigsen (Eds.), *Activity theory in practice: Promoting learning across boundaries and agencies* (pp. 140-159). London: Routledge.

Hanford, S., Houck, J., Iler, E., & Morgan, P. (1997). *Public and private school collaborations: Educational bridges into the 21st century.* The Forum for Public/Private Collaboration: Teachers College, Columbia University. Retrieved from http://www.eric.ed.gov/PDFS/ED411387.pdf.

Higham, J., & Yeomans, D. (2010). Working together? Partnership approaches to 14-19 education in England. *British Educational Research Journal, 36*(3), 379-401.

Hughes, J., Campbell, A., Hewstone, M., & Cairns, E. (2007). Segregation in Northern Ireland – Implications for community relations policy. *Policy Studies, 28*(1), 35-53.

Huxham, C. (Ed.) (1996). *Creating collaborative advantage.* London: Sage.

Knox, C. (2010). Sharing education programme: Views from the White Board. Retrieved from http://www.schoolsworkingtogether.com/documents/Views%20from%20the%20White%20Board%20May%202010.pdf.

Liechty, J., & Clegg, C. (2001). *Moving beyond sectarianism*. Blackrock, Dublin: Columba Press.

Lowndes, V., & Skelcher, C. (1998). The dynamics of multi-organisational partnerships: An analysis of changing modes of governance. *Public Administration, 76*, 313-333.

McMeeking, S., Lines, A., Blenkinsop, S., & Schagen, S. (2004). *The evaluation of excellence clusters: Final report*. Retrieved from http://www.nfer.ac.uk/publications/other-publications/downloadable-reports/the-evaluation-ofexcellence- clusters-final-report.cfm.

Muijs, D. (2008). Widening opportunities? A case study of school-to-school collaboration in a rural district, *Improving Schools, 11*(1), 61-73.

Office of First Minister and Deputy First Minister (OFMDFM) (2006). Review of Public Administration. Retrieved from http://www.deni.gov.uk/index/8-admin-of-education-pg/100-review-of-public-administration/100-policy-documents.htm.

Ouseley, Sir Herman (2001) *Community pride not prejudice: Making diversity work in Bradford (The Ouseley Report)*. Bradford: Bradford Council.

Peters, B. G. (1996). *The future of governing: Four emerging models*. Lawrence, KS: University of Kansas Press.

Police Service Northern Ireland (PSNI) (2009). Sectarian attacks reported to police. Retrieved from http://www.psni.police.uk/sectarian_attacks_2008_2009.pdf.

Pollit, C. (2003). Joined-up government: A survey. *Political Studies Review, 1*, 34-49.

Powell, R., Smith, R., & Reakes, A. (2004). *Network learning communities: An evaluation of the EAZ strand: Final report*. Slough: NFER.

Ribchester, C., & Edwards, W. (1998). Co-operation in the countryside: Small primary school clusters. *Educational Studies, 24*(3), 281-293.

Rudd, P., Holland, M., Sanders, D., Massey, A., & White, G. (2004). *Evaluation of the Beacon Schools initiative: Final report*. Retrieved from www.leeds.ac.uk/educol/documents/00003864.htm.

Rutherford, D., & Jackson, L. (2006). Setting up school partnerships: Some insights from Birmingham's Collegiate Academies. *School Leadership and Management, 26*(5), 437-451.

Sharing Education Programme (2010). *Welcome to the Sharing Education Programme*. Retrieved from http://www.schoolsworkingtogether.co.uk/.

Sharpe, P., Higham, J., Yeomans, D., & Mills, D. (2002). *Working together: The independent/state school partnerships scheme*. Retrieved from www.leeds.ac.uk/educol/documents/00002223.htm.

Sherif, M. (1966). *Group conflict and cooperation: Their social psychology*. London: Routledge & Kegan Paul.

Tett, L., Crowther, J., & O'Hara, P. (2003). Collaborative partnerships in community education. *Journal of Education Policy, 18*(1), 37-51.

The Cantle Report (2001). *Community cohesion: A report of the independent review team*. Retrieved from http://resources.cohesioninstitute.org.uk/Publications/Documents/Document/Default.aspx?recordId=96.

Thorpe, R., & Williams, I. (2002). What makes small school federations work? An examination of six instances of small school federation in Wales. *The Welsh Journal of Education, 11*(2), 3–24.

Turner, J. (2005). Independent-state school partnerships, *Educational Journal, 82*, 28-29.

Woods, P. A., Levacic, R., Evans, J., Castle, F., Glatter, R., & Cooper, D. (2006). *Diversity and collaboration? Diversity pathfinders evaluation*. DfES Report No. 826. London: Department for Education and Skills.

AFFILIATIONS

Karen Carlisle
School of Education
Queen's University
Belfast, Northern Ireland

Joanne Hughes
School of Education
Queen's University
Belfast, Northern Ireland

BRUCE ANTHONY COLLET

10. REFUGEE EDUCATION AS A GAUGE OF LIBERAL MULTICULTURALISM

Iraqi Students in Jordan and the United States

INTRODUCTION

Will Kymlicka (2007) writes of a global "veritable revolution" in relations between states and ethnocultural minorities, as advanced by new multicultural models of state and citizenship. Schools represent key transformational sites in this revolution, as they constitute spaces where minority groups might receive greater school access, identity recognition and accommodation for their particular needs. This chapter focuses on the education of Iraqi refugees in Jordan and the United States. It offers a case for the extension of multicultural policies in Jordan toward the greater realization of human rights of Iraqi refugee students in that country. Working from interviews and focus groups conducted in Amman, Jordan as well as the greater Detroit area of Michigan, and drawing from Will Kymlicka's groundbreaking work on multicultural citizenship as well as his work on the global diffusion of multicultural discourse and policies, this chapter defends multiculturalism as a platform within which fundamental human rights may be realized. Construed as a set of specific public policies, multiculturalism is positioned here as a path that effectively addresses issues regarding social inclusion.

The reason for focusing on Iraqis pertains to the particularly vulnerable position that they find themselves within Jordan. As this chapter details, Jordan's status as non-signatory to the principal conventions governing the international refugee regime has resulted in a tenuous legal and social standing for Iraqi refugees. Most Iraqis cannot obtain citizenship in Jordan, and must continuously renew their residency permits. They are further barred from receiving public assistance, and up until 2007 faced significant obstacles toward enrolling their children in the public schools. Even presently, Iraqi children who have missed three or more years of schooling are still prevented from re-entering the public school system. Moreover, those Iraqi students who do attend the public schools often suffer harassment and discrimination by both their (non-Iraqi) peers and teachers, particularly if they are religious minorities. Further, most Iraqis cannot lawfully work. As this chapter illustrates, Jordan's challenges to embracing multiculturalism exacerbate the effects of these conditions on the daily lives of Iraqis there.

H. Biseth & H. B. Holmarsdottir (eds.), Human Rights in the Field of Comparative Education, 147–169.
© *2013 Sense Publishers. All rights reserved.*

While this chapter discusses the schooling of Iraqi refugees in both Jordan and the United States, it does not involve a cross-national comparison in the sense of striving for empirical regularities between the two countries (Ragin, 1987). Rather, the United States provides an illustration of how refugee students can indeed benefit from policies supporting liberal multiculturalism. Given their very different social, economic, political and cultural conditions, and their very different histories and geographic locations, a one-to-one comparison between Jordan and the United States is neither sound nor viable. The chapter recognizes Jordan's difference from the U.S. and the considerable challenges Jordan faces in embracing liberal multiculturalism. The most notable of these challenges as they pertain to this study include regional insecurity, a lack of human rights guarantees for refugees, mono-cultural curriculum, inadequate teacher preparation, and the propagation of multicultural rhetoric divorced from actual multicultural policies. The chapter also recognizes that the United States is far from a bastion of human rights, and that featuring as a model any U.S. practice of multiculturalism needs to be greatly specified and qualified. In all, the entry strives to offer an argument that is sensitive to these unique country circumstances and conditions. While not all of Jordan's challenges to embracing multiculturalism are within its control, several of them are, and they could be tackled more aggressively. Doing so would provide the country with an opportunity to improve the schooling of its Iraqi youth, and to more fully embrace its present commitments to honoring human rights.

ANALYTIC FRAMEWORK

Liberal Multiculturalism and Human Rights

Will Kymlicka conceptualizes multiculturalism as a set of public policies that attempt to reformulate relations between ethno-cultural minorities and the state through the creation of new laws, policies or institutions. He contrasts this framing of multiculturalism quite sharply with brands of multiculturalism characterized as feel-good celebrations of ethno-cultural diversity, or what Alibhai-Brown (2000) has depicted as the "samosas, steel drums and saris" approach. For Kymlicka (1995, 2007, 2010), multiculturalism is part of a larger human rights revolution concerning both racial and ethnic diversity.

According to Kymlicka, the human rights revolution that followed on the heels of the Second World War has functioned as both an inspiration as well as a constraint for multicultural movements. With respect to the former, prior to the Second World War, strongly illiberal and undemocratic relations had characterized ethno-cultural and religious diversity in the west. Racialist ideologies explicitly propounding the superiority of select peoples and cultures and their right to rule over others had driven hierarchical relationships such as the conqueror and the conquered, colonizer and the colonized, master and slave, settler and indigenous, and so forth. Spearheaded by the United Nations, the post war era witnessed the birth of a new ideology of racial and ethnic equality, formulated in reaction to ideologies that had fueled violent and oppressive relations (in particular those spawned by Hitler's regime). The new assumption of human equality generated a number of important political movements "designed to contest the lingering presence or enduring effects of older hierarchies" (Kymlicka, 2010, p. 100). These movements occurred in a series of waves, characterized by: (a) the struggle for decolonization, concentrated in the period 1948-1965; (b) the struggle against racial segregation and discrimination, initiated and illustrated by the African-American civil rights movement between 1955-1965; and (c) the struggle for multiculturalism and minority rights which had emerged in the late 1960s. Each of these movements draws upon the human rights revolution and its basic ideology of equality (Kymlicka, 2007, 2010).

Inasmuch as the human rights revolution has been a source of inspiration for multicultural movements, it has simultaneously acted as a constraint on the allowable goals and means of these struggles. Historically marginalized groups must also, in the name of human rights, renounce their own traditions of exclusion or oppression with respect to gender, race, sexual orientation, religion and so forth. Kymlicka asserts in fact that states are quite unlikely to accept strong forms of minority rights if they have a realistic fear that granting such rights will lead to "islands of local tyranny" that might jeopardize human rights and liberal democratic values (Kymlicka, 2007). The key to citizenisation, Kymlicka writes, is not to suppress differential claims to minority rights, but rather to filter and frame them through the language of human rights, civil liberties, and democratic accountability.

According to Kymlicka (2007, 2010), three patterns of multiculturalism have emerged in western democracies, each of which have been defended as a means to overcome injustices perpetuated by earlier hierarchies, and to help construct fairer and more inclusive democratic societies. These include new forms of empowerment for indigenous peoples such as the Inuit in Greenland or the Maori in New Zealand, new forms of power-sharing and autonomy for sub-state national groups such as the Quebecois in Canada and the Basques and Catalans in Spain, and new forms of multicultural citizenship for immigrant groups. Of the three, the last is most germane to drawing relations between multiculturalism and the education of Iraqi refugees.

Kymlicka (2007) writes that historically "countries of immigration", or countries which legally admit immigrants as permanent residents and future citizens (for example, Australia, Canada, New Zealand, and the United States), had adopted strongly assimilationist approaches to immigration. Immigrants were encouraged and in fact expected to fully assimilate into the host society, and in the process discard their existing cultural ways of life and identities. Since the late 1960s however, there have been dramatic changes in these countries' approach to immigrants. Most notably the changes have included the adoption of race-neutral admission criteria, resulting in an increase of newcomers from non-European societies, as well as the adoption of a more "multicultural" conception of integration which expects many immigrants to want to express rather than repress or discard their cultural identities, and one which accepts an obligation on the part of public institutions such as the police, schools, and the media to accommodate these identities. Banting, Johnston, Kymlicka, and Soroka (2006) identify eight policies most common or representative of immigrant multiculturalism:

- Constitutional, legislative, or parliamentary affirmation of multiculturalism, at the central and/or regional and municipal levels;
- The adoption of multiculturalism in school curricula;
- The inclusion of ethnic representation/sensitivity in the mandate of public media or media licensing;
- Exemptions from dress-codes, Sunday-closing legislation etc. (either by statute or by court cases);
- Allowing dual citizenship;
- The funding of ethnic group organizations to support cultural activities;
- The funding of bilingual education or mother-tongue instruction;
- Affirmative action for disadvantaged immigrant groups. (pp. 73-74)

As evident, two of the three policies, the adoption of multiculturalism in school curricula and the funding of bilingual education or mother-tongue instruction, pertain directly to schooling. Hero and Preuhs' (2006) work on language and immigrant policies expands item number seven, the funding of bilingual education, to also include English as a Second Language (ESL) instruction. Their rationale for including both bilingual as well as ESL as a legitimate multiculturalism policy is that both programs provide additional educational opportunities of multicultural recognition that would not otherwise be provided under an assimilationist model.[i] The same reasoning may also be applied to the adoption of multiculturalism in school curricula; namely, that this adoption counters an assimilationist logic that denies minority groups rights to cultural identity and belonging.

As much as historic countries of immigration have moved in the direction of adopting the above policies, they unfortunately have not all been equally strong in doing so. In a multi-nation empirical study of multicultural policies, Banting et al. (2006) find that Australia and Canada have been strongest by adopting six or more of the eight policies, while the United States and New Zealand have been modest by adopting only three to five.[ii] As explained further below, Kymlicka notes that the trend toward a more multicultural approach has been largely rejected outside of the traditional New World countries of immigration. Here, newcomers have not been seen as potential citizens, but rather as "guests", "visitors", or "foreigners".[iii]

Banting et al.'s (2006) framework of immigrant multiculturalism appears at first most relevant to migrants who voluntarily come to their host countries with the expressed intent to stay for the long term. Voluntary migrants (or traditional immigrants) desire to integrate and to gain citizenship. Refugees may be included in this group, though not necessarily. Indeed, some refugees see their host societies as only temporary abodes, and hope to return to their homelands when circumstances and conditions allow. However, many other refugees do migrate with either the intent to resettle permanently, or find themselves in situations where return to their homeland has ceased to be a viable option and where their chances of third country resettlement are quite low, and so become *de facto* long-term residents. I will argue that the latter has in fact become the case for thousands of Iraqi refugees living in Jordan.

Challenges to the Global Diffusion of Liberal Multiculturalism

Kymlicka (2007) writes of two levels at which a "veritable revolution" of multicultural models of state and citizenship has been experienced around the world. The first concerns the global diffusion of the political discourse of multiculturalism, circulated by international networks of non-governmental organizations (NGOs), policy-makers, and scholars. Here international organizations may sponsor seminars, publish reports, or train local educators, bureaucrats, media personnel or other NGOs in the task of accommodating a multiethnic and multicultural population. The second concerns international legal (or quasi-legal) norms, embodied in declarations of minority rights that have served to codify multiculturalism. Kymlicka (2007) asserts that these norms are being pushed at both the international as well as regional levels (for instance, the United Nations (UN) 1992 adoption of a Declaration on the Rights of Persons Belonging to National or Ethnic, Religious and Linguistic Minorities, or the Organization of American States' 1997 draft Declaration on the Rights of Indigenous Peoples). While declarations are not judicially enforceable, states are nonetheless increasingly being monitored and judged for how well they comply with these norms.

The use of the term "global" with respect to the global diffusion of multiculturalism needs some qualification. History indicates that certain fundamental conditions must be in place for multiculturalism to take root. While Kymlicka (2010) writes that we do not yet have a systematic account of all the preconditions necessary for successful multicultural citizenship, he nonetheless identifies core factors, the most important of which involve the desecuritization of state-minority relations, and the presence of a human rights consensus. These conditions have disproportionately been met by western states, which, at least in the post war era, have enjoyed the privilege of regional security and opportunities to build strong democratic political cultures. However, in much of the post-colonial world[iv], multiculturalism has had a far more difficult time taking root.

As Kymlicka (2007) notes, the challenges that post-colonial states face in adopting multiculturalism are spearheaded exactly by the two key factors that have facilitated the acceptance of liberal multiculturalism by Western states; namely, regional security and human rights guarantees. Regional security positively impacts the acceptance of multiculturalism by lessening the chance that minorities "are perceived as potential fifth-columnists, or collaborators with neighboring enemies" (p.255). Human rights guarantees in turn advance multiculturalism by offering protections to minority group members from discrimination by the larger society. Kymlicka draws particular attention however to protections to minority group members from human rights abuses *within* the group. Hence human rights guarantees also ensure that minorities who receive autonomy will respect human rights when exercising their powers. Yet post-colonial states have been hampered both by serious geo-political issues, wherein neighboring enemies aim to destabilize the state – often by recruiting to their cause minorities within that state, and by the lack of a strong democratic political culture and well-functioning state institutions that might protect the rights of minority group members.

Kymlicka (2007) notes other challenges unique to the post-colonial world. These include distrust of international organizations that are promoting minority rights, where there exists a widespread perception that International Organizations (IOs) "are internationalizing rights precisely in order to destabilize certain countries" (p. 258). The challenges however also include what he terms "colonial legacies of ethnic hierarchies" (p. 261), wherein certain minorities within the post-colonial world continue to enjoy the privileged status they had been granted by their previous colonizers, as well as demography, where there exists no clear majority group controlling the state and using this control to diffuse its language, culture, and identity (and hence less of a viable basis on the part of minorities for claiming cultural protection). While Jordan faces nearly all of the challenges addressed above (demography perhaps being the exception), the Iraqi exodus into Jordan brings to the fore the two key factors of regional security and human rights guarantees.

THE IRAQI REFUGEE CRISIS

Iraqi Refugees in Jordan

Jordan has historically served as a place of refuge for forced migrants in the area, and in fact has the highest ratio of refugees to indigenous population of any country in the world (Chatelard, 2002a, 2002b; Collet 2010; Zaiotti, 2006). There has been a regular flow of Iraqi refugees into Jordan not only for purposes of asylum, but also for trade and commerce. The 2003 U.S. invasion of Iraq however produced a swell of refugees that has grown to crisis numbers, many of whom have ended up in Jordan. The exact total number of Iraqis in Jordan is not easy to obtain. This is in part due to the reluctance of many Iraqis to register with the United Nations High Commissioner for Refugees (UNHCR) once they are in country (Collet, 2010; International Crisis Group [ICG], 2008). However, observers also note that at least in the recent past Jordan may have inflated the number of Iraqis living in the state so as to attract and retain international aide (Chatelard, 2010; Seeley, 2010). Presently, the UNHCR estimates that as many as 500,000 Iraqis may be living in Jordan, the vast majority residing in Amman (UNHCR, 2009, 2011).[v]

Jordan has signed neither the 1951 United Nations Convention Relating to the Status of Refugees, nor its 1967 Protocol, the two main instruments defining the refugee protection regime under international law. The state has nonetheless allowed migration from neighboring states under the pretense of Pan-Arabism, although this has not necessarily lead to the granting of asylum much less citizenship rights among its Arab migrants (Chatelard, 2002b; Collet, 2010; Zaiotti, 2006). To assist with refugees coming into the country, in April 1998 Jordan signed a Memoranda of Understanding (MoU) with the UNHCR. The MoU establishes UNHCR's legal basis for involvement in Jordan with persons of concern. It includes the 1951 Convention Refugee definition and therein addresses the critical principle of *non-refoulement*, or non-forcible return to possible persecution (Article 33(1)), which the country is obligated to adhere to under international customary law.[vi] The MoU provides the overall legal basis for the stay of asylum seekers in Jordan, pending refugee determination undertaken by the UNHCR. Convention Refugees are provided a maximum of six-months stay, during which a "durable solution" must be found. These durable solutions include integrating into the host country, resettling to a third country, or voluntarily repatriating to the country of origin (ICG, 2008; UNHCR, 2008). A robust network of agencies and organizations serve Iraqi refugees in Jordan. The International Catholic Migration Commission (ICMC) for instance surveyed in 2007 the work of five governmental organizations, 17 local agencies, and 13 major international agencies and international organizations, as well as semi-governmental organizations, and various other initiatives and foundations (Duncan, Schiesher, & Khalil, 2007). During the period of 2007-2009 Jordan also received nearly $400 million of aide directed toward Iraqi refugees, the lion's share coming from the United States (Seeley, 2010).

Despite rhetoric from various government ministries presenting the state as "multicultural", Jordan's domestic policies both explicitly and implicitly treat Iraqi refugees at best as guests, and at worst as foreigners and in some cases as undesirables. Iraqi refugees and asylum seekers fall under legislation applicable to foreigners; they cannot lawfully work, and must obtain time-limited residency permits which they can regularly extend for a fee.[vii] Further, refugees are barred from receiving state public assistance (Collet, 2010; ICMC, 2007; ICG, 2008). While Iraqis began flooding into Jordan following the 2003 U.S. invasion, only since July 2007 have they been allowed to enter the public schools, and the Ministry of Education continues to bar children who have missed three or more years of schooling from re-entering formal education in the country (Zehr, 2008).

Public perception of Iraqis has tended to revolve around competition for scarce resources. Jordan has one of the smallest economies in the Middle East, owing in large part to an insufficient supply of important natural resources, including water and oil. In 2010 the official unemployment rate was 12.5%, although the unofficial rate is closer to 30% (Central Intelligence Agency, 2011). Hence many Jordanians view their Iraqi guests as siphoning from an already much strained infrastructure and economy. In addition, local media have portrayed Iraqis as "predators" who have been the agents primarily responsible for driving up the prices of goods and properties in the country (Chatelard, 2010). For these reasons as well as their generally precarious legal standing in the state, many Iraqis in Jordan maintain a low public profile, fearing government harassment and possible deportation.

Iraqi Refugees in the United States

The United States is not party to the 1951 UN Refugee Convention. However, it is signatory to the 1967 Protocol, which expanded the scope of the UN refugee definition (Hathaway, 1991). Presently, the 1980 U.S. Refugee Act constitutes the legal basis for refugee admissions to the United States. According to the United States Department of State (USDS), the Act "embodies the American tradition of granting refuge to diverse groups suffering or fearing persecution" (USDS, 2001, p. 637).

Iraqis who reside in Jordan and who wish to resettle in the U.S. must first register with a UNHCR office. The one stated exception to this concerns Iraqis with U.S. affiliations (e.g. certain categories of Iraqi refugees who assisted with U.S. efforts in Iraq), who have the option of applying directly to the U.S. Refugee Admissions Program without the need for a UNHCR referral (USDS, 2011). The UNHCR office makes case-by-case determinations regarding whether third country resettlement, be it to the U.S. or another country, constitutes the best solution. If resettlement to the U.S. is determined, the UNHCR works with the Department of Homeland Security and Resettlement Support Centers in case processing. Upon their arrival to the U.S., refugees are placed with a private volunteer agency, or 'volag', that has signed a cooperative agreement with the State Department. With affiliates throughout the U.S., volags are responsible for assuring basic services for refugees during their first 90 days in country, including arrangements for food, housing, clothing, employment, medical care, counseling, and others. Refugees who resettle in the U.S. are also eligible for cash and medical assistance during their first eight months in the country, and for employment assistance, social services, and English language training for up to five years after their initial arrival (U.S. Department of Health and Human Services [USDHHS] 2011a).

While Iraqis may fare better in the U.S. than Jordan, far fewer of them actually make it there. On March 11, 2008 the United States House of Representatives held a hearing on the Iraq War focusing on the U.S. obligation to assist the then 4.5 million Iraqi refugees and Internally Displaced Persons (IDPs). The Democrats insisted that the U.S. had a duty to provide aide for the refugees' survival in Jordan and Syria and, as Adelman (2008) notes, "even allow a few into the U.S. since the proximate cause of 'this human tragedy' is the invasion of Iraq and its aftermath" (p.181). Unfortunately, the U.S. has fallen far short of this obligation.[viii] While the number of Iraqis coming to the U.S. has increased over the years since the 2003 invasion, it remains that approximately 2.5% of the total number of Iraqi refugees in the world have resettled to the United States (Sassoon, 2009; USDS, 2011). Neither the Democrats nor the Republicans, Adelman (2008) observes, have recognized the "desire, need or responsibility of the U.S. to resettle large numbers of Iraqi refugees" as significant numbers of minorities are thought unlikely to be able to return home given the ethnic and religious cleansing rampant in Iraq (p. 182).

METHODS AND PROCEDURES

The data presented in this chapter represent the culmination of two plus years of conducting interviews, focus groups, and formal and informal meetings with Iraqi refugees and the people who work with them. Between the spring of 2008 and the fall of 2010 I regularly traveled to the Detroit metropolitan communities of Southfield and Madison Heights (hereafter simply referred to as Detroit). Detroit and its suburbs play host to one of the largest Arab populations in the United States. While the 2000 U.S. Census found 124,263 people of Arab decent living in the Detroit metro area, estimates are that the population has now approached 200,000. Around 35% of this population is of Iraqi origin (Baker & Shyrock, 2009; Shyrock & Chih Lin, 2009). Within this period I also traveled to Amman, Jordan on two occasions to conduct research; once for the month of July in 2008, and then again for the month of July in 2010.

There was considerable overlap regarding the types of people I interviewed in Detroit and Amman. In Detroit I interviewed four staff members at a prominent resettlement agency, as well as two staff members from two additional agencies serving Iraqi refugees. I also interviewed clergy at one of the major Chaldean churches in Detroit, as well as a member of this church who assists Iraqis in their resettlement from Jordan. [ix] Finally in Detroit I conducted four focus groups with Iraqi refugee public secondary students (a total of 18 attendees) representing three Detroit high schools. Many of these students had lived in Amman, and had attended either primary and / or secondary public schools while there. During my trips to Amman, I interviewed seven leadership staff from seven well established non-governmental organizations (NGOs) serving Iraqi refugees. I also interviewed clergy at a Chaldean church, and I spoke with an independent Jordanian researcher. Finally, in both my 2008 as well as 2010 trips to Amman I was involved in an additional research project sponsored by my university that was aimed at understanding perceptions of Arab identity and Jordanian citizenship. This project involved interviews with officials from the Ministry of Education, the Ministry of Political Development, the United States Embassy, and the National Centre for Human Rights. As several of the questions we asked mapped closely to my own research, I have included that data in the analysis. All interviews and focus groups in both Detroit and Amman were conducted in English. Table 1 below summarizes the data collected from different groups in each context.

Table 1. Data sources by country

Jordan	The United States
Non-governmental organization staff	Iraqi students
Church clergy	Resettlement agency staff
Independent researcher	Aide organization staff
Ministry of Education officials	Church clergy
Ministry of Political Development officials	Community member
United States Embassy staff	
National Centre for Human Rights staff	

All interviews and focus groups in both Detroit and Amman were held in locations comfortable and agreed upon by the participants. Pseudonyms have been used to protect the identities of the study participants, and organizational names have been masked. Following Boyatzis (1998), I employed thematic analysis of the data, initially coding inductively to discern broad themes and the general "story" the study participants were telling, and then coding again deductively using the analytical framework. While a clear narrative emerged from the data, there are nevertheless limitations to the kinds of generalizations one can make from a study of this type. The findings are thus presented in the context of the larger body of research literature and policy reports concerning the plight of Iraqi refugees.

DATA PRESENTATION AND ANALYSIS

Challenges to Multiculturalism as Challenges to Iraqi Schooling in Jordan

A discussion of the challenges Jordan faces with respect to adapting multiculturalism, and how these challenges relate to the schooling of Iraqi refugees, must begin with some demonstration of the degree to which actors at both the international as well as national level are working to implement such policies in Jordan in the first place. Despite the considerable obstacles addressed further below, there is evidence that major international organizations, through their programs and publications, are diffusing a political discourse of multiculturalism in Jordan. For instance, the United Nations Educational, Scientific and Cultural Organization (UNESCO) is deeply involved in the protection of cultural diversity in Jordan, including such interventions as the safeguarding and identification of cultural and natural heritages, poverty reduction, and intercultural dialogue (UNESCO, 2008). The Five-Year Program Cycle of the United Nations Children's Fund (UNICEF) in Jordan in turn follows a "rights-based, gender-sensitive and life cycle" approach at all levels of programming, with a specific concentration on children and women, including those from marginalized communities (UNICEF, 2011). Thirdly, the UNHCR's main objective in Jordan is to maintain and expand the protection space for refugees and asylum seekers, and the agency's assistance programs for Iraqi refugees, from basic health to non-formal and informal education extend to Iraqis some of the same basic rights and privileges already enjoyed by Jordanians. Organizations such as International Relief and Development (IRD) receive funding from UNHCR to provide outreach services for Iraqi refugees, including building awareness of refugee rights (IRD, 2008; UNHCR, 2010).

Jordan is also involved in the codification of multiculturalism, having ratified, acceded, or been succession to a number of major international instruments relevant to minority and indigenous rights. These include the International Convention on the Prevention and Punishment of the Crime of Genocide (1948), the International Convention on the Elimination of All Forms of Racial Discrimination (1965), the International Covenant on Civil and Political Rights (1966), the International Covenant on Economic, Social and Cultural Rights

(1966), the Convention on the Elimination of All Forms of Discrimination against Women (1979), and the Convention on the Rights of the Child (1989) (Minority Rights Group International [MRGI], 2007).

Yet as much as there exists interest in multiculturalism on the part of both national and international actors in Jordan, the country still faces significant challenges toward more fully realizing these interests. Some of these challenges, such as facets of regional insecurity, are less within the direct control of state. Others however, such as human rights guarantees, are within greater state control. These challenges intersect with the schooling of Iraqi refugees in important ways.

Regional Insecurity
Iraq continues to be a very dangerous country, particularly for women and other groups such as religious minorities. One of the most significant educational consequences this insecurity has had for Iraqi youth in Jordan has been missed schooling while residing in Iraq. Rena, a Detroit-based mental health worker who is herself an Iraqi refugee states that most of her Iraqi clients had missed schooling in Iraq due to the war. She describes the effect that the war had had on access to schooling:

> The parents, especially say the mothers, okay, and kids were locked for many years – six, seven years – from 2002 until let's say until they left. Most of them they tell me that for several years, like [an] average five to like seven, eight years they were locked inside the homes in Iraq because of the war and the suicide bombing and stuff, so the kids did not go the school regularly on a daily basis.

Missed schooling in Iraq has put many Iraqi children significantly behind their Jordanian peers in school. UNHCR and UNESCO, in cooperation with the Jordanian Ministry of Education, have partnered with other organizations (notably QuestScope) to provide remedial education for Iraqis who have missed school (QuestScope, 2010). However, Ministry policies concerning school registration have also posed a challenge for Iraqi children. For one, prior to a decree issued by King Abdullah II in late July 2007, most Iraqi children were largely barred from entering the public schools as they lacked the required residency status, and so many children who had come into the country prior to this time continued to remain out of school (Zehr & Mousa, 2008). Additionally, the Ministry of Education bars children who have missed three or more years of schooling from re-entering the public education system (Zehr, 2008), which has led to an overall increase in the number of out of school Iraqi children.

Regional insecurity issues are reflected in Jordan's border policies. Beginning in November 2006, Jordan began barring the entry of single Iraqi men between the ages of 17 and 35 into the country (Adelman, 2008; International Crisis Group [ICG], 2008). Many observers have interpreted this restriction as a response to the November 2005 hotel bombings in Amman which killed 60 people, and for which three Iraqis were held responsible (ICG, 2008). In addition, in May 2009 Jordan began requiring Iraqis to apply for visas before traveling to Jordan, making it more difficult for them to enter the country (U.S. Committee for Refugees and Immigrants [USCRI], 2009). The restriction on men entering Jordan places additional financial strains on Iraqi families already in the country. Several study participants noted that the inability to pay for basic school fees and supplies was one of the major challenges to enrolling children in schools. While the UNHCR now provides assistance to Iraqis in this area, in 2010 only 31,000, or approximately 6% of the total Iraqi refugee population, were actually registered with the agency (MRGI, 2011).

A second security issue presenting itself at the border concerns screening Iraqis for religious identity. The U.S. Committee for Refugees and Immigrants [USCRI], the International Crisis Group, and Human Rights Watch [HRW], have all reported Iraqi Shi'ite being singled out and in some cases turned away at the Jordan border (HRW, 2007; ICG, 2008; Sassoon, 2009; USCRI, 2007). Jordan is a Sunni dominant country, and public anxiety regarding Shi'a Islam has been fueled by the Kingdom's warning of a "Shi'ite Crescent" emerging in post-war Iraq, concentrated particularly in the south of the country (Chatelard, 2010; Sassoon, 2009).[x] Here Shi'ites may well be perceived as collaborators intending to weaken Sunni dominance. For these reasons, and a lack of knowledge about Shi'a Islam more generally, those Iraqi Shi'ite who do make it into Jordan have been vulnerable to harassment and discrimination in the schools from both students as well as teachers (ICG, 2008; MRGI, 2011). Adil, a program-manager at an Amman-based NGO describes the situation:

> Jordanians do not know what Shi'a is about, and it was very recently, [the] last few years, when we start[ed] being exposed to Shi'a. Because this is a Sunni dominant society, and for them having lots of Shi'a and all that was open after 2003. And this is where Jordanians start being more knowledgeable about that. Okay, there is Shi'a, but they don't know what Shi'a is about. So yes, lots of cases were reported of harassment [of] students in the schools because of their religions.

Sabah, a Jordanian researcher and activist, further describes violence experienced by one Iraqi Shi'ite she had been working with:

> There is a case of a Shi'ite boy, and I was trying to convince him and convince his parents to send him back to school. Since, you know, it's not every day you go to them and say, yes, there are centers that are capable to pay for the fees, school uniforms, books, so when you have this chance why not grasp this opportunity and send them to school instead of wasting those years? Because they are not here stuck for a month or two months, they are stuck here for years. I spoke to a Shi'ite woman, and the boy has undergone surgery, an operation on his jaw, because he was in a fight, Jordanian kids beat him up and broke his jaw. After that, uh, he got scared, he quit school because he is Shi'ite.

Border responses to regional insecurity hence have reverberating consequences for the acceptance of multiculturalism in the country generally, and the extension of rights to cultural identity and belonging amongst Iraqi refugee students in particular. As a further illustration, Minority Rights Group International reports that Iraqi Sabean Mandaeans have found it difficult to attend schools because of "extreme societal discrimination and pressure to convert to Islam" (MRGI, 2011). What is particularly telling about these conversations is not only the troubles experienced by particular minority groups within Jordan (Shi'ites and Mandaeans), but more generally that religion, particularly Sunni Islam, matters a great deal both in the society and in the schools. As discussed further below, this has an important bearing on the manner in which multiculturalism has been framed by the state.

Human Rights Guarantees

Jordan's status as non-signatory to the principal conventions governing the international refugee regime has made Iraqi refugees living there particularly vulnerable to ever-shifting economic and security conditions in the country. This makes Iraqis vulnerable to discrimination. Iraqis lack clear legal standing in the country and the state has no domestic procedures for status determination, and hence provides no legal refugee definition. Moreover, the state has no legislation or mechanism that could provide protection to asylum seekers or refugees (UNHCR, 2008). As indicated above, policies guiding Iraqi's entry into Jordan have rather been formulated on an *ad hoc* basis, and have fluctuated with security concerns (Chatelard, 2002a; Zaiotti, 2006). This precarious climate has caused Iraqis to be quite cautious if not distrustful of both the state as well as international organizations, particularly the UNHCR. This is captured in the following exchange with a program manager, Kabil, at an Amman-based NGO:

> My understanding is that Iraqis…they might perceive the UNHCR as an agent of the government and as a place that's going to collect information on them or send them back to Iraq
>
> Kabil: [Iraqis feel] more secure not to register.
>
> More secure not to register. So they believe it's more secure not to register?
>
> Kabil: Maybe … Even if he's registered or if he gets his ID (UNHCR identification card),[xi] even this ID can't protect him.

Iraqis who overstay their visas in Jordan and who do not pay visa extension fees risk deportation. As well, the Residency and Foreigners' Affairs law stipulates that all foreigners must notify the authorities of their residency and of any movement (USCRI, 2009).[xii] The above concerns have resulted in reluctance on the part of many Iraqis to enroll their children in the schools. Parents are afraid to make it known to schools that they don't have legal residency (Zehr & Mousa, 2008). The precarious situation of Iraqis in Jordan has also pushed many Iraqi parents to either withdraw their children from schooling or to not enroll them at all out of expectations that they will soon be resettling to a new country. This happens despite the fact that less than 1% of the world's refugees are ever resettled in a third country, and that from 2009-2010 there was a relative decline in the number of UNHCR registered Iraqis who actually resettled (National Centre for Human Rights [NCHR], 2010; USDS, 2009). Further, a 2010 UNHCR poll found that Iraqi refugees were reluctant to return to Iraq permanently. For instance, in a survey on the Iraq-Jordan border among some 364 families (representing approximately 1,450 individuals), the UNHCR found that none were returning to Iraq permanently. Generally, the UNHCR has stated that it does not consider the security situation in Iraq adequate to facilitate or promote returns (Reliefweb, 2010).

Child labor has also constituted a human rights concern that intersects with schooling. It is very difficult for Iraqi refugees with residence permits to legally work in Jordan, and nearly impossible for those without them. Many Iraqis nonetheless work illegally, and there is a trend in Jordan for Iraqis to engage their children in illegal work, meaning that hours normally allocated for schooling and study are being used to help support households. Iraqi children are particularly vulnerable to exploitation and abuse under such conditions, including an increasing number of Iraqi girls working as prostitutes (Swett & Webster, 2010). One NGO worker based in Amman stated that the government was "turning a blind eye to Iraqis working", and at least one focus group student (a male) reported having worked under rather difficult conditions as an assistant in an auto shop while living in Amman.

Jordan has ratified the Convention on the Rights of the Child, which prohibits in Article (32) the exploitation of children in work (UN, 1989). The country has also ratified the International Labour Organization (ILO) Convention concerning the Prohibition and Immediate Action for the Elimination of the Worst Forms of Child Labour, which identifies the jobs in which children may not be allowed to work (ILO, 1999). Nonetheless, the National Centre for Human Rights (NCHR) in Amman states that children have been working in jobs in violation of the ILO Convention, and reports that children have been subject to hazardous working conditions, battery and verbal abuse, sexual and immoral practices, and long hours without adequate pay (NCHR, 2010). The NCHR states in their 2010 Annual Report that the role of the Ministry of Labor "is still weak and fragile in the area of inspection to reduce the phenomenon of child labor" (p. 119). As a socially and politically marginalized community that the government has turned a blind eye to, it would appear that Iraqi refugee children are particularly vulnerable to the above rights violations. The phenomenon of Iraqi families sending their children to work in the above conditions raises questions of human rights abuses within the Iraqi diaspora, and yet absent of well functioning state institutions, Jordan can offer children few human rights guarantees.

Additional Challenges
There are challenges relating to multiculturalism articulated by the study participants that extend beyond the areas Kymlicka relates to post-colonial states. These include both the curriculum used in Jordan's public schools, and the readiness and sensitivity of Jordan's teachers to work with Iraqi refugee students. However, they also include something a bit less concrete; namely, rhetorical statements given by various government ministries regarding the implementation of multiculturalism within institutions and society. There were mixed reports

regarding the extent to which the existence of Iraqi refugees in the country has changed in any way the official public school curriculum. For instance, Sabah, the Jordanian researcher, states the following:

> In regards to curriculum, it is the Jordanian curriculum. This is the problem. We have another problem; we tried to ask [the Ministry of Education] about their curriculum because we have kids who are coming from Baghdad who have a different curriculum. Okay, you have to know something. Iraqis here, they are guests, they are here temporarily. Don't expect them to integrate into the society. There is no way, like to change the curriculum. Curriculum is for Jordanians, and those residents who have residency who live in this country.

In contrast to Sabah's statement, Education Ministry officials stressed the infusion of diversity and multiculturalism into the curriculum (see below), although there were no references made to specific content reflecting the presence of Iraqi refugees. To its credit, the Ministry of Education has sought to include human rights education within its social education textbooks. However, this is an area that is still underdeveloped, and in need of greater clarity, integration and overall direction (Al-Edwan, 2010). It is quite clear from the interviews with Education Ministry officials that any initiatives within the curriculum, be they concerned with multiculturalism and/or human rights, be constructed within an Islamic framework. Sunni Islam is the official religion in Jordan, and the formal curriculum and general school culture within Jordan's state schools advances an Islamic worldview.[xiii] This is not an issue that a Sunni Iraqi might find terribly problematic. However, it is a factor that certainly affects minority religion communities. For instance, study participants expressed that some Iraqi Christian parents as well as their children were concerned about the religious programming within Jordan's public schools. Father Thomas Denha, a minister at a Chaldean church in Amman, reports that many Iraqi Christians feel excluded from the public schools' emphasis on the Koran, and Iraqi families come to him looking for more Christian-based education, which his church provides.

The readiness and sensitivity of teachers to work with Iraqi refugee students has also constituted a challenge to multiculturalism. This extends beyond the particular forms of religious discrimination noted earlier. The study data indicate that Jordanian teachers may make Iraqi students quite conscious of their overall identity as refugees, or as "guests". What emerged strongly within the focus groups for instance were occurrences of singling out Iraqi students in Jordan for being Iraqi. For instance, Mary, a 16-year-old female in the 12th grade, and Hanna, a 17-year-old female in the 12th grade stated the following about their experiences with Jordanian teachers:

> Now the problems that you had with the teachers, were they just limited to being able to understand them, or were there other issues?
> Mary: Yeah.
> Like what?
> Mary: Like 'you're Iraqi and why you came here? You made – the Iraqis – made the prices up in Jordan' and stuff like that, you know.

Yeah ...
Mary: Because they think we have a lot of money, the Iraqis.
Is that something they would say in front of the other students?
Hanna and Mary: Yeah.
Continuously, or just once in a while?
Hanna: Continuously. When they like to do (it), (then) they do it –
Mary: Yeah.
Hanna: They don't care, the teachers, you know, (about) the other teachers or about the students themselves.
They didn't seem to care about how that made you feel with respect to the other students, like how the other students may look at you?
Hanna: Never.

Regarding the level of support the students felt they had received from Jordanian teachers, Joseph (age 16, 12th grade), stated the following; "Like they say 'you're Iraqi, I could kick you out of this country". Joseph also reported having experienced some harassment from his Jordanian as well as Palestinian classmates ("They always make fight with me"). These interactions with teachers and peers highlight the students' overall status as refugees while in Jordan, and perhaps make evident the degree to which government-controlled information flows regarding Iraqis (who they are, what they represent) might be influencing the views of the general public. Chatelard (2010) depicts such information flows as a part of a hegemonizing state-driven rhetoric that shuts out competing perceptions of Iraqis' presence in Jordan (as represented, for instance, by Iraqis themselves).

A final challenge area, and one that spans across those heretofore discussed, concerns the representation of multiculturalism by various ministry officials. Generally, ministry officials provided statements that eclipsed explicit reference to human rights commitments or specific sets of multicultural policies. For instance, in a 2008 meeting with the Office of Curricula and Textbooks, Education Ministry officials stressed the importance of respect for other cultures and cultural values in their materials, and the "multicultural friendly environments" of their curriculum and textbooks. Further assertions were made regarding the importance of tolerance, peace, cooperation, integration, and "respect for other religions". However there was no mention of specific curriculum policies that might accommodate the needs of ethno-cultural minorities. Similarly, in a 2010 meeting with the same office, officials spoke of the integration of diversity and multiculturalism, and the importance of others' cultural identities, again without reference to specific policies or human rights doctrines. An interesting exception to this pattern of offering general and sometimes rather vague accounts of multiculturalism occurred in a 2008 meeting with the Ministry of Political Development. When asked about the rights of the approximately 700,000 Iraqi refugees then living in Jordan, officials stated that the Iraqis were "non-citizens receiving rights as all other citizens". The clearly false nature of this statement perhaps most directly exposes multicultural rhetoric as multicultural challenge. A positive representation of multiculturalism sounds good to Western ears, and is undoubtedly helpful to circulate within the international aide community. However, rhetoric of this nature also glosses over the articulation of multiculturalism as a set of policies that might more firmly ground the state in its commitment to human rights.

A Qualified Illustration: Multiculturalism and Iraqi Schooling in the United States

As noted earlier, the purpose for presenting some information regarding multiculturalism within the United States is to illustrate that multicultural policies can in fact be of benefit to refugees, and most notably for our purposes, Iraqi students. Using the United States as an illustration must however be qualified. Firstly, as Adelman (2008) notes, the United States was the "proximate cause" for the Iraqi refugee crisis in the first place, and thus bears some connection to at least a few of the challenges that Jordan faces in realizing multiculturalism, such as regional insecurity. This alone does not have anything directly to do with the quality or degree of multiculturalism in the U.S. However it does raise concerns regarding the consistency to which the U.S. has attended to the protection of ethno-cultural minority groups on an international scale, and in the Middle East in particular. This draws attention to the more general point of the country's foreign relations in the Middle East as they bear on human rights concerns. Here there exist several issues of concern, including the use of torture in detention facilities, public accountability for the use of CIA drone strikes, and lucrative contracts with states that are known to commit human rights abuses (HRW, 2012). Finally, while the U.S. has adopted multiculturalism, as Hero and Preuhs (2006) as well as Banting et al. (2006) find, it has done so only moderately, and still lags behind the stronger states of Australia and Canada. So there are some important reasons not to valorize the U.S. too highly, and to be specific regarding where and when to turn to the country as an example. Nonetheless, as the following demonstrates, Iraqi refugees are able to benefit from multicultural policies currently in place in the United States.

It must be reiterated from the onset of this discussion that most Iraqi refugees are not expressing a desire to return to Iraq. Once approved for resettlement in countries of immigration such as the United States, they are admitted as permanent residents and are on track toward gaining future citizenship. Data from this particular study indicate that young Iraqis are crafting future plans that involve remaining in the United States, and not returning to their homeland. As Iraqis are residents rather than guests in the U.S., they can legally work and are receiving rights entitled to all other residents. This diminishes significantly the challenge of paying for school fees, supplies, transportation and so on. Immigrant admission and naturalization policies do not in themselves constitute multicultural policies (Kymlicka, 2007), however there are other policies in the United States specifically designed to accommodate immigrant ethno-cultural groups.

Multicultural Curriculum, and Bilingual and/or ESL Instruction

There are two particular areas where individual states within the U.S. do enact policies matching those identified by Banting et al. (2006) as representative of immigrant multiculturalism, and which have a direct bearing on schooling. These are multiculturalism in school curricula, and bilingual and/or English as a Second Language instruction. This is evident within Michigan's public schools, and is seen in particular within the greater Detroit area. With respect to multicultural curriculum in K-12 schools the Michigan Department of Education's Curriculum Framework makes direct reference to facilitating multicultural awareness and teaching multicultural content in several areas, including social studies, language learning, and literature (Michigan Department of Education, 1996). Michigan is also host to a number of organizations and universities that sponsor initiatives infusing multicultural content and awareness into the public school curriculum, such as multicultural lesson plans developed by the Michigan Diversity Council (MDC) as well as the library at Michigan State University (MSUL) (MDC, 2011; MSUL, 2010).

Immigrant and refugee students, such as Iraqis, benefit from multicultural curriculum through the validation they receive of being members of ethno-cultural minority groups, as well as the enhanced awareness others gain of ethno-cultural diversity. However, for immigrant and refugee students in particular, learning about their host society is also a multicultural experience. Focus group participant Hanna for instance mentioned American History, among all her classes, as her favorite in school. Hanna's interest in U.S. history may well reflect the pro-integrationist stance of the society more generally. Put another way, were Hanna's school to regard Iraqis as foreigners who were in the country only temporarily, her interest in American society might be considerably diminished. Iraqi students' interest and enthusiasm for schooling is also facilitated by bilingual and/or English as a Second Language instruction.

The United States federal government does not currently specify an official language, and Michigan in particular has not adopted an official language (U.S Department of Education [USDE], 2011). Language instruction nonetheless is geared toward the acquisition of English proficiency, and schools may use either or both bilingual as well as English as a Second Language instruction to get there. Schools within Michigan are provided resources under the Title III program of the federal Elementary and Secondary Education Act (ESEA) to help ensure that children who are limited English proficient, "including immigrant children and youth", attain English proficiency, and meet academic achievement standards (USDE, 2011). Several focus group participants in this study spoke favorably of their ESL and bilingual instructors. In fact, the majority of students indicated that these teachers were amongst their favorite, as the teachers displayed the most sensitivity to and understanding of the students' backgrounds and learning needs. For instance, Grace, a 17 year old female in the 10th grade, reported the following about her school and ESL teacher:

> It is a good school for Iraq – especially for the new Iraqian (sic). We have one teacher. She always helps the Iraqians ... like if anything happens to Iraqians she always fixed it (sic) and tells them like how to graduate, how to make credit for the school, like help them after the school. Like when we have that parents talk to the teachers like she always translates, brings another

teacher to translate for her ... She teaches ESL students; low-intermediate, high-intermediate, and advanced.

Grace, along with Mansour, a 17 year old male in the 10th grade, and Adnon, a 15 year old male in the 9th grade, in turn spoke highly of bilingual teachers at their schools:

Mansour: We got four teachers speaking Arabic and helping people.
So four teachers who speak Arabic there?
Mansour: Yeah.
Adnon: The English teachers, they explain English very good.
Mansour: Yeah, they translating (sic) the lessons we don't understand. Like the lesson, it's in English, we don't understand, they explain it to us.
Adnon: I can ask anything, and they will they explain to us.
Right. Do you (Grace) have that?
Grace: Yeah, we have – her name is Miss [ ], she's an Iraqi teacher. She always translates for the new coming group.

The above two accounts demonstrate in particular important relations between pro-integrationist immigration policies and multiculturalism. Allowing Iraqis to legally work gains them access to jobs within the schools, and their involvement in the schools, notably as teachers and translators, in turn strengthens multicultural efforts. While there are several areas where the United States certainly could improve with respect to immigrant multiculturalism, the above does demonstrate some areas where multiculturalism is working to the benefit of Iraqi students.

CONCLUSION

This chapter has shown that human rights underpins liberal multiculturalism when the latter is construed as a set of specific policies, and that liberal multiculturalism, cast as a set of policies, can benefit the schooling of refugees. The challenges that Jordan has faced in adopting multiculturalism overlap quite significantly with the challenges Iraqi refugee students are facing in the country's public schools. It follows that Jordan may improve the schooling of its Iraqi refugees by addressing some of the challenges it faces in embracing multiculturalism.

Such a call for action is likely to be met with resistance. Firstly, there is the question of whether Iraqi refugees really "qualify" as a group that could benefit from any form of immigrant multiculturalism in Jordan. After all, Iraqis are treated at best as "guests", and are largely shut out from meaningful participation in society. Moreover, as a result of these conditions, many maintain a low profile in Jordan, hoping for their eventual resettlement. Their situation is similar in some ways to long-term residents who live in traditionally non-immigration countries of Europe, and who are excluded from basic rights and entitlements. Here, as with Iraqis in Jordan, foreign-born populations are placed in the category of temporary foreigners, barred from receiving citizenship, and told that their "real home" is their country of origin. These policies are enacted with the intention of forcing them to return home. Drawing from Walzer (1983) to dub these groups as "metics", or *de facto* long-term residents who nonetheless face exclusion from the polis, Kymlicka (2007) includes as illustrations illegal North African migrants in Italy, Kosovar asylum seekers in Switzerland, and Turkish students or guest workers in Germany. As Kymlicka discusses, it is increasingly being recognized that policies excluding these groups from full participation in society are ineffective; "Metics who have lived in a country for several years are unlikely to go home, even if they have only a precarious legal status" (p. 76). Kymlicka notes that this is particularly true if metics have married and had children in their adopted country, at which point "it is their new country, not their country of origin, which has become their home" (p. 76). Iraqis holding out for third country resettlement may differ from these populations inasmuch as they still desire to push on. However, the odds are unfortunately not in their favor. As noted, only a small percentage of Iraqi refugees actually resettle to a third country. Coupled with the fact that a very small percentage are choosing to return to Iraq, Iraqis in Jordan too have become *de facto* long-term residents.

Secondly, as Kymlicka (2007) notes regarding the issue of metics in European contexts, the issue of adopting multiculturalism can barely arise until such groups "move out of the category of temporary foreigners and move into the category of permanent residents and citizens" (p. 76). The Jordanian government has stressed that Iraqi refugees are not eligible for citizenship. However granting Iraqis permanent residency, and just as importantly a legal right to work, would signify a concrete step toward implementing multiculturalism. The right to work would undoubtedly also result in redirecting many Iraqi children from having to work to returning to school. This would curtail some of the most serious human rights violations occurring in the country. There are other challenge areas intersecting with education also within the state's control to change, including the elimination of screening for religious identity at the border, and greater awareness and sensitivity amongst school teachers and staff toward religious minority groups such as Shi'ites and Mandeans. These changes could be reflected in both teaching practices as well as curriculum materials. Implementing these changes would allow the state to shift from engaging in multicultural rhetoric to creating multicultural *policies*, and an opportunity to more fully enact the international instruments relevant to minority rights it has already committed to.

NOTES

[i] The authors note the following: "while LEP, ESL, and Bilingual Education programs in the American context are not necessarily thought of as primarily aimed at cultural recognition, they do support the differential needs of ethno-cultural minorities. Thus, in light of possible policy alternatives, these programs add a layer of recognition to education policy, even though they also have, to varying degrees, program elements that are aimed at assimilation" (p.134)

[ii] Kymclika notes that while the United States does not have an official policy of multiculturalism at the federal level, there exists a broad range of multiculturalism policies at lower levels of government such as states and cities.

[iii] Some observers have questioned Kymlicka's perhaps too narrow focus here, arguing that Scandinavian countries or the United Kingdom might also be included.

[iv] Kymlicka uses the term "post-colonial states" to distinguish countries in Africa, Asia, and the Middle East from the post-communist states of Eastern Europe, the democracies of Western Europe, and the New World European settler states. He gives recognition to the fact that it is nonetheless an inexact label, given that some states in Africa, Asia, or the Middle East were never officially colonized.

[v] Iraqi refugees in Jordan do not live in "refugee camps", but rather in urban areas scattered among local population.

[vi] The 1951 Convention relating to the Status of Refugees. The Convention's mandate reads that refugee include any person who as a result of events occurring before 1 January 1951 and owing to a well-founded fear of being persecuted for reasons of race, religion, nationality, membership of a particular social group or political opinion, is outside the country of his nationality and is unable or, owing to such fear, is unwilling to avail himself of the protection of that country; or who, not having a nationality and being outside the country of his former habitual residence as a result of such events, is unable or, owing to such fear, is unwilling to return to it (UNHCR, 2007, p.16).
According to the UNHCR, the Convention remains the cornerstone of the international protection regime (UNHCR, 2006).

[vii] Refugees and asylum seekers fall under legislation applicable to the 1973 Residence and Foreign Affairs Law No 24, which grants the Minister of Interior the authority to determine on case-by-case basis who may be deported (Collet, 2010a).

[viii] In 2003, the year of the U.S. invasion, 295 Iraqi refugees were admitted into the country. This number dropped to 65 the following year. In 2005 the number went up to 186, and made a very modest increase to 189 in 2006. In 2007 the number increased to 1,605 and in 2008 jumped to 12,755. In 2009 18,709 Iraqis were admitted into the country, and between 2010 and September of 2011, an additional 21,482 Iraqis resettled to the U.S. (U.S. Department of Health and Human Services [USDHHS], 2011b; USDS, 2011).

[ix] Most these interviewees were also themselves Iraqi refugees.

[x] The "Shi'ite Crescent" is a geo-political term describing a Middle East region where either the minority or the majority population is Shi'a. The crescent is thought to include Iraq, Lebanon, and Syria. The term has been used to describe the potential for political cooperation among these areas.

[xi] The UNHCR issues a series of identification cards of different types and colors to refugees and asylum seekers, depending on their status with the agency (i.e.; awaiting interview or recognition status). All of the identity cards are stamped by the Jordanian interior ministry and are good for six months (USCRI, 2009).

[xii] Authorities have reportedly tried to block Iraqis from visiting shrines dedicated to historical Shi'a figures (USCRI, 2009).

[xiii] Ministry of Education officials state that Christians can opt out of taking Islamic education courses. However, the teaching of Islamic values is not restricted to religious education courses alone as Islam and teachings of the Koran pervade the entire school curriculum and culture.

REFERENCES

Adelman, H. (Ed.). (2008). *Protracted displacement in Asia: No place to call home.* Burlington, VT: Ashgate.

Al-Edwan, Z. S. M. (2010). Human rights principles in the social education textbooks of the elementary stage in Jordan. *European Journal of Social Sciences, 15*(2), 117-126.

Alibhai-Brown, Y. (2003). *After Multiculturalism.* London: Foreign Policy Center.

Baker, W., & Shryock, A. (2009). Citizenship and crisis. In Detroit Arab American Study Team (Ed.), *Citizenship and crisis: Arab Detroit after 9/11* (pp. 3-32). New York: Russell Sage Foundation.

Banting, K., Johnston, R., Kymlicka, W., & Soroka, S. (2006). Do multiculturalism policies erode the welfare state? An empirical analysis. In K. Banting & W. Kymlicka (Eds.), *Multiculturalism and the welfare state: Recognition and redistribution in contemporary democracies* (pp. 49-91). Oxford: Oxford University Press.

Boyatzis, R. E. (1998). *Transforming qualitative information: Thematic analysis and code development*. Thousand Oaks: Sage.

Central Intelligence Agency (2011). *World factbook for Jordan*. Retrieved from https://www.cia.gov/library/publications/the-world-factbook/geos/jo.html

Chatelard, G. (2010). What visibility conceals: Re-embedding refugee migration from Iraq. In D. Chatty & B. Finlayson (Eds.), *Dispossession and displacement: Forced migration in the Middle East and North Africa* (pp.17-44). New York: Oxford University Press.

Chatelard, G. (2002a). *Jordan as a transit country: Semi-protectionist immigration policies and their effects on Iraqi forced migrants*. Working Paper No. 61, United Nations High Commissioner for Refugees. Retrieved from http://www.unhcr.org/3d57aa757.html.

Chatelard, G. (2002b). *Iraqi Forced Migrants in Jordan: Conditions, religious networks, and the smuggling process*. Paper presented at the WIDER Conference on Poverty, International Migration and Asylum, Helskinki, 27-28 September, 2002. Retrieved from http://www.wider.unu.edu/publications/working-papers/discussion-papers/2003/en_GB/dp2003-34/.

Collet, B. (2010). Refugee policy in Jordan and Iraqi refugee access to Jordanian schools. *World Studies in Education, 11*, 21-36.

Duncan, J., Schiesher, D., & Khalik, A. (2007). *Iraqi asylum seekers in Jordan*. Report of the ICMC-USCCB Mission to Assess the Protection Needs of Iraqi Asylum Seekers in Jordan, December 2007. Geneva: International Catholic Migration Commission.

Hathaway, J. (1991). *The law of refugee status*. London: Butterworths.

Hero, R., & Preuhs, R. (2006). Multiculturalism and welfare policies in the USA: A state-level comparative analysis, in K. Banting & W. Kymlicka(Eds), *Multiculturalism and the welfare state: Recognition and redistribution in contemporary democracies* (pp.121-151). Oxford: Oxford University Press.

Howell, S., & Jamal, A. (2009). The aftermath of the 9/11 attacks. In Detroit Arab American Study Team (Ed.), *Citizenship and crisis: Arab Detroit after 9/11* (pp. 69-100). New York: Russell Sage Foundation.

Human Rights Watch (2007). The human cost of war: The Iraqi refuge crisis. Testimony of Bill Frelick before the Congressional Human Rights Caucus, November 14.

Human Rights Watch (2012). U.S. foreign policy. Retrieved from http://www.hrw.org/united-states/us-foreign-policy.

International Catholic Migration Commission (2007). Iraqi asylum seekers in Jordan: A report of the ICMC-USCCB mission to assess the protection needs of Iraqi asylum seekers in Jordan. ICMC-US Conference of Catholic Bishops. Retrieved from http://reliefweb.int/node/263902.

International Crisis Group (2008). Failed responsibility: Iraqi refugees in Syria, Jordan and Lebanon, ICG Report No. 77, International Crisis Group, Washington D.C.

International Labour Organization (1999). Convention concerning the Prohibition and Immediate Action for the Elimination of the Worst Forms of Child Labour. Retrieved from http://www.ilo.org/public/english/standards/relm/ilc/ilc87/com-chic.htm.

International Relief and Development. (2008). *Outreach services: Identification and protection services for Iraqi refugees* Retrieved from http://www.ird.org/what/programs/jordan_osir.html.

Kymlicka, W. (2010). The rise and fall of multiculturalism? New debates on inclusion and accommodation in diverse societies. *International Social Science Journal, 61*(199), 97-112.

Kymlicka, W. (2007). *Multicultural Odysseys: Navigating the new international politics of diversity*. Oxford: Oxford University Press.

Kymlicka, W. (1995). *Multicultural citizenship: A liberal theory of minority rights*. Oxford: Oxford University Press.

Michigan Department of Education (2011). *English language learner programs* Retrieved from http://www.michigan.gov/mde/0,1607,7-140-6530_30334_40078-,00.html.

Michigan Diversity Council (2011). *About the Michigan Diversity Council.* Retrieved from http://www.michigandiversitycouncil.org/what-we-do.

Michigan State University Libraries (2010). *Multicultural/diverse children's literature.* Retrieved from http://staff.lib.msu.edu/corby/education/multicultural.htm.

Minority Rights Group International (2007). *Which countries have ratified international statements?* Retrieved from http://www.minorityrights.org/556/which-countries-have-ratified-international-statements/which-countries-have-ratified-international-statements.html.

National Centre for Human Rights (2010). *Seventh annual report of the national center for human rights: Human rights situation in the Hashemite kingdom of Jordan for 2010.* The National Centre for Human Rights, Amman, Jordan.

O'Donnell, K., & Newland, K. (2008). *The Iraqi refugee crisis: The need for action.* Washington, DC: Migration Policy Institute.

Questscope. (2010). *Homepage.* Retrieved from http://www.questscope.net/.

Ragin, C. (1987). *The comparative method.* Berkeley, CA: University of California Press.

Reliefweb (2010). *UNHCR poll: Iraqi refugees reluctant to return to Iraq permanently.* Retrieved from http://reliefweb.int/node/370377.

Sassoon, J. (2009). *The Iraqi refugees: The new crisis in the Middle East.* New York: I.B. Tauris.

Seeley, N. (2010). The politics of aid to Iraqi refugees in Jordan. *Middle East Report, 40.*

Shryock, A., & Chih Lin, A. (2009). Arab American identities in question. In Detroit Arab American Study Team (Ed.), *Citizenship and crisis: Arab Detroit after 9/11* (pp. 35-68). New York: Russell Sage Foundation.

Swett, S. & Webster, C. (2010). US dodges obligation to help Iraqi women trafficked into sexual slavery. *The Nation.* Retrieved from: http://www.thenation.com/article/154080/us-dodges-obligation-help-iraqi-women-trafficked-sexual-slavery.

UNICEF (2011). *UNICEF in Jordan – Five-year programme cycle.* Retrieved from http://www.unicef.org/jordan/overview_425.html.

UNESCO (2008). *UNESCO country programming document for Jordan.* Amman, Jordan: UNESCO.

UN (1989). Convention on the Rights of the Child, 20 November 1989, United Nations Treaty Series, vol. 1577, p. 3. Retrieved from: http://www.unhcr.org/refworld/docid/3ae6b38f0.html.

United Nations High Commissioner for Refugees (2011) *2011 UNHCR country operations profile – Jordan.* Retrieved from http://www.unhcr.org/cgi-bin/texis/vtx/page?page=49e486566.

United Nations High Commissioner for Refugees (2009). *UNHCR Jordan – Assistance and protection 2009 mid-year report.*

United Nations High Commissioner for Refugees (2008). *Hashemite kingdom of Jordan country operations plan 2008-2009.*

United States Committee for Refugees and Immigrants (2011). *Homepage.* Retrieved from http://www.refugees.org/.

United States Committee for Refugees and Immigrants (2009). *World refugee survey 2009 – Jordan.*

United States Department of Education (2011). *Office of English language acquisition homepage.* Retrieved from http://www2.ed.gov/about/offices/list/oela/index.html.

United States Department of Health and Human Services (2011). *Benefits and services.* Retrieved from http://www.acf.hhs.gov/programs/orr/.

United States Department of Health and Human Services (2010). *Refugee arrival data by country of origin and state of initial resettlement.* Retrieved from http://www.acf.hhs.gov/programs/orr/data/refugee_arrival_data.htm.

United States Department of State (2011). *Iraqi refugee resettlement.* Retrieved from http://www.state.gov/g/prm/c25771.htm.

United States Department of State (2010). *U.S. refugee admissions program reception and placement (R&P) program agencies FY 2010.* Retrieved from http://www.state.gov/g/prm/rls/146403.htm.

United States Department of State (2005). *International religious freedom report 2005.* Retrieved from http://www.state.gov/g/drl/rls/irf/2005/index.htm.

Walzer, M. (1983) *Spheres of justice.* New York, NY: Basic Books.

169

Zaiotti, R. (2006). Dealing with non-Palestinian refugees in the Middle East: Policies and practices in an uncertain environment. *International Journal of Refugee Law, 18*(2), 333-353.

Zehr, M. (2008). 'Culture of fear' afflicts Iraqi education system. *Education Week.* Retrieved from http://www.edweek.org/ew/collections/jordan/.

Zehr, M. A., & Mousa, Y. (2008). The lost years. *Education Week.* Retrieved from http://www.edweek.org/ew/collections/jordan/.

AFFILIATIONS

Bruce Anthony Collet
College of Education and Human Development
Bowling Green State University
Ohio, USA

CONTRIBUTORS

Mina Afkir is a Professor of linguistics at the Faculty of Letters and Humanities, Hassan II University, Casablanca, Morocco. Her research focuses on children's literacy acquisition in the Moroccan context and how it interacts with the diglossic language situation of the country as well as with socio-cultural factors. Her other research interests include linguistic diversity and cultural plurality, focusing on language contact, language attitudes, and language change in the Moroccan multilingual and multicultural space, which has witnessed many transformations due to the social and political changes the Moroccan society has been experiencing. She has published papers both nationally and internationally, and is currently writing on a book entitled *Literacy Acquisition in a Diglossic Speech Community: Bridges between Home and School.*
E-mail: mina_afkir@yahoo.com.

Madeleine Arnot is a Professor of Sociology of Education and Fellow of Jesus College, at the University of Cambridge, UK and Director of the DFID funded Youth, Gender and Citizenship project in Kenya, Ghana, India and Pakistan and has conducted EU funded research on gender awareness amongst student teachers and on adolescent masculinity, UK research on democratic pedagogic rights and gender education policy. She has published extensively on a wide range of social justice and equality issues over the last 30 years including *Educating the Gendered Citizen; Education, Asylum and the 'Non-Citizen' Child: The Politics of Compassion and Belonging* (with H. Pinson and M. Candappa) and *Gender Education and Equality in a Global Context* (ed. with S. Fennell). She is Editor of the *British Journal of Sociology of Education* and a member of the BAICE Executive Committee.
E-mail: mma1000@cam.ac.uk.

Mano Candappa is a Senior Research Officer at the Institute of Education, University of London, UK. Her research focuses on children and childhoods, migration and forced migration, and issues around social marginalization and human rights. She has collaborated with EU partners on research on human trafficking and asylum; and directed UK research for a range of funders including research councils, national and local government and voluntary sector organizations around the experiences of refugees and asylum-seeking children and families. Recent publications include *Education, Asylum and the 'Non-Citizen' Child: The Politics of Compassion and Belonging* (with Halleli Pinson and Madeleine Arnot).
E-mail: m.candappa@ioe.ac.uk.

Karen Carlisle is a Research Fellow in the School of Education at Queen's University, Belfast. She holds a BSc in Psychology from the University of Ulster

H. Biseth & H. B. Holmarsdottir (eds.), Human Rights in the Field of Comparative Education, 171–176.

and a Ph.D. on collaborative approaches to teaching and learning from the School of Education at Queen's University, Belfast. Her main research interests and areas of expertise are professional engagement in collaborative working, inter-school collaboration and the role of education in divided societies. She has undertaken research and published on these themes. In collaboration with colleagues in the School of Education, Dr Carlisle has also been involved in multi-institutional projects both in the UK (University of Oxford and Birmingham) and Europe (UNICEF/Former Yugoslav Republic of Macedonia). Recently she has been involved in two research projects – an examination of inter-school collaboration in Northern Ireland and a longitudinal study of the impact of cross community contact on pupils' social attitudes. Dr Carlisle also works closely with practitioners and pupils in a supportive capacity within the area of inter-school collaboration as a mechanism for improving community relations. Dr Carlisle has developed an extensive knowledge of the Northern Ireland education system, the key stakeholders and practitioners in schools across all sectors. She has also been involved in the organization and facilitation of workshops, training seminars and capacity building events within the School the School of Education. In her capacity as a researcher Dr Carlisle contributes to the teaching at Masters and PhD level. Her teaching broadly deals with issues related to conducting research in Northern Ireland schools and inter-school collaboration in a divided society.
E-mail: carlislek108@gmail.com.

Bruce Anthony Collet is an Assistant Professor in the College of Education and Human Development at Bowling Green State University (Ohio, U.S.A.). His main research interest concerns forced migration, religiosity, and schooling in host societies. He also writes about religion and minority populations in secular school contexts, and comparative and international education research and theory. Collet has conducted research in Jordan, S. Korea, Canada, and the United States, and has published both in the U.S. and internationally. He is an Associate Editor with the journal Diaspora, Indigenous, and Minority Education, and is a Scholar with the Centre for Refugee Studies at York University in Toronto.
Email: colleba@bgsu.edu.

Susan J. Courey is an Associate Professor of Special Education at San Francisco State University and the Mild/Moderate Program Coordinator. Her work in Human Rights education is an extension of providing education and services for individuals with disabilities. She specializes in preparing teachers to work with students with disabilities. Research interests include Human Rights Education, Autism, mathematics education and using music to teach mathematics.
E-mail: scourey@sfsu.edu.

Paulí Dávila is a Professor of History of Education at the Universidad del País Vasco/Euskal Herriko Unibertsitatea UPV/EHU. His research work has centered on the History of Education in the Basque Country, with special emphasis on educational policy, literacy, teacher training, national curriculum, textbooks,

vocational training, religious orders, etc. He has published several books, book chapters and articles. He has also focused his attention on the study, development and application of the Convention on the Rights of the Child and international organizations, highlighting in particular the educational aims underlying the Convention, as well as on the study of childhood seen from the point of view of history. He is the main researcher of the group for Historical and Comparative Studies in Education, recognized by the Basque Government and member of the Unity of Education and Research "Education, Culture and Society (UFI 11/54)" of the University of the Basque Country.
E-mail: pauli.davila@ehu.es.

Mariana Dias is a Professor of Sociology of Education and President of the Pedagogic Council at the School of Education of the Polytechnic Institute of Lisbon (Portugal). She has conducted research in Portugal, England and the United States of America and has been visiting professor in European and American Universities. Dias has published internationally as well as in Portugal in the field of educational policies and school administration. Her primary interest is in the role of education in relation to social inequalities and she is currently developing research in the field of school improvement in deprived areas and working as a consultant in the national network for priority education in Portugal. In addition, she has participated as an expert in several governmental programs and is presently involved in the evaluation of Portuguese primary and secondary schools.
E-mail: marianad@eselx.ipl.pt.

Joanne Hughes is professor and Director of the Centre for Shared Education at Queen's University, Belfast. Her main research interests and areas of expertise are community relations policy, inter-group contact theory, and the role of education in divided societies. She has published widely on these themes, and much of her work has an international comparative focus. Professor Hughes has been keen to promote the applied value of her research and she has worked extensively with policy makers, government bodies, community groups and organizations in Northern Ireland and in other divided jurisdictions internationally.
E-mail: joanne.hughes@qub.ac.uk.

Pamela LePage is an Associate Professor of Special Education at San Francisco State University in San Francisco CA, USA. Her main research interests are in teacher education. She is especially interested in the moral development of teachers and the development of moral communities in teacher education. She is also interested in the social inclusion of children with high-level autism. Pamela LePage has published extensively in books, refereed journals and conference proceedings.
E-mail: plepage@sfsu.edu.

Luis María Naya is a teacher of Comparative Education at the Universidad del País Vasco/Euskal Herriko Unibertsitatea UPV/EHU. His main lines of research

have revolved around the use of Information and Communication Technologies, minority languages in education systems, children's rights and the right to education. He is a member of the group for Historical and Comparative Studies in Education, recognized by the Basque Government and the main researcher of the Unity of Education and Research "Education, Culture and Society (UFI 11/54)" of the University of the Basque Country UPV/EHU. He has produced many publications, coordinating books inter alia *El derecho a la educación en un mundo globalizado* (2006) [The right to education in a globalized world], *La Educación y los Derechos Humanos* (2005) [Education and Human Rights], *La infancia en la historia: Espacios y representaciones* (2005) [Childhood in history: Spaces and representations].
E-mail: luisma.naya@ehu.es.

Ana María Montero Pedrera, Ph.D., is a Professor at the University of Seville, Spain. Her research focuses on education policy, educational systems and educational thought. Montero Pedrera collaborates with universities in Brazil, Colombia and Chile and she has published both in Spain and abroad. She has participated in European projects, R & D projects of the Ministry of Education and Excellence Projects in Andalusia. She is an Erasmus coordinator with the University of Angers (France), Porto and Guarda (Portugal), Istanbul (Turkey), Bologna, Florence and Rome (Italy). She is a member of the Scientific Committee of Spanish and Latin American magazines and various national and international scientific societies.
E-mail: pedrera@us.es.

Halleli Pinson is a senior lecturer at the Department of Education, Ben-Gurion University, Israel. Her research focuses on citizenship education, youth identities, education and conflict and the education of refugee and asylum seeking children. She has conducted research on these themes looking both at policy discourses and young people's experiences in Israel and the UK. Recent publications include *Education, Asylum and the 'Non-Citizen'Child: The Politics of Compassion and Belonging* (with Madeleine Arnot and Mano Candappa) which won a Society for Educational Studies prize 2011.
E-mail: halleli@bgu.ac.il.

Vedat Sevincer is a researcher and project manager at a media literacy center and education foundation in Norway. His research focus ranges from media literacy to citizenship education, human rights, and multiculturalism. In addition to research in Greece, Norway and Turkey, he has been involved in several educational and media projects. Some of his academic work has been published in English and Turkish publications.
E-mail: vedats@tnp.no.

Catarina Tomás is a Professor of Sociology of Childhood and Education at the Higher School of Education of the Polytechnic Institute of Lisbon and she is researcher at the Research Center for the Social Sciences (CICS) of the University of Minho (Portugal). Her research focus is on children's rights. She has conducted research in Portugal, Brazil and Spain. Tomás has published internationally as well as in Portugal. She develops research and community projects particularly focusing on children's participation. She is a member of The European Network of Masters in Children's Rights and The Mediterranean Network on Children's Rights. E-mail: ctomas@eselx.ipl.pt.

THE EDITORS

Heidi Biseth is an Associate Professor at Buskerud University College (Norway) and a Senior Advisor in Education at Save the Children Norway. Her research focus is on democracy, human rights, and multiculturalism. She has conducted research in Denmark, Norway, South Africa and Sweden. In addition she has been involved in several projects engaging in a range of countries in Africa, Asia and Europe. Biseth has published internationally as well as in Norway. She won the 2011 Dr. Judith Torney-Purta Outstanding Paper Award in Citizenship and Democratic Education for the paper "Citizenship Education in Scandinavian Multicultural Schools: A Comparative Study of Students' and Teachers' Perceptions". The paper is published in *Citizenship Teaching and Learning* (2012). Engaged in children's access to education worldwide, Biseth works with development projects, particularly focusing on monitoring and evaluation. Furthermore, she is engaged in teacher education with a particular focus on how teachers promote democracy and societal participation. She is working with the development of teaching materials in Norwegian within this area and also engaged in one of the Council of Europe's initiatives to develop materials on the use of social media and democratic participation. Biseth is an international convener for the World Congress for Comparative Education Societies in Buenos Aires, June 2013.
E-mail: post@heidibiseth.no.

Halla B. Holmarsdottir is a Professor in Multicultural and International Education at Oslo and Akershus University College. Holmarsdottir has been working with education and development for roughly 20 years, focusing in particular on Africa and Asia. She is the scientific coordinator of the Gender Equality, Education and Poverty (GEEP) project and a member of the project on Education and Sustainable Development in a Post-Conflict Southern Sudan (NUCOOP). Both projects involve a consortium of several institutions and researchers and are funded by the Norwegian Ministry of Foreign Affairs. Her academic competency is within both humanities and social science, which has contributed to an interdisciplinarity in her work. She has served as the UNESCO liaison representing the World Council of Comparative Education Societies (WCCES) from 2005-2012. Furthermore, she has co-edited (with Mina O'Dowd) the collective volume *Nordic Voices: Teaching and Researching Comparative and International Education in the Nordic Countries* (2009) and has recently co-edited (with Vuyokazi Nomlomo, Alawia Farag and

Zubeida Desai) edited a volume entitled *Gendered Voices: Reflections on Gender and Education in South Africa and Sudan* in addition to publishing several articles in international journals.

E-mail: Halla-Bjork.Holmarsdottir@hioa.no.

CPSIA information can be obtained at www.ICGtesting.com
Printed in the USA
LVOW101801220313

325640LV00006B/452/P

9 789462 091504